WHY ON EARTH?

Why on Earth?

Biography and the Practice of Human Becoming

Signe Eklund Schaefer

[signature: Signe Eklund Schaefer]

SteinerBooks | 2013

2013
STEINERBOOKS
An imprint of Anthroposophic Press/SteinerBooks
610 Main St., Great Barrington, MA
www.steinerbooks.org

Cover and book design: William Jens Jensen
Cover art: Karin Schaefer
Diagrams 1–6: Angelica Hesse
Back cover author photograph: Robin Zeamer
Permissions acknowledgments: page 243

LIBRARY OF CONGRESS CATALOGING-IN-PUBLICATION DATA

Schaefer, Signe.
  Why on earth? : biography and the practice of human becoming /
by Signe Eklund Schaefer.
     pages cm
  Includes bibliographical references.
  ISBN 978-1-62148-040-2 (pbk.) — ISBN 978-1-62148-041-9
(ebook)
  1. Self-actualization (Psychology) 2. Four temperaments. I. Title.
  BF637.S4S3414 2013
  299'.935—dc23

                                                2013017253

CONTENTS

"What liberates is the knowledge of who we were, what we became; where we were, where into we have been thrown; where to we speed, wherefore we are redeemed; what birth is, and what rebirth." —VALENTIUS, second-century Gnostic

For Chris

PREFACE

For many years I have been active with what is loosely called *biography work*, a term that embraces an experiential approach to understanding human development. This is not an abstract or academic study, but a practice in reading into our life stories, coupled with the opportunity to listen to the journeys of others. Living destiny questions are explored through biography exercises, artistic practice, nature observation, inner contemplation, and small-group conversation. Behind the specific exercises lie larger themes: What does it mean to be a woman or a man today? How do different life phases shape my experiences? What accounts for such varied ways of being and acting? What in my life story expresses something uniquely mine, and what is more universally human? In my own experience the fruit of this kind of biography work is an ever-expanding interest and enthusiasm for life itself, and for the process of human becoming.

While I was writing this book and living deeply with those large questions, I was often asked, "What is your book about?" My reply, "Life," would invariably provoke puzzled expressions or wry chuckles. The scope of the book is broad, and each chapter could be expanded to a book in its own right. However, my aim is to offer a wide view, touching briefly on different aspects of being human that have challenged and moved me over the years, trusting that readers will delve further into the particular topics that interest them.

My hope with the book is that it may be a kind of speaking partner for readers. The ideas in it were born through conversations over many years with friends and colleagues, students, and teachers. So much of what I offer here has arisen in that in-between space of mutual exploration. I want this idea exchange to continue; my wish is that what is written here may stimulate your own further questioning and life reflection.

My thinking has also been much stimulated by the work of Rudolf Steiner, and, indeed, many of the conversations referred to earlier were efforts to understand his ideas on human nature and development. The concepts and pictures he articulated at the beginning of the twentieth century are complex and thought-provoking. The path of Anthroposophy he offered is for me a journey of on-going discovery. In this book I have tried to share some of Steiner's ideas in a way that lets them build and deepen as the chapters progress. I bring his work into the book with the conviction that the insights he offers can help us shine light on life questions and urgent social concerns that are ours to meet now, in the twenty-first century.

Signe Eklund Schaefer
March 2013

CHAPTER 1

LIFETIMES OF INTENTION

All my life I have pondered questions of human development. As a six-year-old, I remember wondering, "Why do we live?" and feeling quite sure that we must live more than once, or life just did not make sense. Our experiences had to be part of a larger development than just one life would allow. I do not remember how I worded this to myself or if I even tried to articulate it to my parents, but I am quite sure that if I did try, they would have told me not to be silly. Although my family was warm and loving, conversations were grounded on reason and logic. My father was a scientist, my mother an avowed agnostic, and religion was not part of my childhood.

Perhaps it was the prevailing mood of scientific inquiry in the family that led me around that same age to set up an experiment with myself. I felt that there was "another" world beyond what I could see and touch, that in some way this world I could experience with my senses was only a dream. So I decided to close my eyes tightly and pinch my arm as hard as I could in order to "wake up" in that other place. I did this very seriously. When I opened my eyes, I was surprised to see that I was still in my familiar bedroom. Nevertheless, I did not conclude that I was wrong. Rather, I remember thinking very clearly, "I must be only dreaming that I pinched myself, so this can't take me to that other place. I'll have to find another way someday." Then I skipped back into my childhood and do not remember concerning myself with such questions for many years.

But I have always believed in the possibility of development, of people's ability to grow and change. By ten I had worked my way through all the biographies in the children's section of the library. I puzzled over why people did what they did, or why they did not do what I thought I would have done in their situations. Then as a young adult I devoured developmental theories of childhood, and even more, the ideas of adult life phases. I read widely, observed others around me, and myself as well, and eventually began teaching classes and workshops on human development and on various aspects of individual biography. This book comes out of that lifelong study and reverence for the journey each person takes.

As the years went by, when I reviewed my courses and the many rich insights offered by my adult students, I would think: "I should write this up." I felt there was a book nestling there in all my notes. But I could not seem to put anything down on paper. There was always the excuse of no time, but deep inside I knew that was not really what was keeping me from beginning. I felt great optimism for our human potential, and I believed that more consciousness of what I saw as universal truths would surely be helpful. Yet all around me I saw suffering, even among very conscious people. How could I write in a way that did not oversimplify life's complexities or come across as somehow falsely positive?

And then, in my early sixties, my own life seemed to implode. At many levels of my being I felt things crumbling. Change was suddenly not something rosy on the horizon, but loss, sadness, betrayal, loneliness. Were all my good ideas about human development just that: good ideas, but empty of sustaining, supporting reality? Did any of it matter anyway? Were we humans in truth no more than the victims of our DNA, or of our educational or social circumstances? I was disheartened, and yet... I could not ignore a small, persistent inner voice calling me to own these new challenges, to enter this new sorrow, and through it to explore more deeply my long-cherished ideas. Aware of the fine line I could cross at any moment into either simplistic rationalization or an indulgence of self-pity, I gradually began to look once again, but now from within my sadness, toward the wholeness of a life. The long road of human becoming again captured my heart, and even these painful twists and turns began to offer new possibilities of meaning.

An underlying idea in all my explorations has been what that young girl knew to be true: we do not live just one life. Rather, we come to Earth again and again, for it is here that we can practice and learn and, over many lifetimes, grow more whole. It is my belief that we are developing what it is to be human and what as human beings we have to offer to the cosmos. I use the word "belief" with caution. I do not refer to some creed or dogma, some institutionalized set of ideas to which I adhere. I could as well have said "conviction," for that is how the concept of reincarnation lives in me. But it is not something I can prove, nor do I feel that proving it is something I should try to do. I do not expect that everyone reading this will agree with me. I only ask for openness to the possibility and a willingness to look with me at some of the different pieces of the puzzle of our life on Earth.

One of my greatest teachers as I have tried to enter the mystery of the human being has been Rudolf Steiner, the early twentieth-century Austrian spiritual scientist and founder of Anthroposophy and Waldorf education. I have found his work deeply inspiring and will be sharing some of his insights in the coming chapters. He speaks of the human "I" on a journey of many lifetimes and also elaborates upon the significance for the "I" of experience between lives, between death and rebirth. He gives the picture that it is there, in a discarnate state, that we review the life just lived and also build intentions for our next life. Looking back on a one-sidedness in one lifetime creates a wish for balancing experiences in the next. There may be, surely will be, things to regret about the life now finished; and indeed, remorse can call forth the possibilities of transformation in a future incarnation. It is difficult not to picture this in too earthly a way, conditioned as we are by ideas of reward and punishment; and yet it is provocative to consider what we might have brought with us by way of challenges, opportunities, talents, and deficits.

Much of the conversation about human development in the twentieth century, and indeed lingering on in the twenty-first, has been caught in the debate between nature and nurture. Are we to be fully understood through our genetic makeup? Is everything we are, and will become, encoded in our DNA? Or are we rather the product of our social influences and experiences: our family patterns, schooling, class, nation, religion—each of these imprinting itself upon the blank slate of our entry into life? It is a problem of our dualistic modern consciousness that we can get caught in an either/or argument and then fail to recognize the legitimacy of both our DNA and our social shaping as factors—but not the full picture—in our evolving story. *Who* is living in the physical body with just this DNA? And *who* is experiencing this particular combination of environmental and behavioral influences? Can we recognize a Self that has in some mysterious way called together the genetic make-up and what I will call the "soul shaping" it needs to take further steps along its way?

There are real laws of the physical body that can explain in awe-inspiring detail the miracle of the material vessel for my earthly experiences. There are also real laws of the soul and how it is shaped by environmental factors. Ongoing research in biology and psychology reveal ever more about our bodily constitution and the makeup of our soul. But living *in* this physical body and *through* these soul experiences is my eternal self, my true "I." I can also call this my higher self; it has need of, indeed has played a part in organizing, just this body and soul configuration for its evolving journey toward human wholeness. Gradually throughout my life, I meet intentions for development that I myself have set into motion. I am not merely a victim of my body, or of my family, or my experiences. I may not be able to understand the reasons why I meet what I do in life, but the question remains whether I can accept my life challenges as belonging to me, as intended and meaningful opportunities for my very specific further development.

I realize that one could read the preceding as a kind of fatalism, with everything predetermined. I do not see it like that. Rather I feel there are certain themes, struggles, even people in my life that I need to meet. They present themselves to my consciousness with a deeper resonance than simple chance. There is some echo, or call, or recognition just beneath the surface of my awareness. Have you ever met someone and felt an immediate, "Oh, hello again!" or perhaps even, "Oh no, not you again!" without any conscious sense of why such a feeling would arise? The people we encounter and the recurring themes that present themselves may bring me joy or sorrow, but in

INTENTIONALITY EXERCISE • Try to imagine yourself before coming to Earth: what did you pack in your bag in order to become the person that you know yourself to be so far? This is not about yourself as some ideal person, but what was really needed for you to be as you are now—outwardly and inwardly? Perhaps you needed a sense of humor, or an abusive parent, faulty eyes, or a particular friend. Maybe a sailboat or chocolate were essential for you. Write down ten or twelve of these intended necessities. You may also become aware of a few things that you seem to have forgotten to pack—like forgetting your toothbrush on a trip. Perhaps you did not bring music, or a relationship to nature, or patience. Can you picture situations when you reached into your bag and realized that this particular thing was missing? As you reflect on what you did pack, you can also reflect on how some of the different things in your bag have affected each other in your life. It is most interesting to share this exercise with a friend or a group, but it is also useful on your own. Be a bit playful; we all experience how we have come with baggage!

some deep way they are mine to meet. What I do with what presents itself is what is not given; here is my earthly work, my opportunity to learn and to become more than I was before, my invitation to step toward freedom.

And yet, I must acknowledge a further concern with this idea of intentionality. It does not and cannot explain the atrocities and deprivations that continue to exist in our world. I do not wish to trivialize the unimaginable suffering that many people endure through war, poverty, persecution, and all manner of abuse and neglect. But although I may not have the wisdom to understand these painful life circumstances, I do not want to ignore that such experiences have meaning. That meaning may not reveal itself to normal comprehension, but in the fuller reality of life between death and a new life, I trust it will offer its fruit and create future opportunities for healing.

This picture of intentionality for development, with which we come into life on Earth, must not be reduced to simplistic conceptions of judgment, retribution, or reward. Our earthly logic cannot fully encompass the mysteries of human development, or even of our individual life journeys. Destiny and karma are words too often used to cover gross rationalization, self-indulgence, guilt, desire, or abuse. But that we misunderstand, or even misuse, concepts is not reason enough to throw them out. How can we hold our questions in such a way that new insights can come, even as the field of inquiry shows itself to be ever expanding? At the very least the word *destiny* suggests a destination toward which we head—an appointment perhaps, but not a predetermined resolution. And so we build our *karma* as we go—in the ways we meet the intentions of our true "I"; our evolving responsibilities and also our burdens become part of our spirit core.

Over the years I have worked with many people on this question of intentionality and I have been deeply moved by the ways people have known that a physical disability, or the hurt they suffered from an alcoholic parent, or a trauma they endured in their teens belonged to who they later became. They recognized a central destiny intention to meet this hardship, and they valued who they became through their experiences. The former drug addict who becomes a strong and compassionate substance abuse counselor would not erase the years of addiction from his biography. The teenage mother who goes on to develop parent education for high school students would not remove her "mistake" from her life story. These people do not consider themselves as victims of their circumstances, but rather as individuals who meet their lives with emerging responsibility and come to recognize how they are growing through their challenges. For most people the metamorphosis will be more subtle, much less visible in terms of career, and still they may sense that the people they are today would not exist without their past experiences.

Of course there are many who do not want to be, or do not value, the person they perceive themselves to be. They see no meaning in their life experiences. And then it is all too easy to get caught up in blaming the deprivations of childhood, the abuses of schooling, the unkindness of parents, or the inattentiveness of a spouse for our unhappiness or our lack of control, for all that seems to go wrong in our lives. And indeed these experiences do play into our evolving habits and our sense of self, but are we only the victim of these events? Could it be that in the wisdom of my sojourn between lives, I had the courage to know that I needed a critical, unloving mother to invite a deeper compassion, a stronger sense of self in me? Is it possible to find within our struggles, a recognition that this belongs to my work, is part of what I came to do on Earth? I know that this can sound so simple, and surely intending to have an uncaring parent runs counter to everything we know children need. However, find a quality you value about yourself as something you have worked to develop, and then follow it back in your biography. Chances are you will come to some experiences along the way that you did not necessarily perceive as positive at the time, but which helped to set the stage for who you have been able to become.

By way of example, here are some things an older student of mine felt he put in his bag as he came to Earth and also what he experienced growing within him through their presence in his life: "a vulnerability to loneliness to awaken my ability to sense the needs of others; a sense of humor to lighten my soul and bring warmth to others; distant parents who led me to appreciate connections; a sense of self that gave me a survival instinct."

These kinds of thoughts can never be used as justification for our own lack of responsibility in the present, but they can offer us insight into our own past. Of course this is not meant to instill past-life guilt. We much too easily jump to ideas of punishment, or also of reward, to explain unexpected or incomprehensible occurrences. The possibilities for transformation that are set in place between lifetimes guarantee no particular outcome. Our evolving destiny is much more complex. We are called to ever-greater wakefulness if we would take up our lives in freedom. There is no direct line to explain the factors in our life—no formulaic A + B = C. The invitations to our development are always multi-faceted.

FINDING OURSELVES THROUGH EACH OTHER

It would be a misinterpretation of the preceding ideas to assume that while we are experiencing ourselves between death and a new birth, we are the sole planner of our future earthly journey, that somehow on our own we plot out our best next trip. The picture that Steiner gives is of an interaction between our higher "I," wise spiritual beings, and the "others" who are part of our story. Later, as we live our days on Earth, we discover aspects of ourselves in meeting the invitations to our becoming offered by the others of our life. Our "I" is not held tightly within us, nor does it somehow hover above us trying to direct our self-appointed actions. Rather, it lives in the people and circumstances we meet; it waits to be incorporated, to be taken up by us, to be allowed to develop in ever-new ways.

We all experience how different sides of ourselves have space to grow through the different relationships in our life. We are not the same person with our mother as we are with a teacher, a lover, a child, or a best friend. Because these others experience different aspects of who we are, they allow us to explore ever-new parts of ourselves. How life changing it can be to meet someone who sees in us something for which we may, as yet, have only the dimmest feeling or hope. Suddenly we can breathe more deeply; we feel we are known, and we can open ourselves to new becoming. This is the miracle side of our relationships: through feeling seen, we are able to grow. Of course there are shadow sides to all of this as well. Our experience of relationships is also fraught with feelings of not being seen, or valued, or allowed to bloom. The significance and the complexity of our relationships is a subject we will return to throughout this book.

When I was a young mother and wondering how I felt about these ideas of intentionality and finding myself through others, I had one of those magic moments when life offers a picture to illuminate this kind of pondering. While puttering in the kitchen one afternoon, I became aware of the children playing "house." My daughter and son had friends visiting, all between three and six years old, and everyone was involved in setting up the coming play. The task of assigning roles was of paramount importance: "You be the Mommy, and I'll be the Daddy, and you can be the big sister, and you can be the little brother, and..." There was serious negotiation being done, and it was clear to all that the game could not begin until the roles were accepted. Watching their earnestness I was suddenly struck with the thought, "That's how it is! There we are in the spiritual reality between lives, interacting with our future people, beginning to build the intentions that will guide our next earthly life, making the arrangements, the appointments that will shape our futures. "You be the Mommy, and I'll be the Daddy, and you can be the..."

But of course, once we get to Earth, we have forgotten the various plans, the complex contracts we have made. Whether we drank much or only a sip of that mythical drink of forgetfulness as we crossed the threshold into Earth life, the wisdom of our spirit intentions can easily elude us. Indeed, how often do we find ourselves asking: "Why on earth am I in this family? Why on earth is this happening to me? Why on earth is it all so hard?" We ask these questions, but we often forget to notice the beginning phrase *why on earth*; it is so easy to ignore that in the very question itself is a hint of a more encompassing reality, of some greater wisdom that might illuminate the question.

Questions of Meaning

Although there are those today who ascribe to all questions of meaning a kind of naïve irrelevance, I remain convinced that a yearning for meaning is a fundamental human endowment. We want to know, to understand, to make sense of our reality. There is an old Hebrew legend that illustrates something of this essential human possibility. After the Creation there were among the angels some who were critical that God had created the human being in His own likeness. They wanted to know why this had been done. As answer, "God assembled the whole world of animals before him and the angels. The latter were called upon to name the different kinds, but they were not equal to the task. Adam, however, spoke without hesitation: 'O Lord of the world! The proper name for this animal is ox, for this one horse, for

- 9 -

this one lion, for this one camel.' And so he called all in turn by name, suiting the name to the peculiarity of the animal. Then God asked him what his name was to be, and he said Adam, because he had been created out of Adamah, dust of the Earth. Again, God asked him His own name, and he said: 'Adonai, Lord, because Thou art Lord over all creatures'—the very name God had given unto Himself, the name by which the angels call Him..."[1]

This story shows the human being as possessing a particular kind of knowing, one with an almost prophetic quality of understanding. Unlike the other kingdoms of nature and in a way unknown even to the angels, the human being is endowed with the capacity to name, to give conceptual form to the world around and within, to recognize and comprehend the created world. And we start doing this as young children.

In my experience this effort to know often manifests through questions. The answer, the meaning, is not immediately apparent, but the search is of paramount importance. The questions need to be brought to consciousness. Could it be that our human longing to know is not just about finding definitive answers, but about the search itself—an ongoing exploration of who we are, and what we are doing here on Earth? We can learn much from the wisdom of the past, but when we stop searching, when we stop thinking in an open, living way, we simply pile up dead facts, worn-out theories, and thought clichés.

My hope with this book is to share some of the questions that have accompanied me through life. This is my effort to characterize my understandings so far, to recognize and name aspects of our human nature as I grapple with them. I do not expect readers to agree with all I have to say, but I do hope that my words might stimulate further explorations for others. I am also including occasional exercises that may be useful for reflection on life experiences, questions, and aims.

1   Ginzberg, *Legends of the Jews;* see also Steiner, *The Meaning of Life,* lecture I.

Modern life can at times seem arid; we can feel isolated and also unable to reach out to others. At least in the developed world, the earlier ways of knowing ourselves that united, but also divided people throughout history are ever less binding. Blood ties, social class, professional roles, religion, ethnicity, and even gender are just some of the characteristics that have a decreasing hold on our sense of identity. I do not mean to suggest that they are unimportant aspects of who we are, but the context of their significance is shifting.

The sense of oneself as an individual is ever stronger. Increasing numbers of people feel a difference between the core of their being, and the fact that they live in a woman's or a man's body, or were born in America or France or Japan. This enhanced sense of self can bring with it both loneliness and a kind of liberating exhilaration. As we begin to know ourselves as an "I," the contributions to our development from our gender, our nationality, our race, or our family become ever more interesting to ponder. These factors are important, but they do not fully define us. Indeed, where we do see people clinging fiercely to the traditional categories of self-definition, we also very often find fear, manipulation, and strife.

Twentieth-century artists often abandoned a frame for their paintings. This experience of stepping out of a traditional context, this loss of the frame, is for me a clear image of our modern condition. It is both a bold gesture of individuality and a challenge to know ourselves, and to be known, in a new way. We have stepped out of the familiar frames that have defined us for centuries. And so we ask: Who am I? What am I to do? Why am I a woman? Do my relationships matter? Does my life have meaning?

With the remarkable growth of the Internet in the twenty-first century, we are regularly invited—perhaps we could also say induced—to step behind a new kind of screen and redefine ourselves in new and statistically observable groupings. In the cyber world we become "known" through our purchases, our "friends" and our "likes" on social networking sites, and by the petitions we "sign." The virtual world takes on an ever-greater reality in our daily lives. Reinvention of one's identity can be a lark, a hope, an escape, or a manipulation. Relationship, truth, and responsibility become concepts to be explored in quite new ways, even as they challenge us to be individually more awake.

Since ancient times, seekers after wisdom were enjoined to "Know Thyself." What can this mean to us now? Natural science offers us wondrous information about our physical bodies and our physical ancestry. Psychology helps us bring to consciousness many deep and important aspects of our soul experiences. Social science provides clues about our cultural behavior and theories about our economic interactions. But none of these gives us a living, integrated, developmental picture of what it means to be a human being, now in the twenty-first century. For me, this question demands that we also look to the human spirit, to what I have referred to as the eternal or higher "I." This human spirit in us is on a long journey of becoming. It, too, has an ancestry, but not one that can be found through genealogical explorations of relatives from the past.

I have always loved the phrase "human being" because I see the verb in it: the process of being, rather than the finished product. Many years ago I had a student who in a moment of frustration with me, blurted out: "Can't you be more patient with me? I'm just a human becoming." I have always been so grateful to him for this gift of language and concept. I, too, feel myself as a human becoming, and the journey we share in this process, with all its ups and downs, continues to fill me with awe and with questions. In the coming chapters, I will be exploring some of these questions and some of the ways our "I" becomes more human here on Earth.

CHAPTER 2

FEMININE AND MASCULINE AND THE QUESTION OF GENDER

"It's a girl!" "It's a boy!" Although ultrasound now offers expectant parents the possibility of a preview of their child's gender, these are still most often the first words to announce a new baby on Earth. Gender is a central aspect of our earthly experience, a fundamental part of our self-identity and of our relationships with others. Gender influences how we learn, colors our career path, inspires our attractions, and is part of whom and how we love. Through gender we meet prejudice and favor, welcome and prohibition. Even if we could put all social conditioning aside, our gender still affords us very particular opportunities, challenges, and limitations.

Yet, in spite of the profound role that gender plays in our lives, do we not also have experiences of ourselves as beyond gender: recognition of inhabiting a male or female body, but still knowing ourselves to be more than what this most basic one-sidedness allows? Perhaps this is not something we think much about until a moment comes when we are suddenly jarred out of our sense of I-ness by someone's prejudicial reference to our gender. This might come when we are told that boys don't cry (but I am crying); or that girls cannot do some task (that I know I can do). We may feel the chafing of an expected role that feels far from our true aims. Perhaps we are excluded, or included, in a social situation based solely on our gender. Most significantly, as made clear by the rise of the women's movement in the second half of the twentieth century and all the legal changes enacted since then and still in process, we may feel our basic human rights compromised because of our gender.

When I was a young mother, in the early days of the women's movement, there was much discussion about trying to raise babies in a gender-neutral way. But very soon I saw that my daughter gravitated toward dolls, to rocking them and cooing to them, while some of my son's first sounds were echoes of the construction vehicles going past our window each morning. And the arrival of the garbage truck was for him a thing of wonder! In our case, both children were given dolls and trucks; both were cuddled and chased after; both were cared for by Mommy and Daddy. Nevertheless, it was impossible not to notice some intrinsic differences. My husband and I realized that even if we tried not to overly foster the children's innate inclinations in ways that might narrow their future interests, to not notice the differences would have been a falsification of observable reality.

How to understand the paradox of seemingly inborn differences of gender and an internal sense of self that transcends division? Of course modern feminism was born of this paradox as increasing numbers of women knew themselves to be capable of activities in the world that were not readily open to women. An emerging, and offended, sense of "I" in the face of repeated experiences of both glaring and more subtle discrimination gave women the courage to step up to the many barricades in education, career choice, economics, and even—or perhaps especially—within their own relationships. The work is nowhere complete; the resistances have been both blatant and muted, and they continue. But there have also been enormous changes, for and in both women and men.

When I recall my own evolving awareness of gender, I remember experiencing the deep disparity between being a person and a woman after the birth of my first child. It was the late 1960s and I was in my early twenties. Suddenly, the world seemed to look at me as only a mother, something that I was very happy to actively be, but that I had not anticipated as the singular characteristic of my identity. What had happened to the student, the teacher, the young person filled with a passion for social justice? Did anyone see her anymore? While I did not particularly feel this sense of limitation coming from my husband, I was shocked to be so often referred to by others as "Chris Schaefer's wife." I felt that being Chris's wife was a matter between us, not really something that was anyone else's business. But in those pre-feminist days, I was even expected to want to belong to the MIT professors' wives' organization called, to my horror, "Technology Matrons." I was twenty-four years old, with hair almost to my waist, and skirts that stopped mid-thigh. Neither *technology* nor *matron* felt like a word that had anything to do with me, nor did my sense of self rely on my husband's profession.

It was after my second child was born, and our family was living in England where I was studying Waldorf education, that I began to actively ask questions about gender, both personally and as a social issue of the times. My interest in Rudolf Steiner's Anthroposophy (spiritual science), and my attention to the emerging women's movement had been developing hand in hand. While I saw the political and economic battles being waged by women as certainly necessary, this was not where my first interest lay. Even then I was looking for the possibility of wholeness in our being human. I could not focus only on the neglected rights of women or the apparent faults of men. I wanted to know what it would mean to bring the feminine—not just in women but in all people and in our culture—into balance with the masculine, which was so clearly in a position of dominance in so many spheres of life, and indeed in our thinking as well. I felt that Anthroposophy and the women's movement had things to say to each other, and I wanted to be part of that conversation.

A friend and I put up a notice at the local college looking for others who might share this desire, and we were overwhelmed and elated when seventeen women showed up for the first meeting. It was the 1970s by then and our group was discovering its own brand of consciousness-raising. Over the next several years, many more groups were formed out of this impulse in England, Holland, Germany, the US, and Canada. In time, we named the work *Ariadne,* after the maiden in Greek mythology—I will tell her story later in this chapter—and we also began a newsletter, offered workshops, and wrote a book.[1]

Something that emerged very soon in the first of those many groups was the need to become clear about the words we were using to

---

1   Matthews, Schaefer, and Staley, *Ariadne's Awakening.*

discuss our questions and experiences. There are several word polarities that overlap in meaning when gender is the theme, and I want to differentiate how I will use them in an effort to avoid confusion. In referring to our physical bodies we speak of female and male. I will return to the question of transgender later, but for now I am speaking of the basic polarity. We know ourselves as girls or boys, women or men because we incarnate into female or male bodies. When we speak of feminine and masculine we are addressing qualities of soul that show themselves in both women and men; their expression is not bound by our physical bodies. Indeed, we are more fully human when we are able to manifest a balance of feminine and masculine qualities; when we are able to recognize and call forth what is needed in different circumstances.

In characterizing feminine qualities, I look to a sense for wholeness, for relationship and connection. There is a roundness, and openness; there is a living relation to time and rhythm. The feminine embraces, nourishes, nurtures. And here we come to the tricky question of value. We all too easily can think something is good or bad because it is feminine, or masculine, when actually the qualities themselves are quite neutral. It is how we manifest them that brings on judgment. For example we can say that nurturance fosters life, but it can also smother if it is too much. Receptivity—another quality I would identify with the feminine—can be abject passivity, or active acceptance. Diffuse awareness is often identified as a feminine quality: the ability to be simultaneously attentive to a variety of dimensions or needs. While this serves imagination and intuition, and of course multitasking, in its extreme form it manifests as being scattered or distracted.

The masculine shows itself in separateness. It supports individuality, but can also go toward isolation and alienation. Penetration is an obvious expression of the masculine and linear direction, intellect, logic, and focus. Discrimination is a needed masculine faculty, but it can also exclude and do harm. The masculine can steward and guide, and exercise a mastery over the physical world—through thoughtful responsibility or with violence. It rays outward, where the feminine gathers in.

We could, of course, identify more qualities that for the moment I am calling masculine or feminine. The point of speaking of them at all is to acknowledge different and necessary realms of one-sidedness; these different qualities play out in our individual lives, in our relationships, and in society at large. The more conscious we can become of how they work, the less likely we are to have them blindly surge through us or catch us in a valuing war or in simplistic judgments. The more we can see how they work within us, the more we may be able to bring balance into how they interweave in our lives.

Later in this chapter, I will look at challenges for balance between feminine and masculine as forces in the evolution of human consciousness, but first I want to share another image of the human being that has been enormously helpful to me in living through my questions.

THE FOURFOLD HUMAN BEING

Rudolf Steiner speaks about the human being from many different points of view. In the previous chapter I referred to one of his pictures of human threefoldness: body, soul, and spirit. Another image he offers is of the human being today having what he refers to as four "bodies." Of course, these are not all visible or material. They can also be thought of as different sheaths of activity.

Only the physical body can be experienced by our usual senses. It offers a structure, a skeleton, a visible form for our life on Earth. The life aspect itself is related to what Steiner calls the etheric body, or the body of formative forces, or, most simply, the life body. It is what enlivens and sustains our material body. If you imagine a sleeping body and a corpse, you can get some idea of the activity of the etheric body: with the sleeping body there is stillness even though life—the etheric body—still permeates the form; with the corpse there is only a physical body, the material, mineral remains of what was once alive. And like all matter this will eventually decompose. In our physical body we share the qualities of the mineral world, while with our etheric body we share the life possibilities of growth and reproduction that the plant world also exhibits.

Beyond our physical/etheric organism Rudolf Steiner also speaks about the astral or soul body that we can experience as something we share with the animal kingdom. Here we enter the realm of sympathy and antipathy, of sensation, impression, and response. It is through our astral body that we experience instincts, desires, feelings of pain and pleasure, joy and sorrow, even thoughts. We are moved, in ways that no stone or plant can be. This body of sensation is influenced by, and also it offers us information about, our relationship to the world we inhabit.

But it is our "I" that receives the information, which recognizes the feelings and the thoughts. It is our "I" that knows. Here is the part of us that is most essentially human. Our "I" holds our uniqueness. It is our "I" that experiences self-consciousness, can imagine freedom, and allows us to learn. Our "I" can know when we make mistakes; it can take responsibility for our actions, our errors, and our self-transformation. It is our "I" that loves. It is through our "I" that our higher self comes to Earth again and again on the long journey of becoming fully human.

The question of gender becomes much more complicated, much richer, and more interesting when we bring this fourfold picture of the human being into the conversation. I do not bring these ideas as a natural scientist with proofs and statistics for support. What I do offer is a broadening of perspective that I have found helpful in my own life and in my work with others. Discussing gender can be fraught with defensiveness and aggression, with prejudice and chauvinism. I am always looking for pictures of the human being that can allow breath and movement into our perceptions of ourselves and of each other.

If one can hold the possibility of repeated earthly lives, then it is not so difficult to imagine the "I," or higher self, as the part in us that does the reincarnating and is thus, in itself, beyond gender. Rudolf Steiner gives the picture of this eternal, undivided "I" experiencing one life as a woman, the next as a man, and so on in a generally alternating pattern, because the experiences in each gender offer different and necessary learning on the road toward wholeness.

GENDER EXERCISE • Try to find an experience in your life, or a quality you have, that would not be yours if you were a different gender, something that is directly related to your being a girl or boy, a woman or man. What has this brought to your life learning, to your biography, to your sense of yourself as a human being in our time?

In fact, he suggests that the experience of life as a woman calls up a longing in the soul after death to know what life would be like as a man. And vice versa.[2] The opportunities, gifts, and challenges offered by one gender in a given time in history are different enough in their one-sidedness to prompt an intention to balance this out in the next life.

In my early work with women's groups, the guiding question that became clear for me personally was: "Why is my 'I' a woman now?" I did not ask this from any sense of distress; rather I felt grateful and excited to be able to bring deepening consciousness to my experiences. The question assumed an eternal, undivided "I," and also that there was intention in my incarnating as a woman for my own further learning and development. In addition it pointed to my sense for the times we live in: it seemed important to me to consider why my "I" wanted to be a woman now, at this time in history when questions of gender were becoming so important. I felt that I had things to learn from the storehouse of my female body; for example, about rhythm, about birthing, holding, and bearing. I resonated with the urgency of the social questions around me—this was a theme for which I was born.

If indeed it is the case that we generally alternate our gender over the course of lifetimes, then gender chauvinism or blame becomes stunningly irrelevant. If as a man I denigrate women, I am revealing something untransformed about experiences of myself in my last life. If as a woman I blame men for the prejudice against women, for the social conditions that devalue all things feminine, then I need to

---

2   Steiner, *Manifestations of Karma.*

include myself in my last life, probably as a man, as part of creating the current situation. To take this further, if as a woman I work to improve opportunities for women with no regard, or perhaps even disrespect, for men in the process, or if as a man I am unmoved by the need for a more balanced world, I may be creating conditions that I myself will suffer in my next life. At the very least, the idea that we weave through different lifetimes as women and as men can help us to open a more responsible conversation about what serves true human development, and about the need for the free expression of both feminine and masculine qualities in individual women and men, and in society as a whole.

And so we come to Earth, into a female or a male body, into the experience of being a girl or a boy. And our physical body shapes what we will experience, what we will learn, and meet. Among some of the more provocative things that Rudolf Steiner offers on this subject is the picture of an "ideal" human body—in terms of its physical, material form—that is never realized on Earth because of the division into male and female. He suggests that the male body goes more deeply into matter than the ideal, and that the female body does not quite reach the physicality of the ideal. Male bodies are denser, more deeply materialized. Female bodies are softer and more pliable; evidence their capacity to allow another life to grow within them. Of course statements like this must be taken as generalizations; every individual will have his or her own unique form, often proving the exception to the broad picture.

Steiner goes on to say that this tendency toward greater density or softness works into every aspect of our physical form, including the brain. He connects the more rigid, "frozen to a certain degree"[3] brain of the man to his capacity to think intellectually, precisely, but also to his difficulty to follow subtle or multi-dimensional ideas and to a tendency to resist the new. "Any man knows that the male brain is frequently an intractable instrument. On account of its rigidity it offers terrible resistance when one would use it for more flexible lines

---

3   Ibid., p. 205.

of thought. It refuses to follow and must be educated by all sorts of means before it can lose its rigidity."[4]

The female brain, according to Steiner, is more flexible, more open to new ideas and to multiple dimensions of reality. He looks around at his own lectures and points to the greater presence of women at places where there is discussion of the soul or spirit. He points to Mary Magdalene as the first to experience the Risen Christ, much to the consternation of some of the male disciples. "The woman, as such, because of the different formation of her brain and the different way in which she can use it, is able to grasp spiritual ideas with greater facility. By contrast the man because of his external physical corporeality is much better adapted to think himself into materialism."[5]

I must confess that when I first read the preceding quotations, I felt a powerful sense of "Yes!" as did many of my women friends. But I forced myself to try to really observe, without prejudice, in what ways such ideas could be true and, more important, useful to discussions of gender. When I looked at my male friends, I often saw (and sometimes suffered) their need to keep a conversation on one clearly agreed-upon level, but I also experienced again and again a sharpness and clarity in their thinking. Looked at imaginatively, they seemed almost able to walk in the corridors of their thoughts; they could build structures (and I do not mean only "castles in the air"!) in which to consider or illuminate ideas. It also felt true that women could more easily experience multiple dimensions—we could laugh and cry simultaneously, follow associations with interest, be deeply serious while still seeing the humor in something, not to mention being able to talk on the phone while also stirring the soup, with an open ear for the children. But the downside of this kaleidoscopic perspective was often a difficulty in holding on to the many flashing, or passing, thoughts. The memory of having had a good idea was there, but what was it exactly?

Very often I could recognize the tendency that "the psychic and emotional predominate in woman and the intellectual and materialistic in man."[6] But it was also clear to me that unbalanced intuitive leaps

<hr/>

4   Ibid.

5   Steiner, *The Gospel of St Mark*, p. 197.

6   Steiner, *Manifestations of Karma*, p. 203.

and emotional connections are as inhibiting to fruitful communication as is a strictly linear thinking that sticks narrowly to "the point." I cannot repeat enough that these characterizations address natural tendencies; they do not take into account the work of self-development exercised by individual men and women. And, of course, it is just this self-development that experiencing the one-sidedness of gender invites.

Since the early days of the women's movement, there have been endless studies done on female and male differences. Some discoveries seem both obvious and illuminating to the preceding ideas. For example, as a generalization, the male physical body has thicker skin than the female; men have greater muscle tone, and they are usually physically stronger. The female physical body is more often softer and rounder, built for receptivity and transformation. "Females also hear better than males: their auditory discrimination and localization is superior at all ages. Males, on the other hand, see better. These sex-typical advantages in sensory capacities are not learned or acquired through particular forms of experience; they are evident in infancy. Even at a few weeks of age, boys show more interest in visual patterns, while the infant girls attend more to tonal sequences."[7] In study after study girls are more verbally fluent while boys are generally better at spatial calculation.

It is interesting to consider the organs of hearing and of sight in this regard. The ear is a kind of vessel; it receives sound, takes it in. In contrast, the eye rays outward. Dr. Karl König, the founder of the Camphill movement for care of those with a variety of disabilities, took this comparison further in a lecture called *Embryology and World Evolution* (long out of print, but discussed at length in *Ariadne's Awakening*): "from the point of view of comparative anatomy, it is so, that the ear and the ovary, the eye and the testes bear a deep relationship to each other...."[8] König also stated,

> The ovary is a relatively stable organ. The testes, the testicle, is a tremendously vital organ. Everything the testes produces is always new. Millions and millions of sperm cells are, one might say, continuously begotten and created within it. It is a

---

7 From Hunt, *Males and Females* (Penguin, 1973); quoted in Matthews, Schaefer and Staley, *Ariadne's Awakening*. pp. 151–152.

8 Matthews, Schaefer, and Staley, *Ariadne's Awakening*. p. 152.

fountainhead of continual and unending vitality. On the other hand, when a girl is born, the ovary already contains the total number of germs [a translation of the German word *keim*, meaning seeds capable of germinating], only some of which will gradually develop in the course of her life.[9]

Can we see a pictorial connection between how the ear receives sound and how the egg receives the darting sperm? And, further, how the eye, as it looks out into the world, offers an image of the darting sperm seeking to enter the waiting egg?

Since Rudolf Steiner's day, and most especially in the last two decades, brain research has become ever more sophisticated, and many differences have been revealed between male and female brains. For example the male brain is eleven to twelve percent larger by weight than the average female brain, but certain areas, such as the deep limbic system with its relationship to feelings and their expression, are proportionally larger in female brains. The area to do with mathematical ability appears to be larger in male brains. Men tend to process things better in the left hemisphere, which is the area of logical, rational thinking, while women use both the left and right hemispheres equally well and have a larger corpus callosum, which plays a role in the rate of transferring data between the right and left hemispheres. Men use mainly the left hemisphere for language, while women again use both sides. It is interesting to question whether research like this can provide a background to communication patterns noted in Deborah Tannen's popular book *You Just Don't Understand*. She points to the phenomena that women tend to use language to share intimacy, to offer support, to build consensus and community, while men are more likely to speak in order to solve problems, to offer advice, or to establish their identity. Painfully well-known patterns of miscommunication might perhaps be alleviated if women and men could acknowledge genuine differences offered by our different bodies.

Of course, research into differences can also make us very uncomfortable and we may fear how it could be misused to further oppress. Equality of opportunity is essential, and worth upholding

9   Ibid., pp. 150–151.

in every imaginable setting, but this cannot really be done by ignoring differences. Clearly brain size, in relation to gender, is not a significant factor in intelligence, any more than average differences in body size govern essential human experiences; and yet a male or female brain may offer different inclinations for our Earth learning, just as the rest of the physical body does. And, of course, we must still consider the interplay within every woman and man of feminine and masculine qualities, and also the role of socialization in gender identity. Always we return to the undivided "I" inhabiting the body, learning, balancing and deepening as a human being through what the body offers.

The influence that a male or female physical body exerts on our earthly lives is illuminated by the experiences of transgendered people. Whether because of ambiguous anatomy or an inner sense of "being in the wrong body," ever more people (or at least more are speaking out) seem to feel they do not fit neatly into the categories of male or female. This particular, and often very painful, destiny has come into discussion, study, and social activism as people who do not easily identify with either gender have begun to articulate their experiences. Their own stories, their struggles for recognition and rights, and also bestselling books like Jeffrey Eugenides' sensitive novel *Middlesex*, offer testimony to the reality of a sense of self not bound by the gender of the physical body, but that still may long for the experiences that one gender or the other, or both, might offer. Through reading and also through my limited acquaintance with people who have had sex-reassignment surgery, I have become aware of the profound sense that many have felt since childhood of not identifying with the gender of their bodies. By going through the long and painful process of making this change, it seems almost as if they are experiencing two lifetimes in one, at least from the perspective of gender. Their "I" clearly experiences something not comfortable, perhaps not anticipated, about the physical body they were born into, and through the medical procedures they endure, they may achieve some semblance of remedying this situation. Others, who opt not to have surgery, may also find a new acceptance of, and relationship to themselves through their transgender identity.

As mentioned, Steiner adds the picture of the etheric or life body to his consideration of the physical body. As long as we are alive, the physical and etheric bodies cannot be separated. But now Steiner brings another extraordinary idea to the discussion of gender: he suggests that a woman has a male etheric body and a man has a female etheric body. Within the oneness of the physical/etheric organism we find an enduring human wholeness, one aspect manifesting more outwardly, the other more invisible part available as inner potential. As Steiner puts it: "Something of the opposite sex lies hidden in each person... one needs to pay attention to normal experiences. In the man the masculine pole works outwards and the feminine lives more inwardly, while in the woman the opposite holds true."[10] Once again, this is not an idea I can prove logically, yet perhaps we can find phenomena that hint at the truth of such a picture.

As already stated, on average men have stronger physical bodies than do women; yet women's endurance for pain, for example in childbirth, is well known. Could this be an indication of the strength of her etheric body? In addition, women live longer than men; is this the male life force at work? Women's physical bodies are more pliable and receptive (one could even say more vulnerable) than men's. Our still one-sidedly masculine culture has not generally seen vulnerability as a worthy quality, and it has often been put down as womanly. Nevertheless, many women have come to value this aspect of themselves and to recognize that vulnerability is what allows life to go forward; there is no receiving of the new without an openness, a yielding of what already exists. Could the openness of the male artist to his muse, or the male scientist to a new discovery, be a picture of an inner vulnerability to receive inspiration, to bring something to birth? Could it be an image of the activity of a female etheric?

Of course I ask these questions fully aware there are woman artists and scientists, and thank goodness that they finally begin to receive the attention they deserve. What I am looking for here are pictures that might show us something about the wholeness of our female/

---

10   Steiner, "Man and Woman in the Light of Spiritual Science."

male human reality. I am not trying to limit any individual to any particular role or to ignore the wonderful breadth of personal expression that has become ever more possible as a result of feminist attention. It seems quite clear to me that it is really impossible to ascribe any particular way of being as the sole possession of women or men, and the picture of the physical/etheric organism actually helps to show why. For example, if we say a man or a woman is courageous, are we referring to his or her physical body or to the etheric? After pointing to the inconsistencies in how one nineteenth century scientist saw humility as a woman's basic quality, while another saw anger, a third conservatism, and a fourth a revolutionary nature, Rudolf Steiner then gave this picture: "...a man becomes a warrior through the outer courage of his bodily nature, a woman possesses an inner courage, the courage of sacrifice and devotion... In considering only one side of the human being, one is subjected entirely to chance."[11]

A further aspect of the physical/etheric relationship in each individual may offer some insight into the experience of homosexuality. Could it be that for reasons of individual destiny, the attraction that a gay man or lesbian feels for another is somehow more strongly rooted in his or her etheric than in the physical body? In such a situation, it would then make sense that through his female etheric a man is attracted to another man, while with the influence of her male life body a woman is drawn to another woman.[12] Why this particular physical/etheric relationship might be part of a person's karmic situation can only be pondered in each individual case; but the phenomenon itself gives credence to the idea that one is born to homosexuality, that this is a reality of one's incarnation and not merely a question of choice. I must reiterate that the physical and etheric bodies are never separate as long as we are alive, and of course, I am not suggesting anything conscious about how they are interwoven. Nevertheless, in acknowledging their inter-connection, we can deepen the conversation about individual differences within the context of human wholeness.

---

11 Ibid.

12 This idea was first suggested to me by Dr. Bernard Lievegoed in a conversation in the late 1970s.

GENDER MODELING EXERCISE • Recall from your childhood at least one woman and one man who had a strong influence on your understanding of what it meant to be a woman or man. How did they look, how did they act, how did they relate to themselves and to others of the same or opposite gender? See them in your mind's eye; or you might even make simple sketches to help you remember more details. What effect did their behavior have on you at the time? How has their influence—including perhaps your resistance to it—found its way into your own ways of being and relating with others?

For all the opportunities and restrictions offered to our earthly experience by our physical/etheric organism, our "I" still has available to it the interweaving forces of masculine and feminine. Who would say that a woman cannot exercise a discriminating intellect, or that nurturance cannot be done by a man? Every woman and man will find her/his own interweaving and mobile balancing of qualities we might label masculine or feminine. One situation asks for me to be clear, precise, and logical; another calls on my capacity of relating, of listening and feeling into someone else's reality. If as a woman I am only feminine, or as man I am only masculine, then I am a very one-sided person with limited capacity to understand otherness. The more I am able to recognize the breadth of the feminine-masculine polarity, and to see how it exists in the world and within myself, the more my "I" can find a means of expression that will best suit my need at any moment. We can say that it is our astral or soul body that feels the surge and pull and possibility of these different forces. With consciousness I can be more of a determining force for how they will act and interact in my daily life.

This kind of conscious attention belongs to any serious path of inner development or soul purification, the importance of which is felt by many people in our times. Bringing order into our soul life, in this case into the interweaving of feminine and masculine forces, is part of any genuine inner striving. The effort to bring balance does not mean banal neutrality, but rather an ongoing, dynamic attunement in the process of becoming more whole and fully human. And, of course, this does not happen in isolation. This effort by individual women and men is being done within the context of a societal challenge to long existing, one-sided masculine dominance, not only of our social structures, but in our very ways of thinking.

FEMININE AND MASCULINE FORCES
IN THE EVOLUTION OF CONSCIOUSNESS

Have you ever stopped to wonder why we experience a division into female and male at all? Beyond a quick response that it allows reproduction, it is one of the greatest mysteries in our human experience. As in so many other areas, here, too, Rudolf Steiner offers some provocative ideas. He speaks of a time before the division into sexes, when the Earth and the then human bodies were much softer and more malleable, were completely different from the physicality in which we know ourselves today. He describes these early "humans" as androgynous and self-reproducing. Over a very long period of time there was a gradual condensation and materialization of the Earth and of these early beings, until eventually they were becoming too densified to go on being self-propagating; gradually female and male bodies came into being. The human spirit was there, gradually inhabiting multiple evolutionary forms on its journey of human becoming. The journey is long and still ongoing.[13]

Steiner further complicates this picture of the division into the sexes by linking it to the gradual emergence of a new physical organ, the brain, that would serve the development of human thinking and eventually allow an individual, self-conscious relationship to the spirit: "Thus man could use a portion of the energy which previously he employed for the production of beings like himself, in order to

13 Steiner spoke in several places about this basic theme, in particular in
    Cosmic Memory, chaps. 5–7. The theme is also addressed in Matthews,
    Schaefer, and Staley, *Ariadne's Awakening*.

perfect his own nature. The force by which humankind forms a think-ing brain for itself is the same by which man impregnated himself in ancient times. The price of thought is our single-sexedness. By no lon-ger impregnating themselves, but rather by impregnating each other, human beings can turn a part of their productive energy within, and so become thinking creatures. Thus the male and female body each represent an imperfect external embodiment of the soul, but thereby they become more perfect creatures inwardly."[14]

Admittedly, this is a bizarre picture and one surely not to be sim-ply believed. But can we consider it like an early creation myth, and imagine that it has something to tell? Then we may find strange clues that give it some measure of credence. For example all these millions of years later, we still have in English the wonderful word "conceive." We conceive a child through the coming together of a man and a woman, and we conceive a thought as an act of union between per-ception and an idea. We speak of "conception of life," referring to both the sexual act that brings a baby to Earth, and also the view we hold of life itself. And a further clue can be found in a phenom-enon recognized by all attentive parents and middle school teachers as part of early adolescent development: just as the young person's body declares its sexual maturity through puberty, there is also the dawning of a quite new capacity for thinking, and a deepening of self-consciousness.

It is interesting to find further clues in the different imagery of the two creation stories of the Old Testament. In Genesis 1.27, God cre-ated the original human being "male and female" in his own image and only later did he create Adam out of the dust, and Eve from Adam's rib (Gen. 2:7, 2:21–12). Incidentally, why was she not created from a finger bone or a kneecap? What does a rib protect? The imag-ery suggests that it was not until after they had eaten of the fruit of the tree of knowledge of good and evil that Adam and Eve really lost their androgynous, undifferentiated, "not ashamed" reality. When Eve took the fruit "to make one wise" and offered it to Adam, she gave away her capacity for self-procreation and stepped toward a multiplying of "sorrow and conception." They "fell" to Earth and

---

14 Steiner, *Cosmic Memory,* p. 90.

took on "coats of skin"—physical bodies surely, not coats made of some animal fur. In their new life on Earth "Adam knew Eve his wife; and she conceived." The story is riddled with the connection between the division into sexes and the capacity to know, to conceive.

I refer to Genesis as a creation story and not as religious doctrine. It is a myth with rich imagery. And so I must ask: are myths real? Perhaps a better question would be: in what ways might myths be real? It is my conviction that myths tell us something true, though not literally so; they also reveal something about the consciousness of the people who told them, about how those people understood themselves and their relationships to each other, to nature, and to a divine world. Myths are never the complete truth, but still what they tell is not just fantasy. They offer a piece of the puzzle of life on Earth. I feel quite sure that sometime in the far future people will speak of the myth of natural science, or more specifically the myth of DNA, or atoms or bacteria. And they would be wrong to think that these "myths" were not of profound importance, and indeed pointing to something true, at the material level so important for the people of the twentieth and twenty-first centuries.

I want to consider the evolution of human consciousness as seen in the interplay of feminine and masculine forces, but first I will return briefly to Steiner's picture, referred to earlier, of a vastly distant past condition of the Earth and human life. I should say that he offers these pictures as the results of what he calls spiritual research—his own conscious clairvoyant perceptions into the Akashic Record—the spiritual memory of times past. I do not have this capacity of perception. Nevertheless, the pictures that I have received from Steiner have so often helped me to see something more clearly in my own reality or have illuminated a long held question. Of course some of his ideas still remain beyond my comprehension; but since he has been right in so many ways, so helpful in opening my eyes and my heart to such valuable dimensions, I cannot easily reject what I do not immediately understand or know from personal experience. It is my hope that you, too, are willing to consider the essence of these pictures, without needing proof for every detail.

When Steiner describes the early, pre-divided androgynous human beings, he suggests that in form, they were more like what would later prove to be the female. The coming of maleness involved a kind of cutting across that original form, and the introduction of a new element. This dynamic plays out in embryonic development as well. For the first few weeks after conception the fetus does not reveal gender, although, of course, the gender of the child has been determined at conception. Without the introduction of a differentiating force, for example androgens that will bring about maleness, the fetus would go on developing as a female.

Rudolf Steiner also builds pictures of the education given to the emerging female and male beings and suggests that it served a severe differentiation. He states that boys were exposed to hardening forces in order to develop will; they had to undergo dangers, face pain, and develop courage. The girls, on the other hand, were to develop a strong imagination, and so they were exposed to the power and beauty of storms or to the strength exhibited in the combat of the males. These observations were intended to foster inner experiences and the capacity of fantasy.[15] As these special powers developed, early women exercised leadership and influence over the evolving social customs. I quote Steiner here at length because the vision into this long ago time is his:

> The development of humankind can be correctly understood only by those who take into consideration that the first progress in the life of the imagination was made by woman. The development connected with the imagination, the formation of memory, the customs that formed the seeds for a life of law, a kind of morals, came from this side. If man had seen and exercised the forces of nature, woman became the first *interpreter* of them [italics Steiner's].... Through her memory, the woman had acquired the capacity to make the experiences and adventures of the past useful for the future. What had proved helpful yesterday she used today and realized that it would also be useful tomorrow. The institutions for a communal life therefore emanated from her. Under her influence the concepts of "good

15   Ibid., pp. 73–74.

and evil" developed. Through her thoughtful life she acquired an understanding for nature. Out of the observation of nature, those ideas developed in her according to which she directed the actions of men. The leaders had arranged things in such a way that through the soul of woman, the willful nature, the vigorous strength of men were ennobled and refined. Of course one must represent all this to oneself as childish beginnings. The words of our language all too easily call up ideas that are taken from the life of the present.[16]

I appreciate that Steiner articulates this warning; we must be so careful not to transpose pictures of long ago onto our current reality. If anything, we are trying now to release our human experience from such stark differentiation. Many women and men today, myself included, can imagine and indeed are practicing toward a new kind of wholeness, a new balancing of feminine and masculine qualities within ourselves. Nevertheless, in reflecting on our long human story, these pictures of Rudolf Steiner's do seem to be echoed in what we know about early cultures around the world where people looked to Great Mother Goddesses for inspiration and guidance.

With the development of the Women's Movement since the 1960s there has been a growing interest in early goddess figures as feminine faces of divinity. Research into comparative mythology, anthropology, and cultural history suggests a time when people looked to Great Mother Goddesses as the creative source of life. (There are many very fine books exploring this theme. Several are listed in the bibliography. One of the best is by Anne Baring and Jules Cashford, *The Myth of the Goddess*.) This was in the time that is naively called "prehistory," which is to say before what can now be called patriarchal times. We see the Mother Goddess remembered in tiny carved figurines of round fecundity like those found in Willendorf, Austria, dating back 20,000 years. We find her in the archaeological discoveries at Çatalhöyük in present-day Turkey, going back 10,000 years, where the wall painting, the clay figures, the burial practices, and architecture of this ancient center suggest her significance.

16 Ibid., pp. 78 and 80 (tr. rev.).

The Great Mother reveals herself as the guardian of birth and death, the healer, the bringer of civilization, the inspirer of religious ritual. The cultures in which she was worshipped appear to have been peaceful, egalitarian, and stable. Matriarchy was a state of consciousness rather than power. In a time before any real consciousness of division, she was the Cosmic Mother of All, bringing an integrated, non-individuated knowledge of the spirit to human beings on Earth. As Robert Graves, the poet and translator of Greek mythology, put it: "Ancient Europe had no gods. The Great Goddess was regarded as immortal, changeless, and omnipotent; and the concept of fatherhood had not been introduced into religious thought... Men feared, adored, and obeyed the matriarch; the hearth which she tended in a cave or hut being their earliest social center, and motherhood their prime mystery."[17]

There are no written records coming from the times of the Mother Goddess. Writing itself, which did not begin until approximately 5,000 years ago, is an indication that the capacity to hold the wholeness of life is beginning to wane; there is a desire to leave a trace, to create a future prod for memory. Slowly consciousness turned more toward a mastery of the physical Earth, and so the world of the Mother began to erode. The stories that were handed on by word of mouth for countless generations began to be written down, and they tell of the gradual shift from the creator Mother world into one where a son or lover appears and begins to assert a new influence, what we can call a new masculine striving. The battles and overthrows in myths express the change in how people were experiencing their relationship to the cosmos, to nature, and to each other.

> At last, in the Bronze Age [3500–1250 BC], we can hear the hymns sung to her and can follow the story of a goddess who is one yet becomes many, who has a sister or a brother, a daughter or a son. She is single yet she marries; she is virgin and mother; and sometimes her son becomes her consort. As before, she gives life and she takes it away. The goddess has many names and many different tales are told about her, but one story is unvarying.... [She] becomes separated from the one she loves, who dies or

17 Graves, *The Greek Myths,* p. 13.

seems to die, and falls into a darkness called "the Underworld." This separation is reflected in nature as a loss of light and fertility. The goddess descends to overcome the darkness so that her loved one may return to the light, and life may continue.[18]

This is not the place to trace in detail the long road from a kind of unconscious unity of human beings with each other, with nature, and with the spiritual world, through the growing power struggles, toward the ever-accelerating mastery over the forces of nature, and the emergence of the individual from out of the tribe or blood group. It is a story expressed in mythology from all over the world, and also traceable in history. Though by no means limited to this perspective, it also reveals much about the journey to find balance between the feminine and the masculine as archetypal forces in human becoming.[19] For now, I want to touch a few images from our Western cultural heritage with a brief look into Egypt and Greece. Although I am now limiting myself to the mythology of the West, I want to reiterate that the Great Goddess was known around the world and by many names: Isis, Tiamet, Ishtar, Gaia, Inanna, Artemis, Ala, Aditi, Kuan Yin, Tara, Spider Woman ... She has worn many faces and been viewed from many sides.

In Egypt it was Isis who was revered as the Great Goddess, and her influence lasted for 3,000 years. Initially she ruled the people wisely with her husband and brother Osiris. But another brother, Set—the evil desert wind—was jealous of Osiris and conspired to get him into a specially made, and much adorned chest, which was then sealed and thrown into the Nile. Isis went on a long search for her lost love, finally recovering his body, and then becoming impregnated as she hovered over it in the form of a bird. Set discovered her in hiding with Osiris and their new son Horus. He snatched away the body of Osiris, and cut it into fourteen pieces that he scattered throughout the

18 Baring and Cashford, *The Myth of the Goddess,* p. 145.

19 For a more thorough exploration of this theme of feminine and masculine as forces in the evolution of consciousness, see Matthews, Schaefer, and Staley, *Ariadne's Awakening,* as well as many other books in the bibliography.

land. Once again Isis journeyed to find the fourteen pieces and bury them with proper ritual. Meanwhile there was suffering throughout the land, and in time Horus began a battle with his uncle. Isis, too, struggled with the other gods to have them recognize Horus as the son of Osiris, and therefore the next ruler. This part of the story marks a great change happening in human consciousness—in a matriarchal culture fatherhood is unimportant; heredity passes through the mother. Indeed this is still part of Set's claim to rulership—that he is the brother of the Queen. When Isis hands over her leadership to her son based on his paternity, she becomes what Erich Neumann refers to as a "good mother."[20] Here the story tells not of the mother's overthrow by the forces of change, but of her yielding. Nevertheless, when Horus captures and imprisons his uncle, Isis releases Set. This infuriates Horus who then rips off his mother's crown, replacing it with cow horns. In defending Osiris's paternity of Horus, Isis seems to know that change must come, but in releasing Set she also shows that the force of limitation has a place in the all. The power of the Mother is fading, but she herself remains true to her essential wholeness. I will return to the figure of Isis in a more modern form in a later chapter.

When we move to the stories of ancient Greece, we see that the change in consciousness, and the gradual emergence of the individual, is much further along. The Greek myths are tales of human heroes with human cleverness battling a waning maternal cosmic influence that is very often portrayed in the form of female monsters: the Sphinx, the Medusa, the Sirens, the Amazons... Like a rebellious adolescent, humanity is asserting its will in order to come out of the mother's all-encompassing domain. Many of the heroes, at some point in their adventures, marry an Amazon queen—both to subdue her and to absorb her lingering influence. Of course it is in Greek mythology that we also meet the rulership of Zeus, no longer a creator divinity but now a power-wielding father god. Even Athena, the mighty warrior goddess who is still revered for her wisdom, was significantly not born of a woman, but from the head of Zeus. Such an image this: not a natural birth, but a conception (albeit through trickery) from the now all-powerful male head.

---

20 Neumann, *The Origins and History of Consciousness*, p. 64.

Again and again in Greek mythology we find tales of individual skill and a new rationality—signs of a developing masculine force—being brought to bear against an assumed, unconscious, more maternal world order. Earlier I mentioned that I was part of a group that gave the name Ariadne to our work with questions of feminine and masculine. Now I want to tell you why we chose this name.

Ariadne was the daughter of Queen Pasiphae and King Minos of Crete. The Queen had had a dalliance with the god Poseidon and after he appeared to her in the form of a white bull, she gave birth to the half-human/half-bull Minotaur. Because of a lingering matriarchal influence on Crete, the King was not able to kill this monster, and so he imprisoned it in the Labyrinth, from which no escape was possible. Meanwhile Crete had won a long-standing confrontation with Athens, and the Athenians were obliged to send a tribute consisting of a group of youths and maidens who were to be put into the Labyrinth where the Minotaur would inevitably devour them. When Ariadne saw the young Athenians paraded by the palace, she was struck by the majesty of their leader, Theseus, son of the King of Athens. She decided to orchestrate an escape and so gave Theseus a ball of golden thread that he could tie to the lintel of the Labyrinth and unwind as he went inside. With this help, he was able to slay the monster and then lead the young Athenians back out to their waiting boat. In gratitude for her aid, Theseus married Ariadne and sailed away with her toward Athens. But after a stop on the Isle of Naxos he left her sleeping on the beach and sailed away. When Ariadne awoke to discover his desertion, she grieved at first, but in time the god Dionysus appeared and wanted to marry her. This proved to be a much more fruitful union; indeed the crown he gave her can still be seen in the night sky as the constellation Corona.

So why did we choose Ariadne as a name for a group looking for new possibilities of balance between feminine and masculine qualities? We saw Ariadne as a new kind of feminine figure—not a mother, but a potential companion, a partner with whom to move into the future. Theseus, the hero pursuing adventure, personified the growing masculine force in the evolution of human consciousness;

in Greek times this was still just coming into development. Humanity was slowly moving toward greater individual responsibility and consciousness, as well as toward a new relationship with the spiritual world. Plato's dialogues and Aristotle's logic offer other pictures of this shifting consciousness; the movement from the ancient Mysteries to the academies invited a new kind of thinking and an intellectual questioning of all previously accepted assumptions. The old instinctive feminine connectedness, seen in this story in the power of the Minotaur, the protected offspring of the Queen, needed to be overcome. But the emerging hero was still finding his feet, and so the higher feminine—which could offer the life-sustaining thread—then needed to "sleep" for a while, to await the fuller development of the masculine force for individualization.

Of course, the hero and the princess are in all of us, and they have been on a long journey together. The question now is whether they can go forward as true companions. When we chose this name in the 1970s we felt that the hero had begun to abuse his power on every front: in his mastery over the Earth, in conflict for its own sake, even in dreams of star wars. The dominance of the masculine in our social relationships and in our thinking was becoming ever more destructive. It was time for Ariadne to wake up and assume a new role in the story; indeed it was time to marry the god. In so many ways we all, women and men, now have the experience that a potentially new kind of partnership is calling.

In the last several decades we have seen many changes in the ways we understand and practice what it means to be women and men. There is no doubt that girls and women have many more opportunities to express their uniqueness than was the case in the past. And so do boys and men. Nevertheless, what I have been calling the masculine hold on culture and thinking—in both men and women—is still strong and resistant to change. There are many more women doctors, lawyers, and bankers; but have medicine, law, and banking become more balanced, more service-oriented, more collegial professions? The answers are of course mixed.

Finally the question of gender balance returns, again and again, to each one of us. How much am I out for myself, willing to cut past others in my rise to the top, in my adherence to hierarchical social structures? When do I blindly accept current peer pressures and cultural habits without bringing to consciousness and action my own moral integrity? Do I practice collaboration and consensus, ecological awareness, or social justice? Do I seek relationships for worldly recognition, power, or prestige? Can I love—not for self-gratification, but as a deed that I offer from a wakeful heart?

Division into gender is part of our human reality, and yet from within and without we are met with imaginations of potential wholeness. Our times invite a growing consciousness of both the value of our differences and the oneness of our spirit. We have been on a very long road toward the development of personal responsibility and the possibility of an inner balancing of what I have been calling feminine and masculine qualities. Sadly there is still much about modern life that would keep us asleep, as the victims of tradition, power, and the manipulations of advertising. Women have much to do in helping humanity toward a more wakeful and livable future. We cannot do it by merely adhering to the long-established ways. Standing in the fullness of our individualities, we must now bring forward what we know about birth and death, about rhythm, about relating and care, and life itself. And this can only happen when in freedom we can choose to work side by side with men, and when men can freely step beyond the long-held, but no longer productive privileges of their maleness. Then we will be able to go forward as true brothers and sisters, as equal companions here on Earth, building the future together.

CHAPTER 3

UNDERSTANDING TEMPERAMENT:
APPRECIATING OUR DIFFERENCES

I would now like to look at the idea of the four temperaments—sanguine, phlegmatic, melancholic, and choleric—because I have found this to be an incredible tool for social understanding. How often do we experience someone else's behavior to be truly puzzling? We wonder what makes the other act the way he or she does. Or perhaps I observe with distress how another receives something I have done quite unconsciously; how it causes unintended irritation, unhappiness, or misunderstanding. Becoming familiar with the temperaments can help us to live more appreciatively and perhaps even more gracefully with our different ways of being.

The concept of the four temperaments has been worked with since at least the time of ancient Greece. Hippocrates (460–370 BC) related differences in human behavior to the activity of four body fluids that he called humors (blood, phlegm, black bile, and gall or yellow bile). In the second century AD, the Roman physician Galen (131–200) looked for further evidence for the temperaments and connected them more closely to the four elements. In the Middle Ages the Islamic physician and philosopher Avicenna (980–1037) deepened the theory of temperaments to include moral and emotional aspects. Throughout the centuries, the usefulness of temperament as a way of understanding human differences waxed and waned until being largely dismissed in the nineteenth century with the spread of materialistic natural science and the growing interest in environmental factors shaping behavior.

At the beginning of the twentieth century Rudolf Steiner brought a new dimension to this ancient concept by connecting temperament

---

EXERCISES TO AWAKEN INTEREST IN THE FOUR ELEMENTS

With paper and pen reflect on each element in turn. Begin with: "When I think of Earth..." and just write for five minutes without editing. Let memories and experiences arise.

Go outside with paper and pencil and look for manifestations of each of the four elements. Where and how do you experience Earth, Water, Air, or Fire—not only in tangible form but also as forces in creation? Make simple pencil sketches.

Write a dialogue between two elements, for example: Earth and Air.

---

to his picture of the fourfold human being. This image of the human being with four "bodies," or four distinct aspects, was briefly considered in relation to gender in the previous chapter; now we will look at it again from a different angle. Steiner describes temperament as something we are born with, as an aspect of our being that will be with us throughout our lives. It arises through the interaction of our four bodies as we come into incarnation, and it is also related to how the four classical elements—earth, water, air, and fire—are working within us. Like the land, the sea, the sky, and the Sun that make our earthly life possible, so the four elements give substance to all matter and to us.

If you think of the earth element, it is not hard to see how this is connected to our physical bodies. Earth as an element does not mean soil, or land, or the planet, but rather what provides substance and structure, holds form, manifests solidity and density, contracts into matter, and succumbs to gravity. With the element earth we see the laws of the mineral world at work. Without the other bodies the physical body is lifeless, weighty, and will eventually decay. We recognize the physical body through our senses; they give us information about this earth element.

Perceiving the etheric or life body is more challenging, but that it is related to the element of water makes sense—the water of life. Again, we are not talking only about "the" water, but about the fluid element: the force that flows and fills and forms and inclines toward equilibrium and animates lifeless matter. Through its streaming it enables the forces of growth and reproduction. As with the etheric body, we see this liquid element come to life in plants as it moves and shapes in a rhythmic flow.

With the astral body we move beyond the human being in space and time, and enter the invisible world of soul. This is the body of sensation, of consciousness. Like the element of air that is uncontainable, reactive, and invisible, so our astral body opens us to all that is around us, receives impressions, and reacts inwardly to sensation or mood. Mobility belongs to this element, and to our astral body—here is levity, a movement upward and outward.

Lastly we come to the element of fire, which shows itself in warmth and passion. It burns and it expands. It attracts even as it keeps us from coming too close. It enkindles, consumes, and transforms. So, too, the human "I," the bearer of our eternal spirit self, manifests as a force for development and direction. Here is the fiery source of energy, the spark of creativity, and the essential possibility for connection and for love.

Our "I" comes to Earth with an inheritance of many lifetimes; it is the bearer of our individual soul/spirit development and aligns itself with our astral body. As these come to Earth they connect with our physical/etheric organization, which belongs to a stream of inheritance offered by our parents and going back through our ancestors. It is Rudolf Steiner's insight that the temperament arises where these two different kinds of inheritance meet within us: "Temperament stands between the things that connect a human being to an ancestral line, and those the human being brings from earlier incarnations. Temperament strikes a balance between the eternal and the ephemeral."[1]

The four bodies are constituent parts of every human being, just as all four elements combine within us. The way that the four bodies interweave is determined by how the two streams of inheritance flow

---

1   Steiner, *Anthropology in Everyday Life*, pp. 70–71 (tr. revised).

together. In the process of this streaming together, one body assumes a more dominant position, and this gives rise to the temperament. Of course, we can all find aspects of all the temperaments in ourselves because we consist of all four elements and inhabit all four bodies; nevertheless, one or perhaps two temperaments will inevitably be more evident.

This may all sound rather arbitrary, and it certainly raises the specter of boxing people into narrow categories of behavior. I hope that as I characterize the different temperaments—inevitably making generalizations that would never all apply to any one person—you will resist this tendency to pin others or yourself into fixed ways of being. No person is all temperament; rather this is one piece of the puzzle of who we are on Earth. And truly it is a wonderful piece to consider, for as Rudolf Steiner says, "Without the temperaments the world would be an exceedingly dull place, not only ethically, but also in a higher sense. The temperaments alone make all multiplicity, beauty, and fullness of life possible."[2]

These four fundamental types of behavior can manifest in endless variations due to the uniqueness of how our particular streams of inheritance meet. The word *temperament* comes from the Latin *temperare*, meaning "to bring into adjustment" or "to mix." And so the temperament is a mediating factor, establishing a singular equilibrium in each of us. I have sometimes thought of the temperament as being like the major-domo in a restaurant, the one who responds first and brings the guest into a relationship with the establishment.

Our temperament shows itself in how we react to the world, in our walk, our gestures, the tone and rhythm of our voice, and in our habit life. We can be more or less self-aware; we can try to attend to excessively one-sided behavior; but we will never be totally free of our unconscious habits of being. Our temperament is not something "wrong" with us, but, to use another metaphor, it is a kind of doorway through which we meet our life. Although there are many temporarily distorting influences to temperament, such as family or work-place mood, a personal crisis, the speed of modern life, media, substance abuse, and even the weather, our basic

---

2   Ibid., p. 76.

QUESTIONNAIRE
TEMPERAMENT: APPRECIATING OUR DIFFERENCES

Answer the following questions for yourself and for a friend or family member. Try to imagine the different situations and observe the likely behavior for each of you. Gather phenomena.

1. How do you begin your day?
2. Describe your desk or work space.
3. How do you go up and down stairs?
4. What are some of your favorite activities? What is it you like about them?
5. You need some new clothes. What do you do?
6. You arrive at a remote lake for a family picnic and discover that the sandwiches were not put in the basket. How do you react? What do you do?
7. You and a friend or family member are going to visit friends for a potluck meal. They expect you at 5:00. When and how do you get ready to leave home?
8. Your room has become cluttered with clothes, papers, stuff ... How do you approach bringing order to this chaos?
9. What do you remember about your last extended family get-together?
10. How do you make decisions?

temperament does not really change. (I will return to the question of the relationship between a child's and an adult's temperament later in this chapter.) If an awareness of temperament is to be useful, it is important to observe behavior carefully and over time. Here is a questionnaire that can be helpful in gathering phenomena about yourself and another. It might be useful to answer this now, before reading further about the particular temperaments.

I want to say something cautionary about observing others, or even oneself, before I begin looking at the different temperaments. We can observe human behavior anywhere—in a line at the cinema, at the grocery store, at a bus stop, or in an airport. An appreciation for the reality of the temperaments can bring much humor and good will between people and help us accept many minor social irritations. In my classes on this subject there was always much laughter mingled with growing self-awareness and a more open acceptance of others' puzzling, or even at times disturbing, ways of being. But in real life it is important that temperament does not become an accusation, or a way of putting someone down. You know, you have heard or may even have said things like this yourself: "He is such a bossy choleric pain in the neck!" "She drives me crazy with her endless distractions, she's so sanguine." "Why are you so slow? Must you be so phlegmatic?" or "What a pessimistic melancholic!"

That our temperament-colored behavior, at times, can be irritating to others is not hard to understand. Nevertheless, I have often thought that when we experience the temperament of another, we are touching into part of what they must bear in life; we are facing part of the life learning and challenge with which they have come to Earth. Remembering this, I know that others are not trying to make my life more difficult when their temperament is strongly evident; they live with their unconscious habits just as I do. Can we find the heart to help each other with these sometimes burdensome ways of being? Can we see a challenge as a glimpse into a "temperament moment," a kind of pure experience of something universally human that the other is manifesting in his or her very particular way?

When we wish to observe the temperaments at work in others, we face a moral obligation to free ourselves from personally colored judgments. In his major work on the path of inner development, Rudolf Steiner speaks very clearly to the challenge we face when we consider another's behavior: "Observing and contemplating our fellow human beings in this way we can easily fall into a moral error. We can lose our love for them. We must do everything imaginable to ensure that this does not happen. In fact, we should undertake these exercises only when we have developed the absolute certainty that thoughts are realities. Then we shall not allow ourselves to think of our fellow human beings in any way that is incompatible with the profound respect due their dignity and freedom. The idea that another person could be merely an object of observation must never, even for a moment, take hold of us."[3]

I now want to characterize the different temperaments. I must emphasize again that no person, of any temperament, would have all the characteristics I mention; there is no exact profile that any individual would fit. In addition, few people exhibit only one temperament. Each of the temperaments has strengths and challenges. Of course, no temperament is "better" than another. Each opens up particular angles of experience and offers rich life learning. Each is one-sided on its own. Together they contribute to the color and diversity in our social interactions. I know that my descriptions may appear as exaggerations; I offer them as pictures of a range of behavior belonging to the different temperaments.

I am mainly speaking about how the temperaments manifest in adult behavior. In a child, the four bodies are gradually coming into being throughout the years up to twenty-one, a subject elaborated upon in chapter 5. Therefore the relationship between the different bodies is not fully realized until adulthood. Children certainly exhibit the different behaviors I will be speaking of, and attending to temperament can be a great aid in working in a helpful way with one child or in a group context. Nevertheless, it is important to not fix your perception of a child into a particular temperament too early since the different bodies, and ways of being, are still in development.[4]

"I'll go first to get it over with"

If the physical body is in a position of dominance, then the person inclines toward a melancholic temperament. This brings a heaviness of mood, a gravity of experience, and a need for groundedness to feel secure. I want to speak first about melancholics because I know how they long to be seen, even as they will not eagerly put themselves

---

3   Steiner. *How to Know Higher Worlds*, p. 64.

4   Two excellent sources on children's temperaments are Marieke Anschutz, *Children and Their Temperaments*; Ann Druitt, "The Temperaments," in Davy and Voors, *Lifeways: Working with Family Questions*.

forward. It is painful, if also all too familiar to them, to be chosen last and to feel invisible. While they might doubt at times what they have to contribute, melancholics wish deeply to be of service. They want to be self-sacrificial, even as they have difficulty getting outside themselves. They want to open their hearts, but they have high standards. Often they expect themselves to be perfect, and so they can end up being very hard on themselves.

Melancholics do not feel that they are pessimistic, and they often find it offensive when others consider them depressed. Life is "complicated" for them, and there is so much that can go wrong. They feel the weight of things and are on guard against a potential threat or danger. Many years ago we shared a house with a very melancholic man who once told me that when he drove down the road, he was always looking for a place to pull over in case someone was coming toward him on the wrong side of the road. Or another example: I once called, perhaps three weeks ahead, to invite a much-loved relative and her husband for Thanksgiving and her reply was, "If we're still married." To my immediate query whether something was wrong, she simply replied, "No, but you never can tell."

If you love a melancholic and he or she knows it, you may be able to share gentle humor around such exchanges. But it is useless, and even hurtful to try to jolly melancholics out of their perspectives. The concern they feel is real. And they genuinely feel the suffering in the world through the inwardness and depth with which they relate to life. Another's discomfort can even affect them physically. Being able to really help someone else can often relieve them of their sense of isolation. Indeed, melancholics often gravitate toward serving professions where their capacity for empathy can be a true healing force. A young child with a melancholic temperament will eagerly go in search of the Band-Aids if another child is hurt, and will be a willing and patient nurse.

Physically there can be a long, lean, bony quality to the melancholic. The gravity of physicality—the burden of being in a body—can give them a downward orientation, even a slight stoop to the shoulders. They see the rocks on the path through weary hooded eyes. They often like to walk, to feel their feet on the ground, while their hands hang loosely and their steps turn in a bit. Connected as they are to their physical bodies, melancholics feel pain more acutely than people of other temperaments do. A friend once said, "I would never jump into cold water. I go toe, ankle...complaining all the way." They are inclined to take up special diets, and are generally very attentive to the state of their physical bodies—to temperature, to aches and pains, to allergies, to hunger. In combing a melancholic child's hair, the pulling really does hurt more than it does with another child, and special care needs to be taken.

The brain is a particularly physical organ, and melancholics tend to be deep thinkers. They ponder things for a long time and tend to hold onto experiences from the past. If you think of the earth element, it is possible to recognize a rock-like integrity in a melancholic and a solidity of purpose. They are methodical, careful, and reflective. They are also loyal friends, even as they do not seek many acquaintances. It is not always easy for melancholics to express themselves, and sentences can often be left dangling between sighs. Groups are often a challenge for them. As one friend said, "I don't do 'we' so well." Yet for the one who has the patience to find the crystal inside the stone, the depth, compassion, and particular humor of the melancholic are true gifts.

The humor of mature melancholics is rich and resonant. They see the multiple meanings in words, and they quietly observe the idiosyncrasies of human behavior. They are able to celebrate paradox and temper the pain of our stumblings. Some of the greatest clowns and comedians are, in fact, melancholics—in themselves and with the characters they portray; picture for example the world-famous mime Marcel Marceau, or Woody Allen, who has played so many variations of himself in his many movies. Through experiencing the confusions, sufferings, and bruises of life, these artists are able to find bearable ways to mirror them back and somehow lift the pathos of being human. They make us laugh at our human shortcomings even as they invite us to think.

"How do I know what I think until I hear what I say?"

With a question like that we are no longer in the world of the melancholic, but have moved toward a very opposite temperament—the sanguine. Here we enter the air, and the experience of levity, and of openness to every passing impression. Sanguines often do think in dialogue, and they love to talk, which they do rapidly, willingly sharing the moving thoughts that fly through their consciousness. They will take up any subject whether they know anything about it or not. Once, after a class, I overheard a very sanguine student say to one of her classmates, "Don't you feel when a teacher asks a question that you just have to answer it, even if you don't know the answer?" Her much more reserved colleague just looked at her kindly, and quietly said "No."

The airiness of a sanguine expresses itself in great mobility. Lively hand gestures accompany words, the step is light, the eyes sparkle, and laughter is always near, especially for their own jokes and funny stories. Young sanguines giggle and chatter together, dangling their feet, fidgeting. It is no use to tell a sanguine child to sit still; they really can't! Sanguines have very lively imaginations and will quickly fill out a story with their own inner pictures. They may also jump to finish your sentence before you yourself are quite sure where you are headed. They are intuitive, extroverted, optimistic, charming, and exhausting.

The astral body is affected by impressions, thoughts, desires; and so a sanguine lives in the swirling sensations and distractions of the moment. Finishing activities is not their strength; in fact, if you have ever been given one knitted sock for Christmas, it was probably given by a sanguine. They mean to finish the other, they really do! And in fact, they benefit from deadlines. They have ever-good intentions to become more organized, but they jump into so many things and begin so many projects that there is never enough time for everything. With all the new ideas that present themselves, they often forget an earlier plan. They make notes to themselves, but then cannot find them; or as one told me recently, "I write on my hand to remind myself, but then I wash my hands without noticing." They are great list makers, and have even been known to put something they have already done on a to-do list, just so they can have the satisfaction of crossing something off.

Sometimes they become quite overwhelmed by their own multiple interests, by the clutter on their desks, by their own flexibility and sociability. It is easy to become over-stimulated. As one very self-aware sanguine once described it, "It feels like a flapping bird inside, beating its wings and looking for value in a large garage sale." Sometimes this sense of "too much" can lead to an inner insecurity and self-doubt. In this moment of introspection and self-critique, the sanguine might consider that he or she is actually melancholic, but the test here is whether that feeling awakens an immediate sense of "oh, how interesting."

Sanguines do have endless interests. They are often very creative. They love beauty, fashion, flair. They like to travel, and they thrive on change. New people, new adventures, new ideas all spark enthusiasm. While they may long for rhythm and order, they actually feel hemmed in by too much regularity. They do not mean to be fickle, but there is always a new attraction. Perhaps you have had the experience of pouring your heart out to a sanguine friend, and just at the most gripping moment, she says, "I really like your earrings. Are they new?" She does care about what you are saying, but she just noticed those new earrings. As one friend said, "I can't give what I give in a steady way. I give my all, and then I move on."

Sanguines are generally kind and generous. Trust comes easily to them; it is patience and perseverance that are hard. Joy is readily available and they long to share it with others. Young sanguines will try to work harder if they feel someone they admire will appreciate it. Living as they do in the present moment, sanguines do not hold onto grudges; neither forgiving nor forgetting is hard for them. They tend to think of themselves as likeable, though as one said very lightly, "but I don't really worry about that anyway."

A mature sanguine can be a gifted networker. They love to bring people together, to connect ideas, to share what they know. One described having a wide peripheral vision and the joy she feels in weaving things together from different places. This does not feel scattered to a sanguine, but synthesizing and fun. Their ability to jump into new ideas, new experiences, and new relationships can at times be dizzying even to them, but they find pleasure in quickness, and perhaps because they take on so much, are resourceful in finding shortcuts. They rarely bog down for long, ever renewing their good intentions and relishing their ability to improvise as they move along through life.

"I enjoy taking my time."

Now we come to quite another way of being, to the phlegmatic, who wants to live comfortably in the flow of time—no rush, no hustle and bustle, with a careful attention to process. Here the etheric body is especially important, sustaining and ordering life, allowing a sense of wellbeing, building the habits of our days. The experience of ease and flow, and rhythm—these are essential to the health of a phlegmatic.

Physically the phlegmatic may manifest something of the watery element. Think of a drop of water, how it is self-contained, clear, and tending toward pear-shaped, almost a world unto itself. Phlegmatics often have a round softness about them. They walk with a slow, easy gait, not wasting energy with any unnecessary movement. The phrase "make haste slowly" was surely coined about a phlegmatic. Rhythm is in them, and they bring order into their homes, their work routines, and their social lives. They like repetition and well-established patterns. They want to know the schedule, the big picture, the steps that must be taken. They need time to understand a task, and then they will set to work with a calm, thoughtful approach.

Sometimes phlegmatics are characterized as being lazy, but I have not found this to be the case. They can be dreamy, and so may miss that there is a task to be done; and they do not usually rush forward with initiative. But once they take on a job they are dependable and persevering. It is important that the parameters of the task be clear. If you send a phlegmatic child to close the windows in another room because it has begun to rain, you might be surprised when you later go into that room to find the outside door open and a puddle forming on the floor. If you then ask the child why he didn't close the door, he will likely reply, "But you didn't tell me to close the door." He set about the task requested, but did not feel the need to look around for anything extra.

Equally, it is helpful to not pile on too many tasks all at once, such as, "Could you please feed the dog, set the table, and empty the garbage." This kind of request list is likely to illicit a balking, "I can't do all those things at the same time." If there is more than one job needing doing, it is best to carefully outline the whole need in a timely and unhurried way. Phlegmatics are helpful and methodical, and can be very thorough, but they are not particularly spontaneous or flexible. A feeling of time pressure or sudden change makes them retreat into themselves. Indeed, change of any kind can arouse resistance, and so needs to be approached with time and care.

Comfort is very important to phlegmatics both socially and physically. Rarely will they be the leaders of an opposing minority. They prefer to be on the sidelines, cautiously observing and digesting what is under consideration. They are often content to listen and do not need to always make comments, though if they do speak up, they may hold the floor for a while. A group of phlegmatics together will make space for each to speak in turn, and have no problem with silences between them. They are generally comfortable in themselves, as long as they are not pushed.

Phlegmatics also care about the comfort of their homes, their clothes, the chairs they sit on. As one friend said, "I've tried all the chairs and beds in my house, and they are all comfortable." A phlegmatic is quite likely to bring a pillow to a long meeting where the chairs are known to be hard. Beauty is also important, along with the welcoming nature and coziness of an environment. Phlegmatics are content at home and need alone time. They like the quiet things of life, reading or knitting, or maybe just sitting. They do not like to be asked a lot of questions, and will avoid arguments if at all possible.

Good food is much appreciated by phlegmatics, and even more important is the leisurely experience of a good meal. They suffer in our modern times when so many meals are taken on the run—this is unhealthy for all of us, but especially so for phlegmatics who naturally eat slowly, savoring each bite, and need time to digest before returning to work. This goes for sleeping, too—they enjoy the comfort of bed and need time in the morning to enter the new day. A dear phlegmatic in my life is often heard saying, "Bed is man's greatest invention."

Phlegmatics have the challenge to be awake, but when they are, they are good organizers and managers. They are also thoughtful, reliable, and much-valued friends. Their calm gives space to others, their patience is a balm, and they have the neatest and most thorough notes if you ever miss a class or a meeting. They are generally sensible, good humored, and harmonious. Their reflective nature allows them to be careful observers, a gift that often manifests in subtle mimicry and also very fine acting.

Phlegmatics are usually tolerant of others and not easily upset—why waste the energy? However, if over time they finally feel insulted or in some way taken advantage of, their natural good will and acceptance can turn angry. Although it rarely happens, when they do lose their tempers, it can be like a tsunami, with seriously destructive power. A teacher friend once told me that he never stops fights on the playground unless one of the children is a phlegmatic, because that child might be unable to stop himself and could become truly violent. Once upset, a phlegmatic does not easily forgive; even long after the actual offense has been forgotten, the negative feeling remains. It takes a lot to disturb their good nature, and the grudge once formed will not easily go away.

Decision making, like all else, is done slowly by phlegmatics. They may be pondering some life question for weeks, months, or even years, never needing to discuss it with the others who might be affected. Then one day the decision comes, and it is irrevocable. I have heard several stories of phlegmatic husbands announcing at breakfast one day that they wanted a divorce, or were quitting their jobs, or wanted to move across the country—to the utter amazement of their unsuspecting partners. These are, of course, extreme examples, but they exhibit that self-contained quality that is the everyday experience of the phlegmatic.

"There's a job to be done and I'm the one to do it"

With an assertive and confident statement like this, we have again moved to another way of being. People with a choleric temperament have an abiding sense that they can face a problem, assess the need, and find a way to move forward. They enjoy work and like to get things done. A perceived challenge is an invitation to jump in and find a solution. As one friend said: "*Can't* is not in my vocabulary."

Indeed, cholerics have a strong will to overcome any obstacle and a strong heart to better the world. They will often be the first to take on a cause or a task.

This directness, this inclination to go straight to the point, can be challenging to people of other temperaments. Cholerics genuinely feel they have the right vision—they see the goal and know what needs to be done, and by whom, to make it real. They do not necessarily perceive themselves as bossy or controlling, although others may often wonder and complain behind their backs, "Who does she/he think she/he is?" The truth is that cholerics feel indispensable to the functioning of the world—in play, in social circumstances, in institutions, in everyday life. As a self-reflective and honest choleric once said, "I'm not bossy; I just have better ideas. My leadership is to allow others to manifest their own strength." Cholerics have the experience that things go better when their ideas are followed, and they do not understand why others do not just agree with them. Choleric children are very familiar with the frustration of wondering: "Why should we waste so much time and energy considering other options of what to play, when in the end, we know my idea will be the most fun?—It always is."

Even adult cholerics suffer this dilemma. Their confidence in the rightness of their own ideas is not simply a question of pride; cholerics experience it as fact. They trust their own strength and sense of direction. When their leadership is rejected, it is felt as a rejection of their very being. Cholerics really do want to be of service, and they are hurt and confused when their leadership is not wanted or criticized. But since it is difficult for them to show vulnerability, others often experience their bombast more than their hurt.

Cholerics have abundant energy, and they do not want to waste it—there is so much to be done! Like the fire that is their element, they radiate enthusiasm and burn with passion for ideas or for the task at hand. By nature they are efficient and impatient. It was surely a choleric who first coined the phrase, "Let's cut to the chase." And if others complain in review about a lack of social process, the choleric is likely to retort, "We got the job done, didn't we?" Nevertheless, cholerics can feel genuinely sad when they realize they have been too

much for others. That is never their intention; they were only following their own intuition, passion, and direction.

Physically cholerics are most often compact and concentrated.
Though not necessarily large, they have a commanding presence and
easily fill a room with their energy. They have a direct gaze from
fiery eyes, straight backs, quick gestures, and quite often fisted hands.
Their tread is firm, heel first, and you may hear them stomping up
stairs from rooms away. Even when they try to tiptoe, the floor shakes!
Waiting can make them restless. They drum their fingers and want to
get going.

Self-reflection is not a natural strength of cholerics, although as
they get older they generally do fear being too forceful. They are often
surprised that others find them intimidating. They may know they
need to work on listening better, or to temper the speed of their ideas,
but this is hard when they trust their intuitions and are so willing to
give their all. Indeed they are most often generous, dedicated, and
hard working. But they do not necessarily take feedback well; and
they will argue back with righteous self-justification, perhaps even
with a scathing critique about the shortcomings of others. This, of
course, makes it hard for some people to confront them. The best way
to hold a mirror to their behavior is to be completely direct. They do
not easily pick up subtle hints.

Trust is very important to cholerics. They consider themselves to
be trustworthy, and they expect the same from others. They can be, as
one said, "pathologically honest." They have a strong sense of justice
and will rise to another's defense without being asked, whether their
help is wanted or not. But just as often, they bring important attention
to things needing to be addressed. They can have quite a rigid code of
honor, and their respect must be won. Respect is an important word
to them—they speak of it, want it, and grant it carefully. When a
choleric loses respect for someone, the relationship becomes difficult.
They can be forgiving, but they will not easily forget what they consider to have been unjust.

Cholerics are serious people, and do not easily let down their mission to make the world better. They live with a sense for the future
and feel that life should be lived at the edge. They have a hard time

being "low-key." They enjoy the intensity of other cholerics, but have also been known to apologize to their families after spending time with someone they experience as more choleric than they are. In that context they can understand, for a moment, why others sometimes think they are "too much" or too caught in their own sense of rightness. Of course, in another moment, they will question that use of *too*—perhaps others are actually too little, or too passive. Who says they themselves should not be the standard? Where is that middle ground anyway?

MIXING IT UP

As stated, it is rare that someone would exhibit only one temperament. Most often we have two that play strongly into our habit lives, sometimes at cross-purposes to each other. The following chart may be useful in helping to identify primary and secondary temperaments. While not impossible, it is difficult to have temperaments that are across from each other, unless perhaps the dominant one is between them, with added qualities toward either side. Usually we have one stronger and one secondary temperament. Sometimes there is one that seems almost absent, and it can be useful to look on the chart at the one opposite from the missing one to see if that might be one's primary one.

Perhaps because the sanguine and the choleric are more extroverted temperaments, while the phlegmatic and melancholic are more naturally introverted, some combinations feel less comfortable together than others. For example, as a mix of melancholic and choleric, one can feel a more inward, sensitive, and reserved nature at times in conflict with an outwardly directed desire to act. Of course our combinations also bring movement and creativity into our habit lives.

There is another way of looking at how we each manifest a combination of temperament characteristics. This has to do with how we express ourselves through thinking, feeling, and willing, the three essential activities of our soul. Of course in real life they are always interweaving; nevertheless it can be very useful to consider how each of these different soul activities presents itself. Perhaps my thinking

DIAGRAM #1 The Four Temperaments

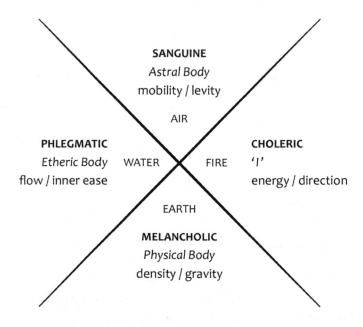

is very sanguine: I easily follow associations, wander off topic, even forget at times what the topic is. But I may also recognize that my feeling is more choleric: I feel things strongly, jump in with my likes and dislikes, and express myself passionately. Or perhaps my thinking is more melancholic and I doubt my perceptions or put obstacles before my decisions; and yet my will may feel quite phlegmatic, as I wait for others to move me to activity or I am content to stay comfortably in the background. Looking at our behavior through this lens can be very illuminating; we may begin to better understand some of our internal conflicts and through the centeredness of our attention bring more cohesion into our daily lives.

As an example of how combinations can play out in real life, I will speak out of my own experience. My husband often bemoans the fact that his sanguine nature pursues multiple interests and responds to the many requests that come his way with a ready "yes," but then it is his phlegmatic side that is left with the task of fulfilling his over-commitments. I know this syndrome as well, but with a variation: my sanguine side also replies positively to much that comes my way, but

TEMPERAMENT EXERCISE • Draw or journal about an experience in your life when your temperament was a primary factor in what occurred, something that you could call a "temperament moment." Be as detailed as you can. Do this with an experience from your childhood and one as an adult.

then it is the choleric in me that suddenly experiences too much procrastination and disorder and so zooms into a flurry of productive activity. Needless to say, there can be challenges when our different ways of taking up a task run into each other—he wants to retreat from my whirlwind of energy, while I impatiently want him to speed it up!

How temperament plays into our relationships is a subject for endless reflection. Do opposites attract or are we drawn to others with similar ways of being to our own? In my experience there is no easy answer to this question because so many different factors play into our attractions and resistances. But it is not hard to see how our unconscious habits—the ways we react, take up a task, or meet a deadline—can become a source of struggle in long-term relationships. Here the idea of temperaments can be a great tool for both self-awareness and appreciation of the legitimacy of difference. In our own self-development we are challenged to attend to the effects, and most especially the excesses, of our temperament. As parents, teachers, partners, colleagues, or friends, our ways of being inevitably exert influence on others.

Children's life habits are strongly shaped by parents and teachers, and they are well served when the adults around them are able to control the excesses of temperamental one-sidedness. The bodies and behavior patterns of the young are affected by what they experience around them—right into the development of willpower, moods, sense of wellbeing, trust, and even breathing. Children are particularly vulnerable, for example, to a flightiness that never finishes a project, to a shadow of doom that hangs over plans and events, to a rigidity of routine that has lost all life or possibility of spontaneity, or to the booming shock of an explosion of words or activity.

Gender is also an influencing factor in how we live with our temperaments, and others may respond differently to how a woman or a man exhibits a particular way of being. For example, many choleric women I know have suffered being referred to as unfeminine because of traditional views of masculine and feminine. Even after years of feminism, many people are more accepting of a choleric man than a choleric woman. Behavior that is seen as strong and showing leadership in one gender is too often seen as aggressive or even threatening in the other. It can be very useful to ask ourselves in what unconscious ways we judge temperament-related behavior as appropriate to one gender or the other; this kind of self-reflection can help free us from the trap of stereotypes and open us to the uniqueness and the gifts of every individuality.

Our temperament can be additionally colored by factors like our nationality or age. I will leave the question of folk coloration to your remembrance of jokes about people from different countries. These are often not very politically correct, and yet they capture something of the different shading that comes from being, for example, French, German, English, or Italian. Our individual temperament does not change, but we can experience that it is tempered by other factors of our biography.

As people grow older it is definitely possible to see how the individual temperament is tinged by an age-related mood. All children have an element of the sanguine: they love to play, they ask a lot of questions, and they live fully in the present moment. Adolescence and young adulthood are when a choleric mood may appear as we make plans for the future and set out on the adventure of life. Middle age with its multiple responsibilities and burdens can bring a melancholy shading; we feel the weight of all we are carrying, including the consequences of our own ways of being. In old age people tend to feel, like the phlegmatic, the need for rhythm and order, and for doing one thing at a time. Comfort becomes ever more important.

I hope it is clear that even as the temperaments offer great riches to our life experiences and interactions with others, they also create challenges for our personal development. An important question for self-awareness is: do I have a temperament, or does my temperament have me? How much of my behavior is the playing out of habits that seem to take me over? When manifesting through unconscious habits, our temperament can all too easily distort our reactions to situations and people. Think for a moment of how we can act when we are overtired and so not really centered in ourselves: we may become bossy and controlling, or distracted and scattered, or dreamy and shut-down, or anxious and isolated. Always we are challenged to stay awake in ourselves, to reconnect to our true center, to be guided by the strength of our "I."

While we will not change our basic temperaments, with conscious attention we can bring a balancing force toward how they manifest. The first step, of course, is to recognize how my temperament plays into my behavior, and we may actually reject this kind of self-knowledge for quite a while. "I'm not really like that... I just happened to do that thing this once." But gradually I may become aware of how this or that habit wreaks regular havoc in spite of my deeper intention. Then I have the challenge to accept that this is part of me. Without acceptance of how I really am, I will not find a way to bring more attention or develop more control toward the future. With acceptance, I can try to find small steps that will build more balanced behavior.

Many years ago I was traveling with two friends, and we were speaking about the excesses of our temperaments and what we could do about this. One friend recognized how readily she takes control of situations, even when this is not needed. So she set herself the task to let the driver drive the bus. This was in Greece where riding on a public bus around hairpin curves in the mountains had an undeniably life-threatening element. But still, to give over the inner desire to control the driver was a worthy and challenging practice—and it brought the benefit of a much less stressful ride. My other friend decided she would find something about which she could laugh at herself at least once a day. And I decided that I would be more attentive to unclenching my fists—that the world would probably continue to function without my constant grip on things!

If we can remember that the different temperaments bring variety and color into our life experiences, we will be able to rise above their sometimes burdensome expressions. They are part of our life learning; part of how we can grow in humility, self-control, and compassion; and part of how we connect to ourselves, to others, and to life on Earth. As I close this chapter, I am reminded of a story—the provenance of which I can no longer recall—of the gardener who kept writing to the Department of Agriculture for advice on how to get rid of a particular weed. After many unsuccessful suggestions, the final reply came with what I consider to be most needed in our approach to temperament: "We have no more advice to give you on ridding your garden of those weeds. May we therefore simply suggest that you learn to love them."

CHAPTER 4

SEASONS OF LIFE: PHASES OF DEVELOPMENT

In the late 1970s, like so many other people, I read the bestselling book *Passages*, by Gail Sheehy; and was inspired to begin my own long exploration of adult life phases. I had already studied child development, and was particularly moved by the works of Jean Piaget and Erik Erikson. Now it was adult development that filled me with questions. I found I wanted more than just phenomenological descriptions of occurrences in different life cycles; I wanted to know why quite disparate lives seemed to develop along predictable pathways. I knew that it could not only be about acculturated life events being similar, but that there must be something deeper at work in the possibilities and challenges for development that people face at different biographical stages.

In these same years, from 1977 until 1981, I eagerly awaited each new quarterly edition of the *Newsletter of the Anthroposophical Society*, for the latest installment of "The Human Life" by George and Gisela O'Neil. These articles, inspired by Rudolf Steiner's spiritual scientific research, provided the depth for which I was searching. (The articles were later compiled by Florin Lowndes as *The Human Life*.) In 1979 my studies were further enriched by the English translation of a bestselling book from Holland, written by the physician Bernard Lievegoed, called *Phases: Crisis and Development in the Individual*.

Here were clear pictures of the human being from the vantage points of biological, psychological, and spiritual development. The one-sidedness I had experienced in so many other perspectives on human life was overcome by this threefold approach. In real life, body, soul, and spirit are always interweaving, and it is somewhat artificial to try to characterize them separately. Nevertheless, acknowledging that difficulty, we can try to appreciate their different contributions to our life on Earth. I feel this is particularly important in an age when so many people consider the human being to be essentially a material, animal body. Psychology, of course, acknowledges the reality of soul (psyche), but all too often the idea of spirit is simply enfolded vaguely into the soul or denied altogether. It is one of Rudolf Steiner's great contributions that he elaborated in a variety of ways on the threefold-ness of body, soul, and spirit. We are invited to continuously shift our perspective, to find ever-new angles from which to view the living human being.

The body provides a vessel for the spirit and soul to exist on Earth. The individual spirit gives the impetus to be here. Through body instincts and sense experiences the soul is informed about physical reality. Through the limbs the intentions of the spirit are fulfilled. The soul is continuously mediating between spirit and body, bridging them and informing our unique personality. Thinking, feeling, and willing are all activities of the soul, with thinking more connected to the spirit and willing finding concrete manifestation through the body. Feeling exists in the center of the soul's activity, exercising sympathy and antipathy, relating us to both spirit and matter.

Characterizations like the preceding can sound so abstract, and every statement invites a contradiction. Body, soul, and spirit are not fixed entities to be quantified or qualified. They exist in life, and in interaction; human life on Earth exists through them. Bernard Lieve-goed offered a simple diagram for how one could picture these three domains of human experience. I have lived and struggled with this portrayal for many years and now offer my own variation.

This threefold perspective can also be shown on a timeline for an individual life—not as a template, but because it shows basic land-marks, with the differing pathways along which our body, soul, and spirit develop and interact. This picture assumes that the individual human spirit or "I" reincarnates, as described in previous chapters—that it comes toward a new life on Earth with its own very individ-ual evolving heritage. Only gradually does it connect with the body sheaths (physical, etheric, and astral) that are developing throughout

DIAGRAM #2   Three Domains of Human Experience

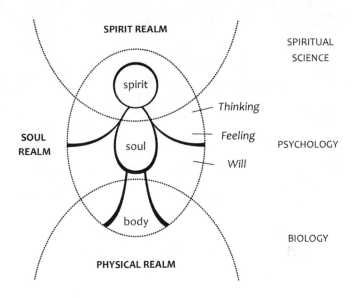

the first twenty-one years. Then in the middle of life this spirit or higher self penetrates and reworks what has come to life for the body and soul. Finally as the individual moves toward old age, the spirit begins to separate—to become free—from the strong connection it has had with the body, until it finally excarnates with physical death.

The biological growth line—anchored through physical inheritance and the parental bloodlines—moves slowly toward maturity. The human child takes its time to become an adult. There is tremendous growth activity from the helpless infant, through childhood and puberty toward the independent twenty-one year old. Then, in a general sense, from the point of view of our physical bodies, we can see a time of relative stability and equilibrium, at least until the forties. After that, even as we may wish to resist it, there is a gradual decline of physical vitality. It takes longer to recover from a cold, or to climb a hill; our bodies ask for some attention. In spite of whatever exercise programs we may follow, as the years go by, our bodies become less vigorous, flexible, or strong. In old age sense organs generally become less acute, and physical forces slowly diminish, until finally the body can no longer sustain further life.

DIAGRAM #3   Timeline Number One

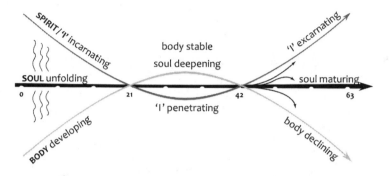

As the biological and spiritual lines of development are coming into being, the soul or psychological domain unfolds between them. Throughout the years of childhood and youth, the individual experiences life on Earth with all its obvious gifts and also its suffering and trauma; and all the while, the soul is emerging, practicing its way into individual thinking, feeling, and willing, laying the foundation for meeting life's challenges and opportunities throughout the rest of life. The "I" inhabits the soul, and this soul dimension will deepen through the coming decades of adulthood. Rudolf Steiner gives names to different aspects of the soul that gradually come alive in the years between twenty-one and forty-two: the sentient soul, the intellectual or mind soul, and the consciousness soul. I will return to this when describing the individual phases in later chapters.

Another insight that Rudolf Steiner brings to this picture of development is the idea that up until the forties, every human being is, from a certain perspective, recapitulating the evolution of human consciousness in general. He suggests that all of humanity is now developing what he calls the consciousness soul, in a way parallel to the phase of individual soul development that takes place in the years from thirty-five to forty-two. I will go into this further in coming chapters, but for the moment I want to introduce the idea of a kind of threshold that we each cross as we enter our forties. From now on we are ever more responsible for whom we are becoming. We are challenged to wake up to the spirit part of ourselves, to take our inner development more seriously, and to know ourselves in an ever more integrated way.

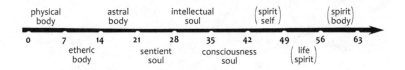

DIAGRAM #4   Timeline Number Two
Seven-year phases

physical body	astral body	intellectual soul	(spirit self)	(spirit body)

| 0 | 7 | 14 | 21 | 28 | 35 | 42 | 49 | 56 | 63 |

etheric body — sentient soul — consciousness soul — (life spirit)

Our soul growth, stagnation, or decline is now dependent on how we live our daily lives. I cannot help but think that this may be the true meaning of the folk wisdom that "Life begins at forty."

If we awaken to this inner dimension, our soul can soar with our spirit as it gradually becomes freed from a dependence on the body. If we identify ever more strongly with our physical self, our material success, or our worldly possessions, then our soul will go with the body along its inevitable decline. This is, of course, neither a strict duality nor a once-and-for-all biographical moment in our forties; rather we meet the opportunity and challenge for inner wakefulness ever and again in the second half of life, and so further shape our soul as we grow older.

From the perspective of evolving human consciousness, the stages of development after forty-two are a kind of premonition of what all humanity will be developing in future epochs. This spirit development is not fully predestined, neither for the individual nor for our human future. It is ours to evolve out of our awakening freedom. It asks for responsibility from each of us, and all of us together, to become ever more conscious stewards of the invisible as well as the visible world. Rudolf Steiner gives names to these future stages of development—spirit self, life spirit, and spirit body—and connects them with the phases from forty-two to sixty-three.[1]

For years this timeline drawing seemed adequate to me, even with its rather vague arrow moving out beyond sixty-three. Then, however, I entered my sixties, and it became unacceptable to have nothing more to offer past sixty-three. I could understand the thought, coming from

---

1   Characterizations of the different bodies, as well as of the soul activities of thinking, feeling, and willing, can be found throughout Rudolf Steiner's work; in particular, see *Theosophy*, chaps. 1 and 2.

Steiner, that after this age and even more so after seventy, we have met the basic pre-birth intentions of this lifetime. From then on we would of course still be dealing with the consequences of those intentions, depending on how we took them up throughout our life so far; but totally new things might have more to do with the future than with the past. The phrase "a child of the gods again" is sometimes used to characterize these later years, although I must confess that there were times in my middle sixties when my inner response to this idea was a wry, "The gods must be crazy!" It did not feel like a time of simple release from the bindings that had, until then, held my life together. Instead, it felt like being both dropped and more tightly bound at the same time.

As I looked for a model of life that could encompass the years beyond sixty-three, I found myself returning again and again to the image of the seasons of the year. Still working with large periods of twenty-one years (three times seven), my picture could easily expand to eighty-four. I continue to look for images that can include the years beyond that, and I consider this search important as more and more people are living into their nineties, and even beyond 100. For now I must let the years beyond sixty-three expand indefinitely. To older readers, I very much welcome contact with you about your experiences, about how you have felt the differences in the phases beyond sixty-three.

As we move through the course of a year, we can experience many changes in the natural world around us. I live in New England and so have a rich encounter every year with the changing seasons. Obviously this is different in other parts of the world. And yet, even in the tropics, where there may be little variety in temperature throughout the year, there are still subtle differences that can be felt—in the life cycles of plants, in the winds and tides, in the quality of the light, in the rainy, dry, and in-between times. Because my personal experience of the Earth's rhythms of growth and decay, life and death, renewal and decline has been shaped by four distinct seasons, I am drawn to seeing a human lifespan from this fourfold perspective.

Each season informs us about the Earth, and gives content to our outer and inner experiences. In a garden, each season has its own gifts to offer and its own requirements of attention. But many human beings now live in large cities and can easily ignore the demands of nature, finding seasonal change more a question of fashion or holiday planning. Central heating and air conditioning are so standard in the developed world that many modern people, hustling between their temperature-controlled homes and offices in their temperature-controlled cars have a limited sense of weather changes, except as an annoyance or as information from an ever-available weather report. Of course I exaggerate here, but only to invite a moment's pause to consider the extraordinary gift that the seasonal cycle of the year offers us.

Sometimes the serendipity of life is such fun. In the midst of working on this chapter, I experienced a chance subway delay after teaching a class in Brooklyn. It offered me two hours to wander in Grand Central Station before returning home to Massachusetts. Normally I speed through with an admiring glance at the starry ceiling, but this time I went exploring and ended up at a photography exhibition of work by the Korean artist Ahae, who over the course of two years took almost a million pictures out of one window in his home. Here were the seasons laid out with great sensitivity and subtlety. The same landscape, sky, animals, birds, trees, bushes, water—the same and yet so different when viewed at different times of the year. The parallel between the developments in nature through the cycle of the year and the changing seasons of a human life from birth to death was very clear to me.

As I write now, spring is just beginning to burst forth. For weeks the days have been unusually cool and wet, and so I have been able to watch the buds on trees slowly expanding, looking ever more pregnant, holding on until just the right moment for blossom or leaf to unfold. The return of perennial flowers reminds me of children playing peek-a-boo. Something starts to show on a sunny day and then contracts back into itself after a frosty night. The warmth of the Sun and the gentle breezes offer promise of life to come. It is as if the air is skipping around the garden. And the delicacy of spring green catches my breath every year—it feels completely new, even on a craggy old tree. Spring, like a young child, stirs our hearts and gives us hope. It is a time of rebirth, of resurrection, and of tremendous growth.

In outer nature what is emerging takes its time. We rush it at our peril. I was once looking at a poppy just as the bud husk fell off and the flower unfolded in front of my eyes. It was a great gift to be allowed to watch this miracle. A few days later I again saw a bud husk perched on the tip of another almost emerging poppy, and I could not resist giving it a gentle flick with my finger so I could observe the unfurling once again. But the time was not right, and that flower never did open. My eagerness had forced the covering off too soon, stunting further growth and through my dismay, teaching me a lesson about timing and about the internal forces at work in life's thresholds.

Although we may celebrate Midsummer Day or toast the birthday of a twenty-one-year old, who of us can pin down the moment when spring moves into summer, or when the young person becomes adult? There is a process, a gradual transition until one day we know we have crossed that illusive line. In the outer world the greens grow richer and more varied, not unlike the life experiences of those in their twenties. The foliage is ever denser and the shadows deeper, as with life in one's thirties. Summer brings verdant lushness, expansion, bright flowers, fruits, and berries. The days are long and the Sun is bright and hot. This is a hot time of life, even as there can also be periods of languid serenity, and a sense of timelessness. Often the air is sultry. Sudden thunderstorms flash by. The years from twenty-one to forty-two are full with finding our way, meeting our important people, developing our work and, for many, building our families. We can feel stretched almost beyond our limits, spread out, and wondering where our center really is.

But then gradually the days grow shorter, cooler; we are drawn in, and we become aware that we have new work to do. The air is crisp and invites us to awaken, to prepare for winter. As we move into our forties, we are indeed challenged to awaken to our essence, and we need courage and a new source of energy to rise above physical decline and know ourselves in a more enduring reality. The leaves of autumn shout their farewell in brilliant hues: a last hoorah, a splendid fling of red, orange, and gold. It is time to gather in the harvest; and as we go through the years from forty-two to sixty-three, life's lessons declare themselves for our reflection. The ground grows harder and the grasses

"We should actually retain the possibility, all through life, of rejoicing in the coming year, because each year charms forth the divine-spiritual content of our own being in ever new forms. I want to emphasize this point. We should really and truly learn to experience our life as capable of development not only in youth, but through its whole span between birth and death."

— RUDOLF STEINER (Sept. 1919)

become brown and matted, but the sky has a clarity unseen in summer. Can we look out with open eyes, and can we experience the promise of resurrection in the beauty and variety of the seedpods that autumn forms, in the kernels of life learning that middle age offers us?

As time moves on, we experience contraction all around us, and the darkness grows. Without leaves the trees look skeletal; twigs show their thorns. In early winter the landscape becomes more visible; the veil of leaves, of abundant life, is gone. We are down to bare essence, and the cold pushes us indoors. And so it is as we move through our sixties and beyond. The life we have lived shows in our health, and on our bodies and faces, even if we vainly thought we could escape the marks of time. Our habits become more fixed, our bodies stiffer. And here, too, we are invited to go inward, to know our spirit core, and to do the work of life consolidation and review. In winter, beneath the hard ground, there is much activity going on, preparing for a new spring. In spite of the apparent dormancy outside, the light grows ever stronger after the Winter Solstice, and the forces working toward renewal are great.

Snows come and the winter world is white, like an older person's hair. There is mystery in the stillness of a snow-covered land. In ancient times people told riddles around a winter fire, trying to penetrate the clues and find the answer at the riddle's core. As we grow older, we—and those who love and care for us—stand before the riddle of our long-lived story, trying to read the clues and understand the mysterious becoming of this particular human being.

To live through the cycle of the year with a consciousness of the seasons—of the gifts and challenges, the rhythms and growth patterns at different times of the year—is a great aid in deepening our sense for human development. Paying attention to the seasonal changes, for example by drawing a tree throughout a year, builds our capacity for perceiving transformation; and this can lead to a deeper appreciation for others' and our own ways of growing. Rudolf Steiner gave many wonderful verses that speak to the exchange of finding oneself in the world, and the world in oneself. Here is one:

> Perceive the secrets of your soul
> In the countenance
> The wide world turns toward you.
> Perceive the living essence of the world
> In the countenance
> Imprinted by it on your inmost soul.[2]

Of course it is important to remember that for Steiner the "world" extended beyond the world of nature to include the invisible realities of spirit as well. Nevertheless, the practice of observing phenomena in the natural world opens up a living experience of development in extraordinary ways.

As we have become ever more technologically savvy, we have been tempted to ignore the rhythms of nature—to supersede them with our human will. Why not have asparagus or strawberries in winter in the northern hemisphere if we can fly them up from somewhere in the south? Or better yet, why not force nature to grow what we want, when we want it? We can do all this, and we do. But in the process, do we lose a capacity to appreciate the particular springtime taste of freshly picked asparagus or sun-sweet strawberries—to anticipate, and wait for, and savor them? I do not mean to fall into nostalgia or to make an anti-technology screed here; I am as grateful as anyone for much that makes our modern world comfortable and full of diversity. But I want to be conscious, and responsible, about the choices I make and the rhythms I am bending. I applaud the expanding movement to buy local produce, and the growth of sustainable farming practices

---

2   Steiner, *Verses and Meditations*, p. 55.

for many reasons, not the least of which is that they invite us into a more wakeful relationship with nature.

Sadly, I cannot help but see in the ways we presume to be masters over nature's timing a connection to what we do with children: how we push them to develop adult behavior and skills at an ever earlier age, and how our kindergartens have turned into hothouses for an intellectual development that is out of season and, for the children, ultimately unhealthy. We have much to learn about the significance of rhythm in nature and in ourselves.

The view of human development that I would like to explore in the coming chapters is based on seven-year phases. Immediately we face the question, "Why seven?" Perhaps it is not difficult to see that seven is a rhythm connected to development. We are used to a week of seven days, a rainbow of seven colors, and a scale of seven notes. Passing through seven steps we seem to come to a new beginning, and we know we have been changed by the journey.

From many directions we meet seven as a significant number—in myths, fairy tales, religious doctrines, and varied esoteric traditions and practices. Shakespeare has the character Jaques, in *As You Like It*, begin a famous monologue with the lines: "All the world's a stage,/And all the men and women merely players;/They have their exits and their entrances,/And one man in his time plays many parts,/His acts being seven ages."[3] And, of course, references to the "seven year itch" abound. There is also the folk wisdom that the cells of our body are all replaced over the course of seven years. While this is not literally true, it is a provocative picture of ongoing change amidst an enduring experience of self. And it is interesting that it is seven, not six or eight, that persists in this "myth."

Many readers will be familiar with the popular television series *Seven Up!* made for the BBC by the British director Michael Apted, which began following the lives of a socially diverse group of children in England, when they were seven years old. The intention in 1964 was to make a one-off statement about the British class system; but

---

3   Shakespeare, *As You Like It*, act 2, scene 7.

the show was received by the viewing public with such interest that the filmmakers have continued to revisit the same group of people every seven years. The latest installment, taking the participants to the age of fifty-six, opened in American movie theaters in January 2013. Leaving behind its original political agenda, the series has become a much admired documenting of human development, following different life stories at seven-year intervals. In spite of hugely varied life circumstances there are surprising commonalities in relation to work, family, ambition, or self-esteem that manifest in the particular phases.

And so I return to the question, "What is so special about seven?" Here again I have found Steiner's research and insights to be extremely helpful, even as they take me into deep mysteries. I mentioned in chapter 1 that Steiner had much to say about the experiences we undergo in the time between death and a new earthly incarnation. In describing this journey between death and rebirth he speaks of seven planetary realms through which we pass, both as we review the life just lived and as we prepare for a new life on Earth.[4] Can we conceive a thought like this without becoming too spatial, too earthly, in our thinking? Can we consider a cosmic existence where planets are not just points of light in the night sky, or even goals for future space probes, but vast domains of spiritual activity influencing all life on Earth, including our individual psyche and our shared phases of development? Even if we would bracket the various planetary names, can we imagine realms of qualitative existence in which we are made spiritually ready for a new earthly incarnation? Can we allow our imaginations to inform our psychological understandings without falling into a trap of astrological superficiality or prescriptive fatalism?

Perhaps it is helpful to look for a moment at the days of the week, this rhythm that influences our social life on Earth in such substantial ways. The names of the different days point to the same seven classical planets that are referred to earlier. Every week remembers an evolution through this world of spirit being and endowment. Sunday has an obvious reference to the Sun. Monday reflects the Moon. To see Tuesday's connection to Mars, we need to look at *martes* in Spanish or *mardi* in French. Similarly to see Wednesday's relationship to

---

4   Steiner, *At Home in the Universe*, "Individualities of the Planets."

Mercury we find *miercoles* in Spanish and *mercredi* in French. Thursday has an echo of Thor's day, the Norse reference to Jupiter; likewise, Friday refers to the Norse goddess Frigg, with her connection to Venus, as well as to *viernes* in Spanish and *vendredi* in French. Saturday clearly sounds its association with Saturn. The question for each of us is: do we experience qualitative differences between the various days of the week—differences that go beyond social practice or tradition? And if so, could this be a clue to deep cosmic influences?

Steiner is by no means the only spiritual teacher to speak of these planetary realms, or to explore this geocentric picture of cosmic influences on the human soul and spirit. The ancient Greeks spoke of seven celestial spheres; they reappear in a variety of forms in the Middle Ages, through Alchemy, and again in the Renaissance. Contemporary psychotherapist and author Thomas Moore also looks to them for his own insights into the psyche. Moore takes inspiration from the work of Renaissance scholar Marsilio Ficino, quoting from Ficino's letter to Lorenzo the Magnificent: "We have an entire sky within us, our fiery strength and heavenly origin: Luna which symbolizes the continuous motion of soul and body, Mars speed and Saturn slowness, the Sun God, Jupiter law, Mercury reason, and Venus humanity."[5]

In looking at Steiner's portrayal of the human being coming toward a new life on Earth, I am reminded of the particularly detailed picture of the preparation for incarnation offered in Plato's *Republic*, in Book X, where Socrates recounts "The Myth of Er." The soldier Er has apparently been killed in battle, but as his body is placed on the funeral pyre twelve days later, it becomes clear that he is still alive. In fact, he has been awake in the world of the dead, observing the passage of souls between worlds. He was spared death in order to return as a messenger, to tell those on Earth what he has witnessed.

He describes watching the newly dead depart from the Earth and also the souls approaching a new earthly life, after a thousand years of spiritual retribution and/or blessing received in consequence of their previous earthly deeds. From all directions they gather in a vast meadow, where those returning to Earth select lots to determine the

---

5   Moore, *The Planets Within*.

order in which they will choose their future lives. There are samples of all sorts of life circumstances: poverty, wealth, fame, beauty, tyranny, cleverness, dullness, health, disease, strength, and weakness. Every possibility is there, and some souls choose wisely, others foolishly, based on the depth of their spiritual learning during the long years between lives. The destiny choices are confirmed as each soul passes by the Throne of Necessity with its spindle of revolving planetary orbs. These are the same classical planets discussed above: Moon, Mercury, Venus, Sun, Mars, Jupiter, and Saturn. The departing souls meet the three Fates, the daughters of Necessity: Lachesis who sings of the past, Clotho who ratifies the present chosen destiny, and Atropos who spins the irreversible threads of the earthly future. From there the souls move on to the River of Forgetfulness where they drink, much or little, before, like shooting stars, they are catapulted to a new life on Earth.[6]

Before returning to the question of planetary influences on the phases of development, I want to share the admittedly rather melancholy ending stanza of a Robert Frost poem that holds echoes of this Platonic myth. The poem is called "The Trial by Existence," and it speaks of the soul's choices before birth and of the intended, though forgotten, struggles that belong to our destinies:

> 'Tis the essence of life here,
> Though we chose greatly, still to lack
> The lasting memory at all clear,
> That life has for us on the wrack
> Nothing but what we somehow chose;
> Thus we are wholly stripped of pride
> In the pain that has but one close,
> Bearing it crushed, and mystified.[7]

The picture builds of intentions made between death and rebirth, as our spirit self is journeying through realms of planetary being. First we divest ourselves of the last life's experiences, encountering in the process the effects of our deeds on others, forming resolutions for

6   Plato, *The Republic.*
7   Frost, *The Poetry of Robert Frost: The Collected Poems*, p. 19.

DIAGRAM #5 Influence of Planetary Journey
on Phases

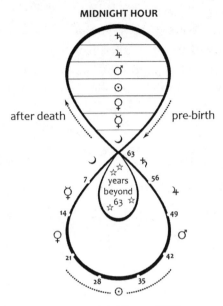

PHASES OF LIFE ON EARTH

atonement, future growth, and ever-greater human wholeness. And
then we pivot back toward Earth again, and on the way we pass once
more through the planetary spheres. Figuratively speaking, we are
now "blessed and dressed"[8] for our future life by the spirit beings
we encounter. They endow us with challenges and opportunities,
with soul qualities and influences that will play out through the different phases of our lives. While all of their influences are working
throughout the whole of our lives, each planetary domain also has
a special relationship to a particular life phase: the Moon—birth to
seven; Mercury—seven to fourteen; Venus—fourteen to twenty-one;
the Sun—twenty-one to forty-two (3 x 7); Mars—forty-two to forty-
nine; Jupiter—forty-nine to fifty-six; Saturn—fifty-six to sixty-three.

I want to emphasize that the movement from phase to phase does
not happen "on the dot" of seven years having passed. It is gradual,

---

8 I am grateful to Maria DeZwaan for this picture, given in conversation.

and yet we can often feel that we have indeed moved on; that something has changed in our relationship to the world, to others, and to ourselves. The seven-year gateposts suggest openings and closings that are more than only personal; in the gestures of growth and change there is something universal happening. If we look only to events, we could dismiss much of the phenomena as culturally biased; but if we look for the inner transitions, prompts, apparent blockages, and shifts in scope that lie behind events, then we may come to appreciate each individual life in both an all-human and a wonderfully unique way.

Over the years I have taught students from every continent (except of course the Antarctic, to which I do, however, have a relationship since my father was a polar explorer!). I have also given lectures and workshops in China, Thailand, Australia, New Zealand, Mexico, Brazil, Canada, England, Norway, Sweden, and all over the United States. Again and again people from very different social backgrounds, ethnicities, and life circumstances have confirmed the basic structure of the phases in their lives. As with the temperaments, no one person experiences all that can be said about the different phases, and yet there do seem to be universal truths at work in how these seven-year cycles manifest in extremely varied life journeys.

This is what we will explore in the coming chapters.

Our birth is but a sleep and a forgetting:
The Soul that rises with us, our life's Star,
Hath had elsewhere its setting,
And cometh from afar:
Not in entire forgetfulness,
And not in utter nakedness,
But trailing clouds of glory do we come
From God, who is our home:
Heaven lies about us in our infancy!
Shades of the prison-house begin to close
Upon the growing Boy,
But he beholds the light, and whence it flows,
He sees it in his joy;
The Youth, who daily farther from the east
Must travel, still is Nature's priest,
And by the vision splendid
Is on his way attended;
At length the Man perceives it die away,
And fade into the light of common day.

WILLIAM WORDSWORTH
"Ode on the Intimations of Immortality"

CHAPTER 5

THE LONG SPRING: BIRTH TO TWENTY-ONE

As we enter the world of child development, can you try to imagine a newborn baby? All curled up, softly sleeping—the fragility is clear, but have you also felt how a baby's presence fills the room? Gazing at a little child easily brings to mind Wordsworth's famous "trailing clouds of glory." We stand before a miracle, and a mystery. Who is this tiny, mighty being? What is he or she bringing to life, and what kind of care is needed that this particular one's intentions can bear fruit on Earth?

Reflecting on your own life, it is always interesting to ask: what world were you born into? Who was there to greet you, and how was the reception? What was the news of the day, even the weather? What mother tongue began to shape your sense of word? What social circumstances and what geography began to inform you about life on Earth?

Or backing up still further, what was your actual birth like? Was it a long, slow labor, or was it induced? Perhaps you avoided the push through the birth canal and came as a cesarean section, or you insisted on coming feet first? Did you come right on schedule, or were you perhaps born early, or a few weeks late? If you know something about your birth, without rushing to interpretation, can you find anything in the gesture of the event that perhaps echoes on, in how you have met other threshold moments in your life?

Let me give an example here from my own birth story. I was born in a state of emergency because I ruptured my mother's uterus at just over eight months. Most babies die if this happens, but my mother was in the hospital for a routine check-up and so they did an immediate cesarean section. Once out I was fine, although my mother was very ill for several weeks. Throughout my life I have longed to meet threshold moments with a gentle, calm approach, but in truth, my changes have often come through sudden and severe crises. For the most part, I have come through all right, even if at times I have created unfortunate havoc along the way. The most recent example occurred as my husband and I were preparing to move out of a house we had lived in for more than twenty years. A few days before the moving truck was to arrive, we were both taken to the hospital, Chris with what turned out to be double pneumonia and I with a closed throat. I awoke three days later to find myself on a respirator in intensive care. Within a couple of days I was on the mend; the move had happened without me, and my adult children's lives were in shambles from all the unanticipated packing, cleaning, care, and worry. It's hard not to notice a kind of pattern here!

Now I return to the question I have sounded: What does the young child need for a healthy start in life? I ask this, knowing only too well that few children are greeted with ideal circumstances. While those of us who are parents have the responsibility to try our best to meet our children's true needs, it is useless to look back on either our own early childhood or on our previous parenting from a position of critical judgment. The more we focus on what did not happen as we might now wish, the more we fall into "victim thinking." Instead, if we can appreciate the ideal, we may come to recognize and accept how its absence has created a challenge, perhaps an obstacle, but also an invitation and opportunity for self-directed development as we go forward in life.

BIRTH TO SEVEN

Any careful observation of young children clearly shows how much they learn through imitation and example. As the Moon reflects the light of the Sun, children reflect the world around them. They mirror the behavior they see and hear—language, attitudes, actions, interactions, and ways of expressing feelings. Too often parents discover this in painful self-recognition; for example, when listening to the harsh or complaining tone their child uses in playing house or talking to a doll. Or they see themselves exaggerated in the way the child shoves the cat off a chair or stomps away from a confrontation with a breathy sigh. More humorously, we may laugh when we see a baby's tongue come out between closed lips when Daddy changes her diaper with his own unconscious facial concentration! Without any direct intention children are absorbing, and being shaped by, the models of human behavior that surround them.

Reading a recent column in my Sunday newspaper I found myself chuckling wryly over this very clear picture of the young child's power of imitation: "There was a phase I went through—I was 6 or 7—when I would get home from school, race upstairs and close my door. I'd don one of my dad's jackets—I preferred a gray pinstripe —balance his glasses on my snub nose and shuffle around in his wingtips. Then I would organize piles of papers on my desk. When the mood struck, I'd pretend to read *The Wall Street Journal*. If my mother came up to check on me, I'd shout, 'Not now, Mom! I'm working!'"[1]

In reflecting on your own early years, and perhaps even on some of your habits that may have carried over from your childhood, can you find ways in which you have manifested imitative behavior? Certainly many parents, in a moment of reprimanding a child, have been shocked to hear their own mother or father's voice. Where did that tone come from, and how did it lie in wait for so many years?

There are important questions that need to be addressed by those who live or work with young children: is the environment—both physical and social—worthy of imitation? Will they experience that the world is a good place to be? Did you when you were a child? Young children are like open sense organs. They drink the world in without protecting filters. Their little bodies, their senses, their brains are coming into being in these early years, and this forming process is strongly influenced by the experiences of daily life.

When I first read Rudolf Steiner's insights on early childhood, I was struck by his assertion that children's developing organs and even brain physiology are affected by the kinds of sensory stimulation around them. Since Steiner's time this has been well researched and validated. Steiner was pointing to the need to protect children from excessive sensory bombardment, to give them a gentle welcome here on Earth; most important, that they be met with warm human care. It has, therefore,

---

1   Christina Alger, "Memory's Office," *The New York Times*, April 29, 2012.

There was a child went forth every day;
And the first object he look'd upon, that object he became;
And that object became part of him for the day, or a certain part
    of the day, or for many years, or stretching cycles of years.

The early lilacs became part of this child,
And grass, and white and red morning-glories, and white and
    red clover, and the song of the phoebe-bird,...

His own parents,
He that had father'd him, and she that had conceiv'd him in her
    womb, and birth'd him,
They gave this child more of themselves than that;
They gave him afterward every day—they became part of him....

The blow, the quick loud word, the tight bargain, the crafty lure,
The family usages, the language, the company, the furniture—
    the yearning and swelling heart,
Affection that will not be gainsay'd—the sense of what is real—
    the thought if, after all, it should prove unreal,
The doubts of day-time and the doubts of night-time—the curi-
    ous whether and how,
Whether that which appears so is so, or is it all flashes and
    specks?
Men and women crowding fast in the streets—if they are not
    flashes and specks, what are they?
The streets themselves, and the façades of houses, and goods in
    the windows,
Vehicles, teams, the heavy-plank'd wharves—the huge crossing
    at the ferries,
The village on the highland, seen from afar at sunset—the river
    between,...

The horizon's edge, the flying sea-crow, the fragrance of salt
    marsh and shore mud;
These became part of that child who went forth every day, and
    who now goes, and will always go forth every day.

                WALT WHITMAN, *Leaves of Grass*

saddened me to observe how this research has been distorted, leading to the mass marketing of sensory stimulators of many kinds and, more distressingly, to what is called—with, to me, linguistic offense— "edutainment" for babies. This comes in the form of electronic toys, DVDs, CDs and flashcards. Programs for learning foreign languages or music appreciation are even available for in-utero "education." Our competitive and materialistically oriented culture finds ever new ways to push the idea of getting a head start in intellectual learning, or of raising a genius, as if this is really in the best interest of the child.

But it is not; instead, this kind of early over-stimulation makes awakening healthy senses much more difficult. It is overwhelming to a young child's sensitivity. Of course there are children who are deprived of needed human contact and healthy modeling, and this neglect must be addressed. But the solution to such deprivation is not more shiny bells and whistles. The modern world provides high pressure enough: almost constant noise, harsh lighting, and endless rushing around fill our days, unless we give attention to creating something else. And then there are all the artificial sense enticements—the flavorings, air-fresheners, synthesized music, talking toys, and, of course, the ever-available screen, whether TV, computer or baby cell-phone app. Virtual and abstract appearances of life abound, when what the young child really needs is real human warmth and the example of adults who enjoy life, learning, being with and caring for others.

In many ways our advanced technological age is not very child-friendly. Too many commercial devices come between the child and genuine human contact: the monitors, clicking mechanical swings, electronic games, talking dolls, TV as babysitter, to mention only the most obvious. And I say this more with sadness than with judgment. It is hard to resist the allure of the latest gizmo or timesaving gadget, especially when time is at such a premium. Indeed, millions of dollars are spent on designing the flashiest ways to catch—captivate, capture—the attention of young children, and through them the wallets of their parents.

To be really honest here, I must tell you that my beloved grandchildren live in Maui, too many thousands of miles away from my husband and me. While we trust that they are where they need to be right now, we miss them terribly and so, even though none of us are TV people, we have resorted to using Skype to stay in regular contact. When our two-year-old granddaughter first saw us on the computer screen, we could clearly see on her face the unarticulated question: How did Ami and Dadu get in there? Eventually she came closer and began whispering to us; it seemed as if to secretly circumvent the strange way we were boxed. Now the children are older and we have all become used to this way of communicating, even as we try to enliven it with stories, songs, and games. Nevertheless, I often feel that when we say good-bye, we all feel strangely more disconnected. I have come to feel that the experience of visiting with the children on Skype is like eating a fast-food meal. We have eaten, but without real nourishment.

Three Mighty Achievements

In addition to all that is learned through imitation, there are three essential human achievements that generally happen before the age of three, and every child accomplishes them in his or her own particular way. As parents we have the opportunity to learn much about the individuality of our child by observing how these archetypal milestones are passed. In looking at our own lives, we must rely on others who may carry the stories of our early years. Are there stories about how you met these challenges, or are there still people who could tell you anything? If so, do the recollections illustrate the beginning of patterns you can still recognize in your ways of being?

STEP 1: Sometime around the age of one, a child stands and then begins to walk. This achievement of uprightness is exciting for both the parents and the child. It is as if there is an irresistible force drawing the child upward. Nothing will keep her down once uprightness begins its pull. He tumbles over, she plops down again and again, and still there is another try. This indomitable urge to be upright is for me a perfect metaphor for the human spirit, and how we keep trying to find our way forward, again and again, in spite of life's inevitable setbacks. Indeed, this image can sustain us through difficult life challenges.

Some children stand very early, even before their legs are strong enough to hold their weight; then, like my son, their legs may bow a bit right into adulthood. Others sit happily, biding their time. None will rise before they are ready, and none can be kept down once the promise of uprightness has taken hold.

The ways of walking are also very individual. My daughter Karin had been standing for many months, and easily walking around low tables or while holding our hands, but she would not let go and walk on her own. Not even one step. Then at fifteen months, in a large room full of people, she rose from a sitting position and walked sixteen steps across the room. Looking around the room with a happy smile, she then deliberately sat back down. Luckily I was there, and I watched in utter amazement, wondering when she could have been practicing since I was with her every day! Of course, from then on she continued walking, in that wonderful angel-held way that toddlers have. The laws of gravity should pull them right down, but they are held up by a greater will.

I want to take this example of Karin's walking to show how these early achievements may herald future ways of being, even though we are unaware at the time. Several years later, when she was five, we were living in Holland and she was going to a local kindergarten. At home we would try to encourage her to say simple Dutch phrases and tell her in English the fairy tales from school, but she strongly refused to speak Dutch to anyone. Her teacher told us she played happily at school, speaking English softly to herself. Then after about six weeks, when I went to pick her up, her teacher greeted me at the door with great excitement: "She speaks fluent Dutch! She started as soon as she came in today and hasn't stopped all morning!" Suddenly I remembered the way she began walking and was also then flooded with memories of other situations where she would stubbornly refuse to do something she had not yet mastered. It was clear to me that this unwillingness to appear less than able was part of something essential about her. She needed to master things in her own time and her own way—no halting steps until she had it right! Over the years when I could remember this, I could better contain my own frustration and try to find gentle and more indirect ways to guide her toward new capacities.

STEP 2: The next great achievement, one that most children carry out during their second or third year, is the miracle of language. Initially babies babble the sounds they hear—cooing, calls, a cat's meow, or revving trucks. Then the babbling begins to imitate human speech patterns and rhythms, complete with inflections, questions, and exclamations. It is most helpful to the child to hear real, beautiful language, including songs and rhymes. The simple rhythms and melodies of a parent's tones surround the child with welcoming warmth. Neither baby talk nor mechanical speech really serves a child coming into language. Even before speaking, it becomes clear through behavior that the child understands ever more words. If a parent looks around and says, "Where is the ball?" it is quite possible that a still crawling baby will scurry behind a chair where the ball has rolled.

Gradually, recognizable sounds begin to emerge out of the child's babbling. Meaning is being expressed, and exchanged, and the child begins to use language as a creative force, often expressing complex concepts in vivid imagery. Young children do not worry if they do not know the right word for something. Instead they extend the usual meanings of words they do know to suit their need. I am often reminded as I take a walk near my home, of the time my four-year-old grandson, visiting from Brooklyn, walked by the local cemetery with his father and said joyfully, "Look Daddy, a little city!"

ç

STEP 3: With ever-more words, the questions begin: "what's that?" and before long, "why?" In his basic book on human freedom, *Intuitive Thinking as a Spiritual Path: A Philosophy of Freedom,* Rudolf Steiner speaks about our fundamental human desire to know; in its primary form this is so clearly evident with the young child. Facial expressions, such as a puzzled gaze—like my earlier example about Skyping with our granddaughter—show us that thought connections are being made. Thinking arises out of movement and speech, not through direct instruction. We do not learn to think at this age by being taught intellectually but because we so deeply want to make sense of, to understand, the world we are perceiving.

We definitely know that children have begun to think for themselves when the word "I" is spoken, usually sometime in the third year, and after the child has discovered the magic of "no." The possibility of negation heralds the beginning of an inner experience of dualism, a sense of self and other; the self now has the power to say "no." All of this is only just beginning in the young child, but it should be clear that "I" is a word that cannot be meaningfully imitated. Up until this moment the child has referred to himself as "Jack," or she has called herself "Annie" because that is how she hears others address her. But one day, through their own thinking, they know to call themselves "I." This is often a glorious moment in a child's development; our daughter ran around the room calling out "I" with a finger pointing to herself and "you" with gestures toward us.

It is difficult to have lasting memories from before the time of saying "I" because it is this sense of self that gives grounding for memory. In the early years the child experiences being part of the wholeness of life. It is interesting to try to find early memories of what can be referred to as "I-knowing"—moments of self-awareness when we stepped out of the more usual participatory consciousness of childhood. A friend once described how in an emergency her mother thrust her younger brother into her arms and said, "Take care of the baby." This was her first conscious realization that she and the baby were not one.

Because as children we live so fully in sense experiences, early memories are most often sensory-based: the feel of a special blanket, the sound of the screen door slamming, or the smells in grandmother's kitchen. What are some of your own first memories?

Coming to a sense of self as distinct from the world around is a gradual process throughout childhood. Tolstoy described with surprise his own lack of early memories of the natural world: "Nature till my fifth year did not exist for me...People must have let me play with flowers, with leaves; they must needs have shielded me from the Sun; but till my fifth or sixth year I have not a single recollection of what we call nature. Possibly one has to get away from her in order to see her, and I was nature."[2]

---

2   Tolstoy, *Leo Tolstoy's 20 Greatest Short Stories Annotated*, p. 18.

I mentioned earlier how children begin to ask questions, and what an important human activity this is. Soon the questions move beyond identification and naming, revealing clearly an insistent longing to know. Can you remember questions that arose in your early years? Did you try to puzzle your way through or did you receive helpful answers from others? When confronted with a child's earnest question, adults can often too eagerly reply with an intellectual or abstract answer. But young children are not looking for lengthy, scientific explanations. They are trying to become oriented here on Earth. The best reply is often to ask the child, "What do you think?" They will then help us see the context in which the question lives for them. I am reminded of the story of the mother who was asked the "where do we come from?" question by her five-year-old and launched nervously into how babies are conceived. But her child soon interrupted her saying simply, "Well, my friend Sophie comes from Boston."

A student of mine once told an amazing story of how she learned about the age appropriateness of explanations with young children. Her husband had recently died and she wanted to help her children— at three and six—understand about his death. She got them each a butterfly box and let them watch the process of transformation from caterpillar to chrysalis to butterfly. She spoke about the soul undergoing transformation. A few days after the children had let their butterflies fly off into the garden, she wanted to check on whether they had understood the parable. The older girl answered her query perfectly, saying "Yes, Daddy's soul is now in another form." Feeling good about how she had handled this, the mother turned to her little one and asked if he understood about Daddy. "Yes," he said, "Daddy's a bug."

Another angle on questions has to do with the ones adults ask children. In our age of wanting to be fair, inclusive, and non-dictatorial, we ask our young children way too many questions: what do you want to wear today? To eat? What shall we do this afternoon? Are you feeling angry? And on and on. While any of these questions might be valid in a particular circumstance, the continual invitation to decision-making is actually burdensome to the very young; and more than that, it stimulates the child's intellect and a kind of egotism that only creates future difficulties. We have all seen the young child who ends up in a tantrum through a confusion of choices. It is possible that we may even remember having been that child. What the child of two, three, or four needs is to feel secure within kind adult supervision. The child really wants to know that the parent has things under control. Clear decision-making in later life is best served by loving direction in the early years.

Gradually the young child has more control over body and limbs, more capacity to communicate with others. Now play becomes an important part of the child's development. Especially from the fourth year on, children naturally play the world around them. Ideally they would not spend time at desks, captivated by tiny digital games, or sit hours in front of TV or DVDs. True play for the young child is will activity and it is most beneficial when it involves the whole body. Children naturally love to run and jump, to skip, and swing. By moving their physical bodies, exploring their environments, and constructing self-created spaces and activities, children are preparing a strong foundation from which to be active and healthy in later life. As they discover and imagine, investigate and predict outcomes, they learn to trust their sense perceptions, and they grow in self-confidence.

Children need time for free play. Do you remember having time and space for playing freely when you were young? Parents or caregivers do not need to organize every waking moment or constantly hover over a child's play. Children need a safe and inviting environment, and of course a worthy world to imitate, but they also need to be allowed to initiate their own play. It is helpful if in their self-directed play they have access to simple objects—colored cloths and cords for tying, pebbles and shells, different sized boards or logs, paper and crayons—with which the imagination can make what it will, every day anew. This is the time for make-believe; fantasy and imagination are true building blocks for future creative thinking. Can you remember living in that world of your own creation, where your dolls could talk, where you were a mighty explorer or a brave princess?

Cloth "Waldorf" dolls have simple faces so that the child can see every expression registering there, and not just a fixed plastic smile. Well-known educational psychologist Jane Healy once said that a good toy should be 10 percent toy and ninety percent child.[3] Sadly, electronic, battery-operated, and many branded or single-purpose toys reverse that ratio, and it is not surprising that children then become dependent on a toy that "does something," or being entertained rather than eagerly engaging in self-generated play.

I have already mentioned the problem of TV-watching during early childhood. The American Academy of Pediatrics has recommended for many years that children under the age of two should not be exposed to TV. Yet we know that TV and other screen activities are the norm—in homes, doctors' offices, airports, and even New York taxis. There is much that can be said about TV and children in terms of the poor quality of programming, the effect of advertising, violence, gender stereotyping, and even obesity; but my primary concern has to do with how TV affects image-making. It is part of our human birthright to be image-makers. This ability is stimulated throughout early childhood as the child builds inner pictures in response to stories, games, or questions that arise. When the TV pictures embody the stories, the child has no incentive to awaken her own inner images. Everything is given, and the child's developing brain becomes more receptive than active.

Many adults have experienced reading a novel and then going to the movie made from it: throughout the film we do inner battle with the director about how a character looked, or spoke or dressed, or what the cabin was like, or how a particular dialogue played out, because in reading the story we formed pictures of our own. In fact, I know many people who will not go to see films of books they have read for just this reason. But if we turn to a book after seeing the film, it is almost impossible not to picture the story based on what we saw on the screen. Children in this early phase of life have no filters to protect them from what comes toward them on the screen; more important, they need time to awaken their own capacity of open-ended imagination before being assaulted with ready-made content.

---

3   I heard this comment at a conference, but Jane Healy, PhD is author
of several books on children and brain development, such as: *Your
Child's Growing Mind* (1986), *Endangered Minds* (1991), and *Failure to
Connect* (1999).

> EARLY CHILDHOOD EXERCISE • Remember a place where you felt
> safe and happy when you were five or six years old. Picture it
> in all its physical details and be aware of any sense memories.
> Observe yourself there as if from outside. What made this place
> special for you? What did you do there?

In what can be seen increasingly as an antidote to much that sti-
fles healthy child development today, Waldorf kindergartens engage
children in archetypal human activities like sweeping the floor,
sawing logs, chopping vegetables, stirring soup, kneading bread,
building a camp, or washing the snack plates. The children experience meaningful action that is of service to others. Perhaps someone
will maintain that sitting at the computer, moving only one's fingers
is fast approaching an archetypal human activity. That would be a
sad consequence for the miracle of our physical mobility. And perhaps even more so for our inner mobility, which is profoundly nurtured by running with the wind, climbing over obstacles, planting a
garden, organizing a dolls' tea party, or sailing a walnut boat down
a stream. It is possible that at the computer a child feels he can con-
quer the world, but there is no real effort being exerted, and no real
resistance being met. The young child needs to meet resistance and
to be physically active to develop the will in a healthy way.

Birth Order and Family Life

Before moving on to look at the next phases of childhood, I want
to make a slight detour into the question of birth order. As a factor in
our family socialization, our placement among siblings or our status
as an only child is one more piece of the puzzle of our emerging personality. Like our gender, it is another aspect of our pre-birth intentionality, and it offers particular life experiences and social learning.

I have found very helpful the model that looks at a repeating pattern of first-, second-, and third-born children, as presented by Karl
König.[4] This means that a fourth-born is a milder first, a fifth again a
second, a sixth another third, and so on. Our birth order is not a huge

---

4   König, *Brothers and Sisters.*

determinant in our life, but it does shape our early social experiences and so influences our ways of relating in later life.

The first-born is, for better or for worse, the center of family attention and the focus of parental learning. The parents are doing everything for the first time, and the first-born, too, has only adults as a model. This fosters an early orientation toward the adult world. First-borns want to please the parents and tend to be serious and more conscious of the world around them. As they grow older they may feel a sense of responsibility toward the family line; they feel the weight of parental needs and values, even as they are the first to meet the barricade of family rules. This can bring a tension: they are impatient to be free, to grow up, while also feeling a duty to preserve the familial status quo. When they do rebel they often make a big noise about it, almost as a declaration of independence. If more siblings come along, the first-born often acts as the bridge between the parents and the children, and this may be done with a fair amount of bossiness. Often ambitious and conscientious, first-borns also tend to be more conservative than later-borns, which shows up in a disproportionate number of them becoming judges, lawyers, and other defenders of the past.

Second-borns come into a busier household and are consequently often freer of parental concerns and values. They may feel second best, they may end up in the middle, but they generally do not care so much about family rules, even wondering why the first-born makes a public commotion about rebelling. Watching his older sister struggle for independence, our son once asked, "Why does she make such a fuss about everything? I won't do that when I'm a teenager." I resisted requesting that he write this in blood, and then watched over the years how he quietly circumvented any rules that seemed to be in his way. Second-borns are often more easy-going, less driven; they bring humor into the family and can be quite interested in community. They take joy in the present and want to live in harmony with the world. And yet they also may be experimental and pioneering. Frank Sulloway, in his book on birth order, *Born to Rebel*, notes that second- and later-borns often introduce revolutionary ideas into science, politics, or religion, or at least are supporters of radical innovation. He interprets this as a learned sidestepping of normal competition with the older, more conventional sibling who was always "first" at home and could never be surpassed on his own terms.[5]

Third-borns come into a world where the two older siblings already have a relationship. Some third-borns receive less attention; some are treated as the "baby"—special and pampered. Relative to their siblings who already have a working relationship and who know how to do things, they often feel like a rejected outsider, longing to find their place and to be accepted but not sure if the older ones can be trusted. This experience may be lonely, but it also fosters independence and originality. Third-borns are generally sensitive, creative, inward, and often very funny. They show a strange blend of being both delicate and strong. König suggests that they have vision for the future, and that proportionately more artists, saints, and heroes are numbered in their ranks.

As mentioned, this pattern of three repeats in larger families. It is interesting to note that often the first and the fourth will have a special relationship. Or the second and the fifth, and so on. Especially in our age of ever-smaller families, of particular note is the only child: a first-born who remains the focus of attention and who carries all the hopes and dreams of the parents. Most "onlies" are quite adult-oriented, even as they may also attach themselves in friendship to a larger family where they can observe how others relate. They often miss having another child with whom to share family experiences and memories. It is interesting to reflect on how the current increase in only children is influencing the manifestations of individuality in society at large, or even in a classroom, a marriage, or a group of colleagues. In China there is now an easing of the one-child policy—and remember that this is usually one child doted on by two parents and four grandparents—in part because of the recognition that an entire generation of "little emperors" has created unexpected social/relational challenges.

It will be obvious that there are many factors that mitigate the preceding generalizations about birth order. Gender is an important factor, and in particular the parents' attitudes toward boys or girls. Being, or having an older sister is not the same as being or having an older brother. Two or three sisters form a different constellation than two or three brothers. The number of years between siblings is also

---

5   Sulloway, *Born to Rebel.*

important: if the gap is larger than six or seven years, you are in some ways dealing with a series of only children. If a child dies, his or her presence in the consciousness of family members will also influence the social development of the other children. And of course today, with the prevalence of divorce and remarriage, we have many combined families, where the new adult relationship catapults the children into a totally different constellation. It is important to remember, for example, that a first-born suffers displacement with the arrival of an older step-sibling. Birth order is by no means the most important factor in personality development, but it does play a role in how we act toward others and feel about ourselves.

Family life in general is a strong force in our socialization during childhood. It is in our families that we first experience care, boundaries, celebration, sharing, anger, forgiveness, happiness, and even grief. Family rhythms and habits of discipline lay the foundation for self-discipline in later life. With our parents and our siblings we learn about relating, about disagreeing, about loyalty, and most of all about love. There is no perfect family today; but happily our times are friendlier to a wonderful diversity of family constellations—nuclear, single-parent, same-sex, combined, extended, and self-determined.

Family members are all on a path of mutual development. We bear each other into life—in all the meanings of the word. Parents bring the child to life, and the child calls out yet unborn qualities in the parents. This mutual midwifery goes on throughout life, even as we also carry each other along in so many different ways. We need each other as we ever and again try to find our bearings. And for the most part, family members can just about tolerate each other! Who among us has never thought when observing the behavior of someone else's child, "I could not bear it if my child were like that"? It is in our families, with all their strengths and shortcomings that we first begin to discover what it means to be a human being here on Earth.

SEVEN TO FOURTEEN

Toward the end of early childhood something extraordinary begins to happen: the child starts to lose his or her "baby" teeth. As these hardest parts of the physical body are gradually replaced by the child's permanent teeth, we can experience that the physical body inherited from the parents has now been fully reworked by the child's own growth forces. Rudolf Steiner points to this change of teeth as an indication of the birth of the child's etheric or life body and so, too, the beginning of a new phase of development and new ways of learning. You can certainly observe how a child's face changes, particularly around the jaw, as the twenty even little teeth eventually give way to thirty-two large new ones that are very individually aligned and spaced. And as this change is happening, it becomes clear how children of this age are stepping into quite a new relationship to themselves and to the world around them.

The world begins to broaden out for the child; elementary school begins in earnest, and adventure calls. As adults we generally have more memories from this mercurial phase of life than from the earlier years. Can you recall what going to school was like? Who your friends were? How you celebrated birthdays? Do you remember how you played? What were your favorite games? What did you choose to do with "free" time? What do you remember about your parents in those years?

In these middle years of childhood the daily habits and rhythms of home and school are gradually influencing the development of the child's rhythmic system. Since birth the child's experiences of mealtimes, bedtime rituals, and all manner of family traditions have been providing order—or chaos—to the days, weeks, and years. Now it becomes ever more important to attend to how the rhythms of daily life impact a healthy working together of the heart and lungs. There is so much that is chaotic in modern life, and children need living rhythms—but not inflexibly fixed routines—as they are building their rhythmic systems and their own habit lives.

Rudolf Steiner advises teachers that in these years they should "teach the children to breathe." He did not mean to introduce yoga exercises or other conscious breath work, but that there should be a healthy and rhythmic breathing in the day's activities—times of contraction and expansion, inner and outer, experiences that are serious and funny, quiet and exuberant. This kind of movement, with others and within oneself, builds health, soul flexibility, and fosters a love of learning. Sadly, too many children spend far too many hours sitting at desks or in front of screens, where their bodies and souls are more often constricted than stretched, more dulled than enlivened.

Can you find memories from your childhood of this interplay between drawing into yourself and expanding out into the world? I remember very clearly getting out of elementary school for summer vacation and how everything seemed to stretch and expand—my legs, the hours for play, the days themselves. And then within those wide-open days how I also cherished curling up under a tree for a few hours alone with a book and my imagination. This is a season-connected memory, but every day the growing child benefits from rhythmic movement between outer and inner experiences.

Deeply related to the development of the rhythmic system is the awakening of the child's feeling life. This, too, needs flexibility. These are the years of "best" and "worst" friends, of what I like and what I hate, of hobbies and clubs, and hopefully ever-awakening interests. Stories and activities can invite imaginations of danger and courage, of hope and despair, of trial and accomplishment. These are, literally, the best years for "learning by heart." Memory is aided by rhythm whether with times tables, songs and poems, or, less helpfully, the endless advertising slogans that may well be with us for the rest of our lives. Who does not remember TV jingles from childhood? We are all living proof of the power of rhythm!

These are also years when authority is very important, and how it is exercised will have lasting impact. Children need boundaries and guidelines to feel secure. You can see this in how they organize their own games at this age. Do you remember how important the rules were for neighborhood games like kick-the-can or hopscotch? Or how upsetting it was when adults bent the rules of a board game for a younger child? "That's not fair!" is a steady cry of the eight-year-old as he struggles to know the parameters for his own behavior.

Parents today are often reluctant to exercise authority, wanting instead to be their child's friend; but that is actually a burden for the child, who needs a parent's wisdom to lead the way. Parental discipline need not be harsh or overbearing. Hopefully it is benevolent, inviting,

---

EXERCISES ABOUT CHILDHOOD

1. Find some family norms, advice, even commandments, that belonged "in our family" (spoken or not). Picture the situations where these would be articulated or understood by all. What made them arise? Who spoke them and who was there? How did you react then? How does this advice live in you now?

2. Find a family rhythm or ritual—something that was regularly repeated (daily, weekly, or yearly). Observe it in your mind/heart's eye. You might try drawing a simple picture of such a family scene, attending to the details that come up. How did you feel about this activity as a child? How does this rhythm live in your life now?

---

and clear. Sadly, when it is non-existent, it fosters not freedom but a confused egotism. Can you remember times when you needed your parent to be in charge, or when you felt the stress of having to support your parent in ways that felt beyond you?

Children are naturally inclined to revere adult authority, as evidenced in statements such as "My Daddy said so"; "My teacher does it this way." The opportunity to feel pride and awe for the adults in their lives is so important. It inspires their own desire to become a grown-up, and also works as an antidote to the cynicism and mockery about the adult world that is so prevalent in children's TV and movies.

Perhaps you will remember a very important time in the middle of this phase, usually between nine and ten when the child experiences an awakening sense of self-consciousness. As opposed to the glorious step into "I" of the two or three year old, this change most often shows itself in a new moodiness, a feeling of isolation, and sadness. What the parent hears are statements like "Nobody likes me," "I don't have to tell you," and the forlorn "Says who?" Many children at this age decide that they were adopted and even secretly hope they were, for then there would still be that lost king and queen somewhere, rather than these now so obviously flawed parents: "I couldn't really belong to these people."

It is a lonely time for the child and a challenge for the parent. Many of us can recall feeling isolated or critical; perhaps we remember sitting under a tree crying for no apparent reason, or wondering how our mother could be so embarrassing. A former student recalled very clearly thinking, "Life's not as much fun anymore." Another shared a picture of himself at nine standing on the school playground, filled with a new sadness as he looked at the other children and realized that they all had their own eyes through which to see the world but that none of them could see inside themselves.

Billy Collins brings a poet's attention to this important transition.

ON TURNING TEN

The whole idea of it makes me feel
like I'm coming down with something,
something worse than any stomach ache
or the headaches I get from reading in bad light—
a kind of measles of the spirit,
a mumps of the psyche,
a disfiguring chicken pox of the soul.

You tell me it is too early to be looking back,
but that is because you have forgotten
the perfect simplicity of being one
and the beautiful complexity introduced by two.
But I can lie on my bed and remember every digit.
At four I was an Arabian wizard.
I could make myself invisible
by drinking a glass of milk a certain way.
At seven I was a soldier, at nine a prince.

But now I am mostly at the window
watching the late afternoon light.
Back then it never fell so solemnly
against the side of my tree house,
and my bicycle never leaned against the garage
as it does today,
all the dark blue speed drained out of it.

This is the beginning of sadness, I say to myself,
as I walk through the universe in my sneakers.
It is time to say good-bye to my imaginary friends,
time to turn the first big number.

It seems only yesterday I used to believe
there was nothing under my skin but light.
If you cut me I could shine.
But now when I fall upon the sidewalks of life,
I skin my knees. I bleed.

BILLY COLLINS[6]

And Annie Dillard, in her memoir *An American Childhood*, captures beautifully the confusion of this time:

> I was just waking up then, just barely. . . The great outer world hove into view and began to fill with things that had apparently been there all along: mineralogy, detective work, lepidopterology, ponds and streams, flying, society.
>
> Children ten years old wake up and find themselves here, discover themselves to have been here all along: is this sad? They wake like sleepwalkers, in full stride; they wake like people brought back from cardiac arrest or from drowning: 'in medias res', surrounded by familiar people and objects, equipped with a hundred skills. They know the neighborhood, they can read and write English, they are old hands at the commonplace mysteries, and yet they feel themselves to have just stepped off the boat, just converged with their bodies, just flown down from a trance, to lodge in an eerily familiar life already well under way.
>
> I woke in bits, like all children, piecemeal over the years... I noticed this process of waking, and predicted with terrifying logic that one of these years not far away I would be awake continuously and never slip back, and never be free of myself again.[7]

Happily this lonely time is a passage, not a permanent state. Once the child has made the transition, there usually follows a lovely,

---

6   Collins, *Sailing Around the Room*, p. 63.

7   Dillard, *An American Childhood*, pp. 10–11.

open time in the very heart of childhood, a fresh breath before the onslaught of puberty. This book is not the place to go into all the nurturing and enriching ways that the Waldorf curriculum serves the needs of the growing child. For readers who are unfamiliar with this developmentally attuned form of education, there are many books referenced in the bibliography. Torin Finser's book *School as a Journey* would be a good place to start.

In any form of schooling it is important to ask if the education serves the child's imagination and nurtures the awakening feeling life. Do the children experience beauty, inspiration, new interests, and a growing sense of confidence? Or is there a daily damping down of the life force that would freely bubble within them? Whether in a rural or an urban setting, are they invited into a living relationship with the natural world? Are they allowed to observe, and find their own wonder-filled questions that will then lead to conceptual understandings, or are they bombarded with abstract facts in preparation for standardized tests? Do they feel an increasing awe for what the human being can do, or are they caught in the magnetism of machines? And how was all of this for you?

In the early days of computers my ten-year-old son and I visited a children's museum where he began to play on one of the available modules. In a kind of preliminary "chat," he made a spelling error in his entry. After an audible sputter, the computer flashed the message, "Just a moment, I'm thinking." He was of course fascinated, while I felt a sudden chill at this subtle usurpation of such an essential human capacity. Since that day in the early 1980s, the allure and the reach of technology has grown exponentially. And children seem ever more to be born knowing how to manipulate it. But they can also be easily caught in its thrall. As parents and teachers are we providing appropriate balancing activities that awaken and encourage what is truly human?

As I write, I am reminded of a recent front-page article in the Sunday *New York Times* about a Waldorf school in Silicon Valley where three-quarters of the parents work in high-tech professions yet choose to send their children to a school without computers in elementary school. As one parent who works at Google said: "We make technology as brain-dead easy to use as possible. There's no reason why kids can't figure it out when they get older." And another spoke of what young students most need: "Engagement is about human contact, the contact with the teacher, the contact with their peers."[8]

Before moving on to the phase of adolescence, I want to look at one more moment in the middle years of childhood, which many readers may remember. For many children between eleven and twelve there is a glimmer of a future interest or even vocational choice. This may not present itself consciously, but in looking back later one can sometimes see the first manifestation of what will become a life theme. William Bryant, who did extensive work with life cycles, speaks about the rhythm of twelve years, which he calls the Jupiter cycle, as "a rhythm of creativity" marked by "moments when 'something clicks,' something meets us just at the right moment, or a new idea or plan suddenly slips into place."[9]

I recently asked a retired biochemistry professor when he began to be interested in chemistry. He laughed with pleasure in describing the thrill, between eleven and twelve, of making tennis ball bombs, even though, he noted gratefully, most did not work very well. In my own case, I moved to Santiago, Chile for one year at the age of eleven and first woke up to my lifelong interest in travel, language, and culture. A more public example is Dave Isay, the founder of StoryCorps, who at eleven set up his parents' tape recorder at a family holiday dinner and interviewed his "larger-than-life" grandmother and other elderly relatives.[10] Under his leadership, StoryCorps has become one of the largest oral-history projects in the world. Between 2003 and 2013, more than 45,000 interviews have been recorded between family members and friends and are now archived at the American Folklife Center at the Library of Congress.

There is still more to say about children around the age of twelve, particularly girls. Many readers will be familiar with the work of

8   "A Silicon Valley School That Doesn't Compute," *New York Times*, Oct. 23, 2011.

9   Bryant, *The Veiled Pulse of Time*, p. 137.

10   Isay, *Listening Is an Act of Love*, pp. 249–250.

Carol Gilligan, who conducted a multi-year study of girls approaching adolescence and the dissociation that often happens in their feeling lives as they try to fit in with the images that surround them of what it means to be a young woman. She observed how bright and lively girls would begin to stifle their unique voices as if in "fear that if they give voice to vital parts of themselves, their pleasure and their knowledge, they will endanger their connection with others and also the world at large."[11] A society-inspired sense of competition creeps into peer relationships, and there is often a loss of self-esteem. Many girls who have loved math and science, for example, suddenly close off this side of themselves. And all this is going on in spite of the many changes in educational practices brought about by feminist attention in recent decades.

Perhaps some of this withdrawal into self belongs to the advent of adolescence itself, but its exaggerated expressions suggest a broader, societal issue. Greater and more subtle attention is needed to correct the large and small ways that parents, teachers, and Madison Avenue continue to promote gender behavior and attitudes that are in direct conflict with healthy self-images for growing girls and boys. The widespread incidence of eating disorders, cutting, depression, bullying, and other destructive behaviors among preteens and teens is a clear indication of the conflicting and damaging nature of too many current female and male representations. Even where there is rhetoric about gender-free opportunity, the images of success are often still permeated with stereotype and bias. Speaking for myself, I find it painful to see young children portrayed in the media in sexually suggestive poses, outfits, and attitudes. This is a sad, indeed often grotesque, materialization of gender differentiation before significant attention to difference is even relevant for the developing young person.

FOURTEEN TO TWENTY-ONE

With puberty, of course, gender differences clearly do begin to manifest. And this transition has occurred ever earlier throughout the last two hundred years in both girls and boys, shifting down an average of

---

11   Gilligan, *The Birth of Pleasure*, p. 15.

two years per century in developed countries. Various factors seem to influence the early onset of physical maturity: childhood obesity, environmental chemicals and hormones, nutritional changes, the stress and speed of modern life, early intellectualization, and even absentee fathers, to name only the most researched factors. Particularly with girls, puberty can now begin as early as seven or eight, long before there is the mental or psychological maturity to really understand what is happening with the body. Boys' choirs are having increasing difficulty keeping twelve year olds because their voices are breaking ever earlier. Contrast this to the average age of eighteen for voice break of boy singers in J. S. Bach's choir in the 1700s.[12]

In considering general life phases, many questions arise when phenomena seem to contradict the basic patterns. Are the seven-year phases still relevant? How can we understand individuals or groups manifesting out-of-phase characteristics? Is it best to work from the ideal or the actual in trying to serve healthy development? When is a phenomenon so widespread that a new conceptual framework is needed? There are no simple answers to questions like these, no ready-made understandings.

In terms of basic child development, I have found it important to pay attention to the difference between puberty as the process of sexual maturation, and adolescence as the process of psychological development. In earlier times puberty and adolescence occurred more or less together, but especially in recent decades the gap between physical and psychological maturity has grown ever greater. Perhaps this widening gap helps to explain the depth of confusion that accompanies the teenage years for so many, and it may also be a factor in the arrested adolescent behavior that so often lingers long into adulthood.

Certainly there is a real change—what I would call a deepening of soul life—that begins somewhere around thirteen or fourteen, no matter when physical puberty occurs. Perhaps you remember that time of confusion, excitement, new hopes, fears, and longings. Rudolf Steiner connects this transition into adolescence to the awakening of the young person's astral body, which brings a new focus on wishes, desires, passions, thoughts, and feelings. Conception now becomes

---

12   Fiona Neill, "Puberty Blues," *Intelligent Life Magazine*, summer 2010.

possible—not only physically but also mentally in a quite new way. I think all parents and teachers of middle school children notice a marked change in how the young people start to look at the world, to ask new kinds of questions, and to grapple with complex thoughts. Slowly the possibility opens up to give birth to their own ideas.

The early teens are a time of many polarities: young people are both world-interested and deeply self-centered; they are newly idealistic and often harshly critical; they feel profoundly alone and unique, even as they are deeply peer-influenced. A friend of ours once suggested that fourteen-year-olds should wear a sign on their heads, invisible to them but in plain view to others, saying "Closed for Reconstruction."

A former student, writing at twenty-three, had this to say about her entrance into adolescence:

> I remember, at age thirteen, having a conversation with myself on the front lawn. I was considering very serious questions about life, truth, what was and was not real. I told myself that something was going to happen to me, I was soon going to become like another person—I would not see through the same eyes. I felt very sure of this and very strongly about wanting to leave myself some clues so I could get back from where I was going to, to where I was then.... I remember one of the things that I felt then was very important was to lie on my back and look at the outlines of the shapes of the leaves of trees. This way I could know which trees were different and which were the same. Such clarity. This was clear truth for me. Other things I can't yet recall, but most strong is the memory of the moment of knowing that "growing-up" meant moving out of a particular world where good and bad and truth were clear, and into a world where good and bad and truth would become blurry.

Young teenagers are contrary and challenging, seething with inner discord, but also dear in their moments of raw openness and passion. It is as if they are walking along an unseen line with childhood on one side and adulthood on the other. At any moment they may hop to either side, and it is the adult's task to perceive which side they are on and then to interact with them accordingly. If they are feeling grown up, they are insulted when we treat them like children; yet if they are for a moment basking in childish behavior, it is pointless to expect more mature actions from them. Can you remember this hopscotch experience as a young teen? What do you recall about how adults responded to your behavior, and also how you felt about the ways you were treated?

Adolescents long for ideals, for a society they can believe in, for authenticity. They are searching for truth, and reason, and some semblance of order within the chaos they experience around and within themselves. If you remember any ideals that arose for you in your teens—the wonder of art, the possibility of political reform, a person exhibiting inspiring courage—did this belief in something beyond yourself offer the promise of hope and safe harbor?

Of course adolescents often wear masks to hide their emerging sense of self. When my daughter would go out with petticoats as skirts, or when she died her hair blue, I would try to remind myself that as a little girl, I encouraged her to play "dress-up." It helped to see that these new outfits were a next step on the long road of self-discovery. I felt privileged to know several young people in the 1980s who went through a punk phase. Although the chains and Mohawk haircuts had an air of seeming menace, these particular young people were bright and kind, warm and loving. I came to understand that part of the motive for this fashion choice was to challenge the adult world to look deeper if we wanted to meet them. They wanted to know if we stopped at the superficial façade, or if we were willing to go through to a more profound reality.

Adolescence can be very challenging for parents. Your beloved child is suddenly critical. In fact there is no one as able as your teenage daughter or son to slip a dagger into your most hidden shame, self-doubt, or hypocrisy. They can be merciless in their criticisms, even as they deeply long for parental acceptance. They act badly and also feel bad about doing so. They are trying to discover who they are, and so they must hit up against the boundaries that have held them through childhood. They rebel in order to find themselves, and most often parents are the battering ram for their self-explorations. They must test every limit. Indeed the young person who does not rebel at all during adolescence may have a harder time finding his or her own voice and sense of personal authority later in life.

Parents, of course, can recall their own rebellions and experiments and want to spare their children the hardships they remember. But a sudden clamping down with new rules often leads to more problems. Attention to discipline, including the example and fostering of self-discipline, is vitally important in the earlier years of childhood. Of course there is still a need for boundaries in adolescence, but it is difficult to introduce them now if they have been absent at younger ages. Now the young people are looking intently for the truth in what we say and do, for whether and how we are living our words of control and advice.

There are so many things to worry about as parents of teens. There are real dangers in the world, and however confident our young people may try to appear, as adults we see their vulnerability. Yet I think we also know that all the worry rarely does any good. We certainly can know this from our memories of being adolescents, when we chafed at what seemed like foolish parental concerns. Many parents describe that it was when their children were teenagers that they really learned to pray. I know for myself that I worked hard to trust in my children's destinies; I tried to feel in touch with their higher selves, or what some would call their guardian angels. Inwardly, daily, I wished them the strength to deal in their own right ways with the many threats and temptations that would inevitably come their way.

The healthy adolescent will move through the negativity and over-sensitivity of the early teens toward a growing capacity of self-reflection, an ability to focus his or her thinking, and even the possibility to listen with interest to another's point of view. As they struggle through their own experience of polarities, they can be homeopathically aided by working with real polarities: black and white drawing or drama like Romeo and Juliet that addresses the conflict between blood-ties and the individual. One teacher friend of mine had tenth graders work with scenes of arguing from several different plays. In developing the different characters the students were able to play out various soul moods and so perhaps bring added perspective to the conflicts in their own lives.

Stories of trials, of striving, and initiation nurture their emerging sense of independence. Lucky the young person who can work with

EXERCISES FOR ADOLESCENCE

Was there someone special you could really talk to in your teen-age years? Picture this person as clearly as possible, and also yourself at the time. What were the particular qualities that this person offered? What made this relationship so important for you?

Can you remember an ideal that awoke for you in these years? How did it present itself? Picture yourself clearly as this was dawning in you. How did it influence your behavior at the time? What happened to this ideal as you grew older?

literature like the story of Parzival, a knight on a quest who must work his way beyond all the inherited advice of his upbringing until he can finally ask from his own heart a question that brings healing to another's suffering. Perhaps you remember reading biographies of people who overcame great difficulties or whose actions or discoveries served social justice or innovation. Self-confidence is also well served by summer jobs, community service, and responsibilities at home.

What is sad is when the pressures of competition usurp a natural desire to learn ever more about everything or to follow after an exciting interest or ideal. Too many young people are caught by the rat race of college admission and miss the true quest for real learning and identity that these years can inspire. Others withdraw or rebel from familial or educational expectations, escaping into substance abuse and the arrested development that accompanies it.

And then there is the lure of love and the draw of sex that can be powerful during these years. Awakening longings accompany a ripeness for love. These are the Venus-influenced years; like the planet for whom she is named, the beautiful goddess of love shines over adolescence in both her sensuous and her more celestial sides. Popular culture offers a steady stream of tempting images and possibilities to the feelings that abound in the yearnings for relationship. And still there can be great tenderness in the miracle of a first

love, even in our time of sexual materialization and the ever-present
teen peer pressures.

Rudolf Steiner offers interesting pictures of gender development in
the teen years. Only at the high school level does he suggest that girls
and boys should be treated in any way differently, and he grounds
this suggestion on the different ways they are coming into incarnation.

As discussed in chapter 2, Steiner says that males are more deeply
incarnated into their physical bodies. Puberty takes longer for them,
and the "I" waits until the early twenties to really connect with the
physical, etheric, and astral sheaths. We can clearly observe the muscle
and bone development that happens in the teenage years, and the gradual firming up of the intellect is also a pleasure to behold. Perhaps you
even remember the joy of experiencing this. But it is harder to know
what is going on in a boy's feeling life—even for him. It is as if the boys
are only slowly awakening to the riddle of life, and they are often lonely,
confused, and shy. They may hide their inner turmoil and yearning by
playing the clown, or even cover it with bullying behavior. Speaking
about the adolescent boy Steiner advises us to respect the "secret con-
cealed in his soul"; it is important not to mock his sensitivity or to ask
him too many personal questions.[13] He really does not know how to
answer them. Rather he can be helped by asking him to speak about
the feelings of a character in a story or play or painting. This one-step-
removed articulation lets him practice attending to an inner dimension.

Sometimes when I watch adolescent boys bumble past me on the
street acting so silly or self-absorbed, I try to remember the words
of the English poet Paul Matthews, who captured very movingly the
hidden tenderness of those years in describing his gradual awakening
to the secret within him:

> When I was fourteen years old, I broke my leg playing Rugby. I
> think it was the Muse that tripped me. I wasn't able to dance at
> the parties that Christmas—had to sit aside watching, suddenly
> awake to my separate presence in the Universe. And when the
> girls came to scribble their names on my plaster their eyes cast
> a glamour upon the light, and changed it.

---

13 Steiner, *Education for Adolescents*.

Then I went back to my boarding school. It was difficult being boys only. Girls…were what we joked about. Boasted about. Or else they were goddesses. Nothing in between. When the neighbouring girls' school joined us in the choir we gawped at them across an unbridgeable gulf. That was the shadow of it (I suffer it still); but maybe it allowed some other gleam to come through.

I began to read Wordsworth. When the other boys went out into the woods to smoke, I went to commune with Nature. It sounds priggish as I write it. Maybe I was so—would have done better to run with the others. Except that she was waiting— "the woman I would marry." The trees were too blatant. The stars were. I wanted to strip them away and find her.

The rain was an aspect of her. When I heard it pattering against the window I would be off and out in it. I could be naked there. Not shy. Not awkward anymore. I would smile a sort of smile to myself.

And I began to write poetry. "The shivering moon hangs silent o'er the trees," was the first line I ever wrote. The false rhetoric embarrasses me now. But at the time it thrilled me. Lying in bed that night I muttered it over and over to myself— knew at last what I was born for.[14]

The adolescent girl is more aware of, and more interested in her feeling life. Her inner world is more accessible to her and all the talking she does with her friends is a way of exploring it. Many boys (and indeed men!) find it truly puzzling how girls can talk together so much: what do they have to say so endlessly? And yet I remember noticing when my children were teenagers how the boys would gravitate to the periphery of the girls' conversations, not quite willing to partake, perhaps even feigning disinterest, but vicariously attending to those female soul searchings.

Steiner attributes the girl's ability to look at her feelings with more self-assurance to the fact that she is less deeply incarnated into physicality. He goes further to give a picture of the girl's astral body sucking her "I" into it, already in her teens. With this earlier connection of

---

14   From an *Ariadne Newsletter* in the 1970s, now printed in a revised form in Paul Matthews' *Slippery Characters*.

her "I," she is more self-conscious and she can more easily understand the moods and motivations of others. He says that it is less important to ask a high school girl how a character in a story feels than to ask her how an engine works, or to describe a historical occurrence, or to bring objectivity into an aesthetic judgment. Always this attention to serving balance.

It is interesting to reflect for a moment on these two gender-based developmental pictures. When the young man's "I" enters the pre-pared physical, etheric, and astral sheaths at around twenty-one, it does so in a clear and distinct way; whereas the girl's "I" is inter-mingled with the development of her astral body. These patterns play on throughout life, contributing to a generalized gender differentia-tion and challenge. For the man it usually takes conscious effort to shine the light of his "I"-attention on his feelings, while the woman may spend much of her life trying to distinguish her sense of self from its entanglement with her feelings. Images like this can veer toward stereotypes, which is certainly not my purpose. But insofar as we do recognize tendencies toward one-sidedness, we can be more active in our efforts to respect these natural inclinations. In addition this can help us appreciate just how much women and men learn from and need each other on our long road toward human wholeness.

The First Moon Node

Turning now to the older teen, we see that there is an interesting rhythm that occurs between eighteen and nineteen. Without entering into lengthy astrological considerations, this eighteen-and-a-half-year rhythm reflects the relationship of Moon, Earth, and Sun as they were at the time of one's birth. Called the first Moon Node, it refers to the Moon's path crossing the ecliptic—the path of the Sun as seen from the Earth—as it did when one entered into life on Earth. Pictorially it is as if we come once again to a cosmic gateway we passed through on our journey to Earth, and it is often a time when the young person feels openness to the spirit intentions of this life. Some people will have particularly significant dreams; others find themselves pondering quite new questions of meaning. It is interesting that in many cultures this is the time of finishing high school and making choices about future work or education. There may be both outer and inner change, perhaps a break with life as it has been, and an opening to a new step, or a new, even surprising, glimmer of a career direction. One young woman who had for years wanted to be older than she was, unwittingly spoke the truth of this rhythm in stating at eighteen and a half, "I feel closer to myself than I have in years."

And of course in these last teen years one's eternal individuality, one's "I" is indeed ever closer. These are the years of pondering, "Who am I?" and wondering if anyone can ever really know me. There may be a growing desire to really meet others as well. I was moved one time when a twenty-year-old friend of my son's told me: "I realize I don't know my mother. I love her, but I don't know her as a person. Now I am interested."

And so the springtime of life moves mysteriously into summer. After long years of preparation it is time to begin blossoming, which leads us to a whole new chapter.

The Recognitions

Not the god, though it might have been,
savoring some notion of me
and exciting the cloud where he was hidden
with impetuous thunderstrokes of summoning
—it was merely you who recognized me,
speaking my name in such a tone
I knew you had been thinking it
a long, long time, and now revealed yourself
in this way. Because of this, suddenly
who I was was precious to me.
  —Irving Feldman, *Collected Poems, 1954–2004*

◊

Is my contact with others anything more than a contact with reflections? Who or what can give me the power to transform the mirror into a doorway? —Dag Hammarskjöld, *Markings*

CHAPTER 6

SUMMER FULLNESS: TWENTY-ONE TO FORTY-TWO

Stepping into adulthood is like entering into the heart of the question "who am I?" The question itself is, of course, a journey of discovery lasting in some ways forever; but around twenty-one, there is often an urgency for some answers or at least for experiences that will open new doors to our emerging sense of self. As mentioned in chapter 1, many of those doors will, in fact, open through the recognitions of others: our friends, colleagues, partners, and advisors help us to incorporate different sides of ourselves, as do, often, those with whom we have difficulties.

Throughout the years of childhood and youth what I have earlier referred to as the body sheaths were gradually developing, preparing the vessel that the eternal "I"—each one's own unique individuality—can now approach more directly. The physical, etheric, and astral bodies have come into being through the different phases of childhood and can now offer housing for the incarnating spirit "I."

Of course the "I" is not born fully awakened or self-aware. It takes us the whole of life to approach its evolving majesty. Throughout these next twenty-one years, this blooming, blossoming, summertime of life—indeed the phase most influenced by the Sun—we find ourselves on a road of self-discovery and self-definition. Although the way may wind through clouds and darkness, the Sun stays high in the sky, offering warmth and light for our self-searching.

Because I have seen so much evidence for it, I have always been moved by the picture Rudolf Steiner gives, referred to in chapter 4, of the "I" gradually transforming the legacy of our first twenty-one years through this next period of life. Each of us has our own story of gifts and deficits coming over from our experiences between birth and twenty-one. The "I" now penetrates into the astral, etheric, and physical sheaths, reworking what has been offered and even what may have become embedded quite unconsciously into our developing being through the years of childhood.

Pivoting around the twenty-first year and then again around the forty-second, we can sometimes experience significant echoes in experiences between twenty-one to twenty-eight, and further between forty-two to forty-nine, from an event that happened between fourteen to twenty-one. Similar correspondences can sometimes be found between seven to fourteen, twenty-eight to thirty-five, and forty-nine to fifty-six, or between birth to seven, thirty-five to forty-two, and fifty-six to sixty-three. It is as if there is a spiraling resonance, a movement of a perhaps hidden theme, beyond an initial outer event into a more inner soul or spirit reverberation in later phases. None of this has prescriptive value, which would be built on speculation, but it can sometimes be useful in considering events that seem puzzling in their immediate context. Often it is possible to recognize a greater will at work behind the seemingly isolated events of our lives. At the very least we can see that these corresponding phases reveal the activity of metamorphosis in our lives.

One aspect of these echoing phenomena has to do with the awakening of new dimensions of soul during the twenties and thirties. As noted in chapter 4, these are the years of soul deepening, when our inner life is enriched by the emergence of our individuality. In these years we are challenged to take up our own process of psychological maturing. We wake up into our unique soul existence, becoming ever more responsible for our own feelings, thoughts, and deeds. Rudolf Steiner elaborates upon this process in referring to the development of what he calls the sentient soul in the years from twenty-one to twenty-eight, the intellectual, or mind, soul between twenty-eight and thirty-five, and the consciousness soul from thirty-five to forty-two.

I do not want to minimize in any way the sufferings from childhood that people carry as a legacy into adulthood. Through neglect or over-stimulation, as a consequence of abuse or manifold hardships to body and soul, we may come to adulthood with a wounded sense of self. For good reason our times offer a great variety of healing

DIAGRAM #6 **Timeline Number Two**
Seven-year phases with echoing connections

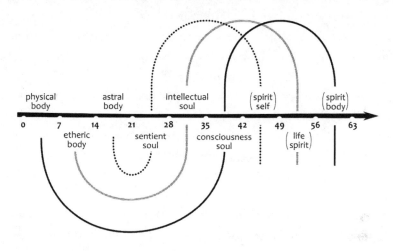

approaches to work with the biographical scars that inhibit healthy psychological growth. My focus in these chapters on life phases is on basic developmental rhythms. I believe that these rhythms unfold in all our lives, in individual ways colored by the joys and sorrows, the opportunities and the deprivations we have experienced. We are never static beings, and we are challenged to be ever more wakeful to the growth that is occurring. As we do our best to bring consciousness to our life stories, and also understanding and forgiveness where we can, I trust that we will be able not only to find our way through the shadows that darken our path, but also to grow in depth and strength. I am reminded here of a poem by Mary Oliver from her book *Thirst*:

THE USES OF SORROW
(*In my sleep I dreamed this poem*)

Someone I loved once gave me
a box full of darkness.

It took me years to understand
that this, too, was a gift.

—MARY OLIVER[1]

---

1   Oliver, *Thirst*, p. 52.

TWENTY-ONE TO TWENTY-EIGHT

Can you remember your twenty-first year? Did you feel an awakening to a new sense of self-responsibility, perhaps manifesting in the desire to begin real work or to shape your own life circumstances? For many people the time between twenty and twenty-two brings significant outer changes: one's own apartment, a first "real" job, college graduation, or the end of parental financial support. Even young people who were already leading independent and responsible lives by their late teens, can often identify a moment around twenty-one when they felt differently about themselves, older and more adult. One friend who had two children by the age of twenty-one, remembers very well the day she went out and bought herself a pair of white boots and knew that her life had taken a decided turn. Friendships often transform, and quite new kinds of people become more interesting. One can feel as if one is shedding aspects of oneself. Many people travel at this age, and in the process discover not only new places in the world, but also new parts of themselves.

One January night when I was twenty, I found myself on a plane over the Atlantic Ocean, on my way to study in Spain. The arrangements had all been made in the flurried two weeks before my departure, because the impulse to go had only just erupted with an insistence that defied my more rational decision several months earlier to remain on a more traditional road to finishing college. I had no idea where I would be staying, but had been told there would be a message for me when I arrived at the Madrid airport. As I looked out the plane window, high above the clouds, I remember thinking: "I'm free! For the first time in my life I'm nobody's daughter, nobody's student, nobody's girlfriend, or friend or sister or anyone already known. People will only meet what I choose to share with them." It was exhilarating! Of course, it was also largely illusion, but as a step in self-awareness and responsibility it was a glorious and important heralding of my "I." A new sense of self was stepping forward and adventure was calling.

Do you recall this time of stepping into adulthood? Did you feel the desire to free yourself from the norms and limitations of your upbringing? Did you find yourself sifting through the advice of parents

> **WRITING EXERCISE** • Write for five minutes beginning with the phrase: "When I was twenty-one..." Just let the memories come, without editing. Was this a time of change for you, of new inner and outer experiences?
>
> At another time you can also do this writing with: "When I was twenty-eight..." or "When I was thirty-five..."

and teachers, trying to discover your own values as you explored new ways of being? The adolescent may have tried on a wide variety of masks, but now there is a stronger wish to step right into different kinds of social circumstances, to find oneself by meeting the world in all its complex ways, to test one's dreams against reality.

Life is the great teacher in the years from twenty-one to twenty-eight, offering us information about who we are as we experience what we do well and what is more challenging. The resistances and reactions of the world are central to our emerging self-definition. What I am able to do, and what I like or I dislike begin to describe who I am. It is important in these years to experiment with different activities and ways of being, to explore different skills, and to learn from the consequences of my efforts. It is hard when one is stuck in a narrow, repetitive job and, of course, even worse when there is no employment to be had. We need the feedback of others; we soar inwardly when we are praised, and a part of us wilts when we are criticized. Finding a balanced self-image is a great challenge throughout these years.

Twenty-first century American culture prematurely pushes concerns about job security and pensions into the twenties, when ideally this should be an adventurous and expansive time, not overburdened by long-term planning. It is fortunate when a young person has the chance to travel or to explore a variety of jobs. Unemployment or the need to move back into one's childhood home are painful because they can narrow the opportunities to test one's wings, to meet new challenges, and to discover new sides of oneself. Even within one steady work or life situation, it is helpful to be able to try out different tasks and be confronted with ever new expectations. At this age the future ideally feels wide open and dreams can reach far; a great many possibilities lie ahead.

When my husband Chris and I were first married, in our early twenties, we had a next-door neighbor with whom we had occasional working-in-the-garden conversations. He was in his early thirties, and every encounter would include the same question to Chris about whether he had yet done his military service. This was the late 1960s, in the middle of the Vietnam War, and we were in fact very relieved that Chris's PhD studies would take him beyond the draft age limit of twenty-six. But our neighbor would slide over this detail and say with earnest conviction: "You want to get your service years over as soon as you can, so that by the time you are thirty, you can be hired by a company with a good pension plan." In order not to offend him, we would quickly go inside where we would marvel at the idea that anyone would organize life around a pension plan. Putting aside the question of whether vocational choices are best determined quite so pragmatically, this exchange illustrates such a phase-based difference of perspective. At his age this kind of rational planning was perfectly appropriate, but to us, in our early twenties, it was unthinkable.

As noted, there is a dynamic relationship between the teen years and the twenties. Throughout the twenties the "I" attends to the legacy of the adolescent years with ever greater consciousness. The self, growing in awareness, now meets the swirl of emotional life that came alive with the awakening of the astral body. Feelings are still a primary motivating force throughout the twenties, as impressions from the outer world are received into the developing sentient soul. Indeed, the experience of these years is strongly colored by how we feel about what meets us. Our feelings are the compass for what is true. I once had a student who began a paper with the sentence: "It's amazing how my father has changed in the last four years." No doubt this was so, but what became clear in the paper was the vast difference in my student's heartfelt perceptions of his father at twenty-three, compared to when he was nineteen.

Gradually throughout this phase our "I" learns to attend to the messages the feelings offer about oneself and about the world. These are years of great passion and energy. One's social, political, and

---

EXERCISE • Doors: In these years from twenty-one to twenty-eight, who opened a door of development for you? Picture this person as clearly as you can, and also yourself both before and after the opening. If you have access to clay, it can be very illuminating to model yourself after this door was opened. How were you then different? What might an observer have seen about you? How did you feel about this opening? Does the experience live on in you in any way?

You can also ponder these questions with the next two seven-year phases in these years from twenty-one to forty-two. See if you can feel qualitative differences in your experiences in the different phases. Were there doors that you opened for yourself? For whom did you open a door?

---

ethical views can be especially strong. Whether idealistic, angry, or radical, they are often fired with self-righteousness, as in the call of my generation to "never trust anyone over thirty." Life touches the soul deeply that it may grow in dimension. It is interesting to reflect on what ideas and what people came into your life in these years. What sparked your enthusiasm? Who opened doors for you? What encouragements and what boundaries shaped your becoming?

Part of entering adulthood is the effort to free ourselves of values and limitations from our upbringing that we feel are no longer necessary or perhaps now even damaging to our emerging sense of self. At the same time we are challenged to integrate aspects of our story and ourselves that are not going to change, such as the shape of our nose, our need for glasses, our temperament, our parents' divorce, or that we grew up in a big city. As we forge our way into the future, we each have our particular strengths and weaknesses from childhood that now appear as landmarks in our biography. With attention we can discover how we are more than those strengths and weaknesses: we now have our independent "I" with which to steer our way and guide our on-going story. Ideally in this phase, young people will feel that the future is open, that changes can be made, and that fulfilling dreams is possible. Even perceived deficits can be faced with a will for development.

In speaking about his own early adult years, when he was a tutor for a family of four boys, Steiner had this to say about meeting something that he then perceived as lacking from his childhood:

> Before I came to this family, my opportunities to participate in children's games had been limited. Consequently, finally, during my twenties I had time to play, since I had to learn how to play and direct the games. I did this with great satisfaction. I think that during my life I have played as much as anyone, but it was not until I was between twenty-two and twenty-eight that I did what is usually accomplished before the age of ten.[2]

A Time of Crisis

As we move our way through our twenties, it is almost inevitable that around twenty-eight, we experience a time of taking stock, a questioning of our direction, even what many experience as an inner and outer crisis. Of course, the word crisis has many layers of meaning within it. It comes from the Greek *krisis* and implies both an instability and a turning point. It is connected to judgment and decision, testing and discrimination—all of which come into play for the young person at this age.

This is a self-analyzing time, a time of asking questions: Am I doing what I want to be doing? What have I accomplished? Who am I now? What do I want for my future? What are my capacities and my limitations? In all the introspection, people look at their relationships as well: Have I been avoiding intimacy? Am I too needy? Do I have room to grow in my relationships? Am I ready to settle down? Or do I need to move on?

As the young person becomes more aware of the consequences of his or her decisions and actions, there is often a wish to make changes. Attitudes are reevaluated and new goals are set. This is a time when many people decide to marry, and also when many divorce. People in graduate school now want a job, and others will decide to return to further study. I worked for many years in adult education, directing a Foundation Studies program for people who were considering becoming teachers in Waldorf schools. There was always a noticeable clump

---

2   Steiner, *Autobiography*, p. 53.

of students between twenty-seven and twenty-nine; after much soul searching, they had arrived at the college, ready to take both outer and inner steps.

This time around twenty-eight can be particularly challenging for people born with strong artistic talents, including those who have trained for many years as musicians, dancers, poets, or painters. Now come inner questions: "How do I go on with my art? How do I make it my own, and not only a gift I was born with?" These gifts that are ours through karmic inheritance now ask to be worked with in new ways, or they recede in importance. Will the gift become the basis of one's life work? How can one's evolving "I" now direct the further nurturing, exploration, and development of one's talent?

A young woman named Etty Hillesum who was active in the Dutch resistance during World War II kept a diary that was found after her death in Auschwitz. Although her life situation was certainly more gripping and traumatic than most, her words capture something archetypal about this age: she describes feeling

> a growing sense of self-certainty. I have matured enough to assume my "destiny," to cease living an accidental life.... And it helps that I am now twenty-eight and no longer twenty-two. Now I have a right to a "destiny." It is no longer a romantic dream or a thirst for adventure, or for love, all of which can drive you to commit mad and irresponsible acts. No, it is a terrible, sacred inner seriousness, difficult and at the same time inevitable.[3]

A Detour through the Soul Orientations

Before stepping into the next phase from twenty-eight to thirty-five, I want to pause to explore another way of looking at our individual ways of being. I do this at this point because it is a perspective that can be very helpful in understanding how we find our work in the world. Both the teen years and the twenties have very much to do with the developing astral body, the part of our makeup that is informed by the journey through the starry heavens between death and rebirth.

---

3   Hillesum, *An Interrupted Life*, pp. 132–138.

In chapter 4, I suggested that along the way through the seven classically known planetary spheres, we are "dressed and blessed" for our coming earthly life. I mentioned that various planetary influences play into the different life phases, and that each of us comes to Earth with our own particular planetary endowment. This shows itself in what can be called a Soul Orientation or Soul Type.

Here is another piece of the puzzle of our individual human nature, another way of seeing how cosmic realities color our unique personalities. Can you imagine that each different planetary being shines its forces on us as we descend toward a new earthly life, blessing each of us with a unique combination of soul qualities that will manifest ever more strongly after puberty, as our astral body begins its activity? Can you consider that when I refer to a planetary being, I am not envisioning some fixed entity but rather the quality of "being" as a verb? The planetary spheres exist as spiritual activity that is vital, broad, and overlapping, and each domain has something different to offer.

Even if the imagination of planetary being(s) is not something you want to consider, this typology is useful in understanding personality differences. These orientations can be thought of as different character types. The endowment I am born with is part of my character, and it shows itself in what interests me, in what I choose to do, and in what soul qualities I have to offer. As opposed to the temperament that lives in our habit body and manifests in our unconscious ways of acting and reacting, the soul orientation shows itself through inclinations, interests, and ways of being we offer into the world. We have been gifted with our soul orientation and so we can share this gift through how we relate to our life tasks. The idea of soul types is a particularly helpful framework for those who work with adolescents and young adults; it can be used as a way to focus conversations about possible career choices as well as a practical aid for self-awareness.

This typology with its relationship to the planets is rooted in Rudolf Steiner's views of human development. I could describe these basic orientations without reference to this background as Bernard Lievegoed does in his book *Phases*.[4] I choose not to do this because for me the background deepens my sense for the value of the approach. There are other categorizations of human personality differences that are popular today, most notably the Myers-Briggs system, which is an adaptation of C. G. Jung's ideas, and several different approaches to the Enneagram, a ninefold geometrically based perspective. In both these systems there are lengthy questionnaires to help people determine their particular type or inclination. These assessments have proven helpful for countless individuals, as tools for self-understanding and also in career guidance. I have appreciated working with both of them. Nevertheless, I find myself wanting to know *why* they work and what forces in human development are involved in creating the different ways of being.

I often think that any typology that gets people to look at their lives has something to offer. I am reminded of a book published many years ago by a friend of mine that was a spoof of the Color Me Beautiful analysis that was all the rage in the 1980s. My friend's book was called *Find Your Seasoning, Find Yourself*,[5] and the categories were parsley, pepper, garlic, and ginger. For all the good humor, there was also much validity in these characterizations of distinctly flavored human behavior. But if these seasonings do depict something archetypal in our ways of being, then I would wager there is some outside force—I would call it cosmic—that is influencing both them and us.

And so I now want to characterize the planetary soul types, the different orientations that manifest in life interests and work and were formed through qualitative outpourings in the different planetary spheres. The different planetary influences can also be seen in many other aspects of life on Earth. For example, they are involved in shaping and supporting the different organs of the body, and their influences appear in tree species or in the varieties of metals, grains, colors, and in the days of the week as mentioned in chapter 4. To go into all these connections is beyond the scope of this book, but I recommend it as a

---

4   Lievegoed, *Phases*, ch. 4. In his book *Man on the Threshold*, Lievegoed does elaborate on the planetary connections (pp. 101–118); for a more detailed description of the different types, see also Lee Sturgeon-Day's self-published workbook, *Planetary Qualities for Working Groups*, in her *Biography Workbooks* series.

5   Hickey and Hughes, *Find Your Seasoning, Find Yourself.*

fascinating further study. Our human passage through these spheres has its individual trajectory, and so we are each uniquely endowed as we journey toward incarnation. Of course we have all been offered gifts from each of the planetary spheres, and yet it is part of our destiny to be more richly supplied with one or two basic orientations.

The Researcher

People with a lot of Saturn forces have deeply inquisitive minds. Saturn is the most distant of the evolutionary planets and those it strongly influences are inclined to go to the depths of what interests them. They will follow a question to its source, steadfast in their desire to explore, to gather all the relevant information, to reach to *how, when,* and *why?* Perhaps you know a mathematician who has lived with a single problem for many years, or an artist who pursues one resounding thread through all her artistic explorations. Both are researchers, patiently considering every angle and open at any moment to new inspiration. This kind of lifelong quest could also be in science, history, or any other field of knowledge. Saturn people are after an ultimate truth, an archetype; their search will be careful, persistent, and orderly. Saturn has been known in mythology as Father Time, with his hourglass in hand—holding the beginning, the wholeness, and the long evolving process, grain of sand by grain of sand.

In groups Saturn people are the ones who remind us of the goal, they help the group to stay on track with a prodding, "Why are we doing this?" or "How would that serve our aim?" Actually, people with a lot of Saturn forces are not readily drawn to work in groups, nor are they ardent team players. They tend rather more toward isolation and may stay removed from immediate concerns. Saturnine people can be somber and brooding, but their devotion and loyalty to the quest is very real. While they may have the problem of tunnel vision, and are not always the most flexible of thinkers, they bring great staying power to a task. It is the path of inquiry itself that fills them with inner enthusiasm.

The Thinker

Very different is the person with a lot of Jupiter forces. In ancient myths Jupiter is the King, the wise one with the all-encompassing view, surveying the land and holding a vision of the whole. People with a lot of Jupiter forces take the broad view, they see the larger system, they appreciate harmony and how things fit within a greater order. Philosophers in any field—ideas, the stars, music, mathematics, or painting—show Jupiter's love of concepts, laws, and logic. Jupiter people are often poor researchers, for the details are not what interest them; they have great vision and a deep will to see larger patterns at work in the world. People who are drawn to long-range planning, systems theory, or institutional and family structures are all likely to have a Jupiter orientation.

In groups it is Jupiter people who draw the threads between the many ideas put forward; their view is from the mountaintop and they look for connections, seeing wholeness from the pieces. Sometimes they can get caught in abstractions or a well-conceived theory and turn away from the nitty-gritty particulars of actually getting a job done. They assume that others will somehow deal with any necessary details. My husband reminds me every day of Jupiter's different qualities: he lives with large social and political concerns and has great gifts in weaving together seemingly disparate ideas, but at least once a week he loses his keys or misplaces his wallet and daily leaves a trail of abandoned clues to show his passage through the house. The general idealism of Jupiter-inspired people shields them from taking momentary obstacles or limitations too seriously. With their love for meaning and the big picture they are often inspiring teachers.

The Doer

Mars, the red planet and inspirer of the mythological God of Combat, offers the human being energy, initiative, and purposeful direction. Here we find the organizers, the entrepreneurs, and those who long to put ideas into practice. Mars-inspired people are courageous, active, and forceful. They are not theoretical; rather it is in real, specific situations that they feel the impulse to bring order, to control, and reshape what is in front of them. Sometimes they can get caught in functionality and run the risk of losing the greater goal. Mars people do not necessarily wait for any outside authorization before responding to a perceived need. Nor are they afraid of conflict; indeed, they like a good challenge and grow through resistance.

Mars people are often the first to speak in a group. They have a strong relationship to words and can use them persuasively. They name what they see and "call it like it is." They are often effective public speakers. Even though the world needs their initiative, their forcefulness can at times be overwhelming for others. Nevertheless, their strength and drive can also inspire hope in those around them. They are hard workers, willing to take on difficult tasks and to find a way through any obstacle.

The Caregiver

If Mars people are speakers, then Venus people are the listeners of the world. They have space in themselves to receive and support others, and can ponder things quietly in their hearts. Their essential caring impulse creates environments of beauty, warmth, and security where life can be nurtured and protected. When you walk into the home of a Venus-inspired person, you feel welcomed and comfortable. Picture the creator of a salon of bygone days: usually a woman, she would prepare the space with a quiet devotion and gracious attention to detail, all in the service of her guests who would arrive to hold forth on their own ideas. People with strong Venus forces are drawn to service professions like nursing, gardening, or early-childhood teaching. They know how to tend to life itself. They care about relationships and are concerned about the feelings of others.

In groups Venus people listen not only to the words spoken, but also to the mood, and they can be particularly alert to unspoken feelings or moments when someone may feel overlooked or ignored. Their great sensitivity to the needs of others can occasionally become overly sympathetic, even at times excessively sentimental. There is a selfless quality in Venus people, although when overextended they can fall into feelings of martyrdom. Venus-inspired environments are warm and nurturing. There may be a danger that they become over-organized or over-protective, but as a counterbalance in our modern hurried and functional world we dearly need the care, comfort, and aesthetic attention that Venus people offer.

John Gray's very popular books about men being from Mars and women from Venus build on gender stereotypes connected to these two related planets. For myself, however, I feel the need to be careful about identifying them too specifically with men and women. Certainly there is a more masculine force in Mars qualities and a more feminine mood to Venus characteristics; but since all women and men have both masculine and feminine aspects within them, as elaborated in chapter 2, it would be wrong to identify either gender too closely with any particular soul orientation. Nevertheless, it is useful to notice how much these particular planetary ways of being need each other: speakers and listeners depend on each other to be able to offer their best. The initiative-takers of the world need those who can nurture their ideas and offer supportive, well-tended venues in which new activities can flourish; and the reverse is also true.

The Innovator

Jupiter, too, has a counterpart in the universe in Mercury; every king needs his fool or jester to balance out a tendency toward self-importance or even pomposity, to bring humor, realism, and social art into the present moment. As a god, Mercury was worshiped by the sailors, the traders, the gamblers, and the thieves—wherever things were in movement, his protection was sought. The ancient Greeks knew him as Hermes, the Messenger of the gods, carrying news on winged feet between Earth and the divine world. Mercury people love to make connections between people and so make skillful networkers and lively salespeople. Medical professionals often use the staff of Mercury, known as the caduceus, with its wings and two intertwining rising snakes, as a powerful image of the will to heal through restoring balance. It is actually a bit of mercurial trickery that the caduceus is so used, since the traditional medical symbol was the rod of Asclepius, with only a single snake. Mercury people are ever adaptable: if one approach to a task does not seem to work, then they are ready with another idea to try. Mercury's influence can be felt in those who bring practical intelligence to the present moment, the specific case; where things are stuck they bring a story, a joke, a prod, or another way to look at something.

Mercury people bring innovation through their love of experiment and their devotion to the idea that change is good—in relationships, groups, communities, or the broader social order. They are quick, artful, and insightful, and were surely multitaskers before the concept existed. The metal mercury, or quicksilver, is a perfect image with its lack of solidity or fixed form. Sometimes this love of movement is too much or too fast and so creates chaos, a situation more problematic to others than to Mercury people. At times Mercury-influenced people seem to skim along the surface of things, or they can embody the trickster with a certain amorality. But with their basic compassion, ready wit, and strong desire to serve development in real situations, they invariably invite life and offer the hope of new possibilities.

The Record Keeper

So much closer to the Earth than any of the planets, the Moon offers a polarity to far-off Saturn. While Saturn reminds us of the once-upon-a-time beginning, the Moon reflects the Sun's light day by day and orders the tides and other vital earthly rhythms to do with reproduction and growth. People with a lot of Moon forces know the importance of rhythm and are inclined to gather, conserve, and mirror back the daily occurrences of life. They have a deep reverence for the past, for continuity, and tradition. Their desire to capture what has been makes them good archivists, historians, librarians, bookkeepers, or journalists. Their will to maintain, reproduce, and support the routines of life can incline them toward the regularity of administrative activities. They can have an encyclopedic memory about statistics, family happenings, or the workings in an office, and they are often staunch defenders of the status quo. Collectors and those with a natural inclination to recycle—clothes, newspaper articles, antiques or buttons—show the Moon influence on their ways of being.

In group settings, people with a lot of Moon are the natural reviewers and evaluators: "Let's look back on what we have done today." They like the regularity of group habits, rituals, and ways of doing things. They are orderly and measured in their approach to new ideas. At times they can get caught in the past, in the way things have always been done, yet the foundation of memory they offer is often stabilizing and supportive. The coldness of the Moon can sometimes be a problem if reflections become rigid, excessively impersonal, or more operational than alive. Nevertheless, the generous reflections of Moon-inspired people faithfully collect and preserve living threads from the past in order to offer them for use in the present and the future.

The Creative Center

The Sun is the center of our universe, and it shines in the heart of every human being. The Sun sphere is centrally important in our journey between lives; we are all blessed with its warmth and light. As opposed to the other soul orientations, there is not a Sun type per se, but rather people with a lot of Sun are able to use their other planetary endowments in a creative way. The Sun brings artistry to the other ways of being; it allows the other qualities to sparkle and to become fruitful in the world. Sunny people radiate creativity and illuminate it in others.

I have often thought of those with a strong Sun force as having what I call a "relationship capacity"; in social circumstances they weave light between people, bringing a balancing force to different one-sided attributes. They ray out enthusiasm, kindheartedness, and forgiveness, warmly inviting the interest and engagement of others. There is much that overshadows our modern lives, and it is those filled with the light of the Sun who help lift us from the bindings of the past. They have the capacity to freely perceive what is needed and can enlighten new steps toward the future.

I want to reiterate that we all have been gifted with capacities from each of the different planetary realms. Nevertheless, perhaps you can feel that you more naturally exhibit qualities from one, two, or even three spheres than from the others. Of course your temperament will color how these orientations manifest, but try to experience how these different typologies address quite distinct aspects of your behavior. Can you see the difference between a person with a lot of Mars and someone who is choleric? Do you know someone who is phlegmatic and yet exhibits a Mars influence—the quiet steady entrepreneur who gets the job done without a lot of fuss? How would a sanguine with a lot of Venus behave differently than a Venus-endowed phlegmatic? How differently would a melancholic with a lot of Moon look from a Moon-influenced choleric? Please allow your perceptions to roam widely, gathering what may seem to be contrasting phenomena. Live with the wonderful uniqueness of everyone you meet, and do not too easily fix anyone into a set temperament or soul orientation.

As mentioned earlier, the orientations often become visible in our working lives. Of course people with any soul type can work in any career, but there are some jobs that would easily become boring or frustrating where the soul qualities are not allowed full expression. It should be clear that a person with a lot of Saturn would probably not be happy as a receptionist for a large company, nor would a Jupiter person shine as an archivist. Likewise a Mercury person would most likely find it hard to spend all day reconciling figures in an accounting office or researching the movements of a sloth. And someone with a lot of Mars might be challenged as an aid in a nursing home—unless he or she could reorganize the supply closet and design a more efficient way to distribute meals.

It can be very interesting to observe how different inclinations play out within a shared profession. For example, at the small college where I taught for many years, I had some colleagues for whom deepening their subjects through ongoing research was paramount, and others who were more drawn to refining the curriculum as a whole and attending to how the different subjects interrelated. Then there were those who happily took on complex projects for the good of the whole—such as overseeing a building project—while others took deep care for the quality of the students' daily lives. Some were interested in developing alumni gatherings and gladly carried college traditions like opening day or commencement, while others bubbled with ideas for marketing and public relations. We were all devoted to adult education and we carried the development of the college collectively; the freedom to share the gifts of our different ways of being, in addition to the specific tasks for which we had been hired, made the whole a richer and more creative place, both for us as colleagues and for the students as well.

TWENTY-EIGHT TO THIRTY-FIVE

After my rather mercurial detour through planetary realms, I now return to the young person who is emerging from the challenges around age twenty-eight. One twenty-nine year old expressed her movement into this next phase with a very characteristic sentiment: "I feel now as if I need to rethink everything." In this next phase our focus does indeed shift more toward how we think about our lives and somewhat away from the emphasis of the twenties on how we feel about everything. Now we can step back a bit from our experiences and reflect more objectively on where we are going.

It is during these years that the intellectual or mind soul is developing within us. The German word that Rudolf Steiner uses for this aspect of our soul is *Gemüts-Seele*, which has no English equivalent but carries the connotation of both mind and heart. I mention this because the intellectual soul encompasses more than the intellect alone; it includes a feeling perception as well. As our "I" gradually reworks the legacy of our etheric development, especially from the years between seven to fourteen, the intellectual soul now begins to provide us with a deepening sense of understanding through thinking. The challenge, of course, is to have our thinking be renewingly alive, and not riddled with clichés and dead, finished thoughts.

If our elementary school years provided life-filled learning experiences, we will be well served for flexible thinking as we move into our thirties. If we spent those earlier years being bored by the dull monotony of school, we may now be challenged to awaken new forces of enthusiasm. The quality of the time we spent playing, or in nature, or in front of screens, as well as the habits of our family life will all now bear their subtle fruits. But we must never forget that we can now be active with our "I," and we can choose to bring interest, change, and balance into neglected or stressed areas from our earlier years. One of my greatest joys as an adult educator has been seeing people open themselves to ongoing learning and in the process overcome limitations stemming from childhood.

I experienced this myself as well. At the age of ten I shut down completely toward music after the chorus teacher advised me to just move my lips rather than actually sing. I had earlier overheard my piano teacher tell my mother that she was wasting her money on lessons for me. At that time there seemed no hope for me, so I just stopped trying. I did later sing lullabies to my children, but I always felt musically cramped. Then in my early thirties I impulsively asked my daughter's piano teacher if she ever gave lessons to inept adults. She very kindly told me to be at her house the next afternoon, and so began a painful, but ultimately wonderful healing of this inhibition from my childhood. Through the years I was further helped by the many faculty meetings that would begin with group singing. I cannot say I have become a particularly good musician, but I did step over a boulder on my path and have most gratefully enjoyed taking part in music-making ever since.

This phase from twenty-eight to thirty-five is sometimes referred to as the "organizational phase" because it is a time when planning draws our attention. This may manifest in the ways we plot out our rise along a career ladder; or it may show in our desire to see if we can handle a mortgage or how we will afford a special holiday; or it may play out in our consideration of whether or when to have a child. At this time of life we very appropriately believe in the rational promise of well-made plans. We walk around with our day planners, and make a date to meet a friend for lunch in three weeks; in our twenties such a lack of spontaneity felt very burdensome.

After what may have been a lot of emotional turmoil in the twenties, we can now feel excited about settling down, building our career, and pursuing a variety of life goals. We analyze relevant facts and generally take a logical approach to decision-making. We actually feel like an adult now, and we have things to do! We live with schedules and to-do lists, and life can be very full. Can those of you who are parents remember when you began to talk about "quality time" with your children? The concept of such a distinction is very characteristic of this phase.

This is generally a healthy and stable phase, but then gradually, as the years go by, we can start to feel consumed by all the practicalities of life. The rationality and order we once welcomed have created too many responsibilities, as well as what can feel like fixed routines. We may begin to miss the drama and passion of our twenties. Those in long-term relationships can feel constrained by their various roles and the many demands of family life. As the years pass, we may experience our behavior falling into well-formed ruts. For some the time around thirty-three, which echoes that lonely confused time between nine and ten, is particularly challenging. We may feel duty-bound, and engulfed by our material life, by all the requirements and earthly possessions that fill our days.

For many women the later years of this phase, and on into the next one, can become particularly challenging: how do we balance the feminine and masculine sides of ourselves, how do we honor a wish for relationships and family with an equally compelling need for personal expression through work? My generation saw the opening up of career opportunities that earlier were rarely possible for women, even as we carried memories of a mom at home. So much has changed in the last forty years in terms of how women can imagine their lives, and yet healthy relationships still need time and attention, and children still need care and energy from loving parents. The wish to "have it all" and all at the same time can be very stressful in these years.

Does one's budding career allow time for an intimate relationship? And what about children? How long can I wait? And what if I'm not in a stable relationship; should I choose to be a single parent? Of course many people will already have children by the time they enter this phase, but for those who do not, these questions can press from the inside with growing urgency. I had a friend who debated throughout this entire phase whether to have a baby, always hoping that a rational answer would come to what was clearly not only a rational question. Men, too, of course, may be trying to bring balance to their feminine and masculine sides; indeed, many younger men have stepped into family responsibilities that would have been unimaginable to their fathers. Perhaps they are now the family cook or they are much more involved in their children's lives on a daily basis. Nevertheless, it is my observation that in these years balance is more an outer question for them, perhaps even brought to consciousness by their women friends. The real inner need for this kind of balancing attention generally comes in a later phase for men.

As we approach thirty-five and the end of this phase, we are experiencing the most deeply incarnated time of life. We have arrived fully onto the Earth, and the weight and pull of our material lives can be very strong, especially in our materialistic culture. Thirty-five is also the turning point when the up-building forces that have guided our physical growth gradually begin to withdraw. From within we may begin to

wonder what more there might be to life than our own known world, or
what might be calling from beyond the needs of the earthly "I."

THIRTY-FIVE TO FORTY-TWO

I would like to begin looking at this next phase with a favorite poem
of mine by William Stafford. I first read it in a newsletter when I was
in my late twenties, and I cut it out and carried it around with me for
years. But I think its deeper meaning really began to resound in me
in my late thirties.

A RITUAL TO READ TO EACH OTHER

If you don't know the kind of person I am
and I don't know the kind of person you are
a pattern that others made may prevail in the world
and following the wrong god home we may miss our star.

For there is many a small betrayal in the mind,
a shrug that lets the fragile sequence break
sending with shouts the horrible errors of childhood
storming out to play through the broken dyke.

And as elephants parade holding each elephant's tail,
but if one wanders the circus won't find the park,
I call it cruel and maybe the root of all cruelty
to know what occurs but not recognize the fact.

And so I appeal to a voice, to something shadowy,
a remote important region in all who talk:
though we could fool each other, we should consider—
lest the parade of our mutual life get lost in the dark.

For it is important that awake people be awake,
or a breaking line may discourage them back to sleep;
the signals we give—yes or no, or maybe—
should be clear: the darkness around us is deep.

—WILLIAM STAFFORD[6]

---

6   Stafford, *The Darkness around Us Is Deep*, pp. 135–136.

It came as no surprise to me to discover that Stafford wrote this poem when he was thirty-nine, and so in the phase I am now addressing. In its multi-layered imagery the poem expresses the mood of the consciousness soul, that part of our soul life now being deepened. I mentioned in chapter 4 that all of humanity is in the process of developing this aspect of our human nature. We are at a crucial edge in our becoming, and the way forward is through our individual awakening and effort—coming to know *the kind of person I am* and you are, beyond the patterns made by others. And yet, there is also a clear impulse to work together with others in new ways, *lest the parade of mutual life get lost in the dark.* It is part of this age of the consciousness soul that the traditional groupings of family, ethnicity, religion, or social group that once defined identity have ever less hold over us. This is both liberating and isolating. Even as our individualities grow stronger, we can feel the resistances to self-responsibility within and around us, and we often cling longingly to group identifications that were once supporting. The extreme expression of this can be seen in the enduring ethnic and religious conflicts that belie a deeper, but hopefully ultimately stronger, emerging sense of global brotherhood and sisterhood.

And so we can feel how the darkness around us is indeed deep. It is the awakening of the consciousness soul within each of us that will take us forward—individually and collectively—into a new sense of our human connection and further toward genuine spiritual awareness. As an all-human development, the age of the consciousness soul is, according to Rudolf Steiner, only about one third of the way along, stretching for more than 2,000 years from its beginning in the 1400s, which may help to explain the sense of living on a precipice that is so prevalent in our times, and especially in this phase from thirty-five to forty-two.[7]

These years between thirty-five and forty-two are when the "I" is reworking the legacy of our experiences from birth to seven, most of which is beyond the reach of our conscious memory. As already mentioned, those early years are often filled with stress, whether from our own family situation or from modern educational practices, nutrition, media, or the over-stimulation of our fast-paced lives. And now *the*

---

7   Steiner explores the broader subject of the evolution of consciousness in many lectures and in his major work, *An Outline of Esoteric Science.*

horrible errors of childhood can in fact come storming out in all manner of disguised ways—a deep loneliness, unexpected confusions and insecurities, self-doubts, and surprising new fears. I remember thinking when the "inner child" movement became so popular in the mid-1980s that this kind of attention to healing childhood trauma was arising just as the first wave of baby boomers was entering into this phase of life.

In these years we also experience ever more the consequences of the choices, deeds, and compromises we have made. The future does not feel as open, and we may wonder if there is still the space ahead for a fulfillment of our dreams. One artist friend, reflecting at that time on the many pressing responsibilities that seemed to eat up her creativity, worded her inner turmoil this way: "Am I doomed to a life of middle-class mediocrity?"

In these years we also become aware of having less physical energy. It takes a bit longer to climb a hill or to get over a cold, and suddenly fine print seems so much smaller. Who am I, if not my youthful energy? Can I come into touch with some more authentic, more essential sense of self? Am I really the hypocrite my teenager so pitilessly accuses me of being? Perhaps my partner, too, is holding up a harsh, unflattering mirror.

So I try a new exercise program, a new job, a new car, or a new relationship. Any of these might be exactly what I need; the crucial question is whether I seek them out as an escape from self-knowledge and responsibility or whether I go toward them learning all I can as I go. It is our will that is being especially challenged in these years and quite specifically our willingness to take on more consciously our own further development. Am I doing what I am really meant to be doing? Many people in these years will begin paying attention to an inner dimension, finally actually taking up an inner practice—no longer as an interesting possibility, but now as an existential need.

These years are not always easy, but they do invite us to experience the virtues of realism. By this phase, we have, in fact, learned a lot about what it means to be an adult, and there can be real comfort in recognizing what we have accomplished through our own efforts. As one student put this, "I may feel like I am in a dark forest, but I now know that I can go through this." We are more in touch with what really matters to us, and we have the option to be less easily swayed by outer demands and the opinions of others. It is with our consciousness soul that we know ourselves as potentially free individuals; not free in the sense of being able to always do what we want, but inwardly free enough to own our lives with all their messy complexities. With this self-acceptance we can look forward to a deeper dimension of self-determination.

We learn to know paradox in this age and are challenged to come away from the dualistic trap of either/or thinking. Conflicting feelings can both be true: loneliness and connection, anxiety and trust, self-doubt and quiet hope. Often the images in poetry express the ambiguity in our experiences so much better than definitive statements. Donald Justice says much about this phase of life in this poem:

MEN AT FORTY

Men at forty
Learn to close softly
The doors to rooms they will not be
Coming back to.

At rest on a stair landing,
They feel it moving
Beneath them now like the deck of a ship,
Though the swell is gentle.

And deep in mirrors
They rediscover
The face of the boy as he practices tying
His father's tie there in secret

And the face of that father,
Still warm with the mystery of lather.
They are more fathers than sons themselves now.
Something is filling them, something

That is like the twilight sound
Of the crickets, immense,
Filling the woods at the foot of the slope
Behind their mortgaged houses.

—DONALD JUSTICE, *Night Light*

REFLECTIONS FOR EACH OF THE PHASES FROM TWENTY-ONE TO FORTY-TWO •
Try to build vivid and detailed pictures of real events and people:

1. Did you experience a turning point in those years? What was
   the outer or inner situation prompting this change? How did
   it come about? Were others involved? What did this call on in
   you? What entered your life through this experience?
2. How did you make decisions in the different phases? How did
   you make plans? And how did you approach difficulties, or
   adjust to unexpected realities?
3. Who were particularly important people for you at this time?
   What kinds of relationships were important to you in those
   years? What was the quality of your different relationships?
4. What learning did those years offer you? How did you face
   and/or avoid what presented itself to your evolving self-
   knowledge? Did you recognize particular "life themes" of
   your own? How did they manifest and how did you respond?
   How did these themes evolve?

The Second Moon Node

Toward the middle of this phase the second Moon node occurs.
As mentioned in the preceding chapter, this is the rhythm of just over
eighteen and a half years that brings the Sun, Moon, and Earth into
the same relationship they were in at our birth. Between thirty-seven
and thirty-eight we may experience important openings and closings
to do with basic life intentions. Our life may take a surprising turn;
we may move, or begin a new study or work, or there may be a change
in a significant relationship. We are in a very earthly time of life, and
yet this gateway to our deepest spiritual aims is for a moment slightly
open. This can sometimes manifest in an unsettling sense of discon-
nect, while for others it brings an important affirmation.

A former student of mine realized that she began her career as
a Waldorf teacher at this age, and then she recalled that at her first
Moon node, as a recent Waldorf graduate herself, she had tried to

apply to a Waldorf teacher training program but had been told to go study and work elsewhere first. In the intervening years the wish to take up this kind of teaching had been all but eclipsed by study, work, and family, only to reappear with new force and new possibility at the time of her second Moon node.

In the following poem W.S. Merwin offers an image of the puzzlement toward our aging process that can enter our consciousness at this Moon node time:

IN THE WINTER OF MY THIRTY-EIGHTH YEAR

It sounds unconvincing to say *When I was young*
Though I have long wondered what it would be like
To be me now
No older at all it seems from here
As far from myself as ever

Walking in fog and rain and seeing nothing
I imagine all the clocks have died in the night
Now no one is looking I could choose my age
It would be younger I suppose so I am older
It is there at hand I could take it
Except for the things I think I would do differently
They keep coming between they are what I am
They have taught me little I did not know when I was young

There is nothing wrong with my age now probably
It is how I have come to it
Like a thing I kept putting off as I did my youth

There is nothing the matter with speech
Just because it lent itself
To my uses

Of course there is nothing the matter with the stars
It is my emptiness among them
While they drift farther away in the invisible morning

              —W. S. MERWIN, *Migration*

And here is one more example of someone opening at this Moon node time to the call, and the first inkling of a significant life theme: at thirty-seven J. W. Goethe secretly slipped away in the middle of the night from the order of his life in Germany to embark on a journey to Italy. Once on the road he wondered in his diary, "Can I learn to look at things with clear, fresh eyes? ...Can the grooves of old mental habits be effaced? This is what I am trying to discover."[8] It was on this trip that he first conceived his idea of the archetypal plant; and he reflected later on "what enthusiasm we feel, when we glimpse in advance and in its totality something which is later to emerge in greater and greater detail in the manner suggested by its early development....having been captured and driven by such an idea, I was bound to be occupied with it, if not exclusively, nevertheless during the rest of my life."[9]

I have been working on this chapter about life between twenty-one and forty-two while visiting my son Stefan and his family on Maui. Every morning as I write, I look out at the sparkling white-capped ocean, the dark mountains off to the side, the many shapes of green growing between, and the blue sky dotted with cotton puffs. Except that often, because I am on the north shore of this paradise island, there is early mist and fog, the sea joins the gray sky, the mountains disappear, the trees become an indistinct dark mass. I try to remember what I know is there, but for the moment the veil is thick. And then it lifts, and again I see clearly the Sun-illumined world. This ever-shifting vista reminds me of these summer years of life—days when everything shines so distinctly and our lives make sense, times when our understanding fogs over and we feel we may lose our way, moments when the hot Sun breaks strongly through, months shrouded in heavy veils. And also days like the miracle rainbows that here on Maui arch above my head, surprising me each time—those magic intervals in life when through the

---

8   Goethe, *Italian Journey 1786–1787*, p. 21.

9   Goethe, *Goethe's Botanical Writings*, p. 162. Thank you to Craig
    Holdredge for pointing me toward this time in Goethe's life.

veil a luminous bridge appears, inviting us to know another world beyond the boundaries of our earthly days.

Everything beckons to us to perceive it,
murmurs at every turn, "Remember me!"
A day we passed, too busy to receive it,
will yet unlock us all its treasury.

Who shall compute our harvest? Who shall bar
us from the former years, the long-departed?
What have we learnt from living since we started,
except to find in others what we are?

Except to re-enkindle commonplace?
O house, O sloping field, O setting Sun!
Your features form into a face, you run,
you cling to us, returning our embrace!

One space spreads through all creatures equally—
inner-world-space. Birds quietly flying go
flying through us. O, I that want to grow!
the tree I look outside at grows in me!

It stands in me, that house I look for still,
in me that shelter I have not possessed.
I, the now well-beloved: on my breast
this fair world's image clings and weeps her fill.

—Rainer Maria Rilke[1]

1   Rilke, *Later Poems*; see also the blog: Giam Life, "Streams of
     consciousness," blog.gaiam.com/quotes/authors/rainer-maria-rilke?page=1.

CHAPTER 7

AUTUMN LIGHT AND SHADOW:
FORTY-TWO TO SIXTY-THREE

To experience the clarity of autumnal light that shines on an *inner-world-space* is the promise, or at least the invitation, of these next twenty-one years. But this will not happen without my effort; if I ignore the call of this emerging dimension of my being, the shadow of aging will begin to dominate my days. Am I able now to perceive the inner nature of my being? Do I experience an enlivened sense of my eternal self, or what may feel to me like an inner birth? Do I recognize the potential, indeed the need to awaken to the spirit working in me? Or am I ever more enveloped by the material aspects of my life?

From the perspective of these questions, forty-two introduces a kind of parting of the ways. My maturing as a full human being is not a given. If I do not heed the challenge for deeper self-reflection, my development as a responsible moral being will be hampered. The more my self-identity is dependent on my physical reality, my power in the world, my material successes and possessions, the more my soul/spirit potential will be bound to the inevitable decline of my physical body. But I have the possibility to become ever more inwardly free, to come to know myself in a new space of inner reality. As mentioned in chapter 4, this is not a transition moment that we meet only once. The coming years will continue to offer encouragements to awaken greater inner attentiveness, even as our habits of resistance to change grow stronger as time goes by.

The first twenty-one years of our life were devoted to preparing our body as a worthy vessel to receive our eternal "I." In the next large phase our soul has the opportunity to deepen and mature. Now in this time beyond forty-two we are also working on our spirit development. Rudolf Steiner speaks of three further sheaths or "bodies" that are not yet fully evolved in our human nature, and he suggests that in these years we are each laying the seeds for this future possibility. Between forty-two and forty-nine our "I" is working on the transformation of our astral body toward what will one day unfold as the Spirit Self. The years from forty-nine to fifty-six anticipate the future Life Spirit, as a reworking of the etheric body, and from fifty-six to sixty-three we prepare the way for what is called the Spirit Body, which involves a metamorphosis of the physical body.[2]

I have mentioned before that this perspective on evolving human nature belongs to a larger picture of the evolution of human consciousness, an idea that is central to Steiner's discussions of the human being. For me personally this conception of evolving consciousness has been like a guiding star, shining the possibility of meaning onto the mysteries of life here on Earth. As mentioned in the previous chapter, humanity is now in the age of the consciousness soul. We are bringing into being this new aspect of the human soul, individually and collectively. Because it is still becoming, we have nothing to fall back on in terms of what was developed during earlier epochs of our human story; we are literally at a growing edge in bringing this part of ourselves alive. This gives a background to the turning point that the forties present: our spirit awakening will not happen automatically but is something each of us is called to take up with inner attention and activity.

When I speak of inner or spiritual awakening, I do not mean to narrowly define how this might manifest or be exercised. Some people's spiritual life is supported by traditional religious practices; others have forged very individual paths of conscious inner schooling. One person's journal writing, music, gardening, or painting is a valued opening to life's invisible dimensions; for another a therapeutic experience is spirit-confirming. My agnostic mother was allergic to spiritual language but, in fact, more spiritually alert and consequent— in her teaching, her garden, her community service, or her attention to social justice—than many lifelong churchgoers. Meditation, prayer,

---

2 For a characterization of the different bodies and their transformations, see Steiner, *Theosophy*, chap. 1.

mindfulness, and conscious reverence are all ways that help people attend more responsibly to what is sacred and evolving in the world and in themselves.

In one of his *Talks to Teachers*, William James, the renowned late-nineteenth-century American philosopher and early psychologist, reflected on a well-known quotation from Charles Darwin about the atrophy, through disuse, of a capacity to appreciate the arts. James makes it clear that the habits of attending to our higher spiritual nature must be practiced, in this example through poetry, music, and other arts. Without our attention as we move into middle age, this bridge to the spirit that the arts provide may lose for us its life-enriching potential and we will be diminished as human beings.

There is a passage in Darwin's short autobiography which has been often quoted, and which, for the sake of its bearing on our subject of habit, I must now quote again. Darwin says: "Up to the age of thirty or beyond it, poetry of many kinds gave me great pleasure; and even as a schoolboy I took intense delight in Shakespeare, especially in the historical plays. I have also said that pictures formerly gave me considerable, and music very great delight. But now for many years I cannot endure to read a line of poetry. I have tried lately to read Shakespeare, and found it so intolerably dull that it nauseated me. I have also almost lost my taste for pictures or music... My mind seems to have become a kind of machine for grinding general laws out of large collections of facts; but why this should have caused the atrophy of that part of the brain alone, on which the higher tastes depend, I cannot conceive... If I had to live my life again, I would have made a rule to read some poetry and listen to some music at least once every week; for perhaps the parts of my brain now atrophied would thus have been kept alive through use. The loss of these tastes is a loss of happiness, and may possibly be injurious to the intellect, and more probably to the moral character, by enfeebling the emotional part of our nature."

We all intend when young to be all that may become a man, before the destroyer cuts us down. We wish and expect to enjoy poetry always, to grow more and more intelligent about pictures and music, to keep in touch with spiritual and religious ideas, and even not to let the greater philosophic thoughts of our time develop quite beyond our view. We mean all this in youth, I say; and yet in how many middle-aged men and women is such an honest and sanguine expectation fulfilled? Surely, in comparatively few; and the laws of habit show us why. Some interest in each of these things arises in everybody at the proper age; but, if not persistently fed with the appropriate matter, instead of growing into a powerful and necessary habit, it atrophies and dies, choked by the rival interests to which the daily food is given. We make ourselves into Darwins in this negative respect by persistently ignoring the essential practical conditions of our case. We say abstractly: "I mean to enjoy poetry, and to absorb a lot of it, of course. I fully intend to keep up my love of music, to read the books that shall give new turns to the thought of my time, to keep my higher spiritual side alive, etc." But we do not attack these things concretely, and we do not begin *today*. We forget that every good that is worth possessing must be paid for in strokes of daily effort. We postpone and postpone, until those smiling possibilities are dead. Whereas ten minutes a day of poetry, of spiritual reading or meditation, and an hour or two a week at music, pictures, or philosophy, provided we began *now* and suffered no remission, would infallibly give us in due time the fullness of all we desire. By neglecting the necessary concrete labor, by sparing ourselves the little daily tax, we are positively digging the graves of our higher possibilities.[3]

The Double

One aspect of the call to a deeper sense of self concerns the increasingly overt experience of what Rudolf Steiner referred to as our "double." As we move through middle age, this shadow part of our self begins to knock on our consciousness with persistent urgency, showing up in all manner of unworthy behavior. In fact, this double began to summon our attention in ever more pressing ways already in the previous phase. As the consciousness soul comes alive in us, we are more able to perceive the manifestations of our double, and

3   James, *Talks to Teachers on Psychology*, pp. 25–26.

this unbidden evidence of our need for development can be unsettling and even shocking. Are we able to face these disconcerting and unredeemed sides of ourselves or will we turn away from this ever-renewing invitation to grow?

The concept of the double is complex. Among the many voices in the development of psychology, Carl Jung's discussion of the shadow offers an important contribution to what can feel like an impenetrable subject. To consider in depth the many angles from which the double can be viewed is beyond the scope of this chapter.[4] What particularly concerns us as we enter middle age is that the double begins to show up wherever our "I" has not been able to work through our body and soul experiences. The double belongs to us, and can be seen as a great teacher if we are willing to take our development seriously. It makes manifest the yet untransformed aspects of our being, our unconscious habits and unattended, even fallen, ways of behaving. Much of this has been accumulating throughout our life; some of it came with us as part of our destiny learning. By midlife it is beginning to surface in our consciousness, and asks for our attention. The double is part of us, not some outside force to be blamed for our transgressions; it is not, however, part of our higher self, although it serves our true development.

Here is one image I hold for the growing force of the double: in living my life over the years I have often met things about myself that I could not accept, or did not want to work on, and so, metaphorically speaking, I kicked them under the bed. By my late thirties, the space is full under there, and things are starting to poke out. Some of the accumulating "stuff" begins to grab at my ankles and trip me up. There is no room left for me to keep shoving away any more. It is time to do some clean-up, to take my own development in hand, to face some of these undigested, unredeemed, or just plain unsavory parts of myself.

What are some of the situations where we meet this double of ours? Do you have moments when you feel deep shame, or when you

---

4   For a detailed look at the double see Lievegoed, *Man of the Threshold*, chapter 8. See also Lee Sturgeon-Day's helpful, *Double Trouble*, in her *Biography Workbooks* series.

experience inner regret over a reaction, a thought, a deed, or judgment? You wonder who was just acting. Where was the good and true you? These twinges of conscience are often indications that the double has been at work. Do you listen to the message, or do you reject it and project your distress outward? Perhaps you have well-established habits, such as tardiness, vanity, or prevarication that you in some way rest within and justify. What about when others say "you always..." or "you never..." and you immediately respond, even if only inwardly, with "I am *not*"...haughty or vacant, intimidating or lazy...? You might even feel quite indignant to be so misperceived, but could it be that the other is experiencing something that you have grown immune to recognizing? Something that is almost like a shell around your best intentions?

Often it is in our relationships—at home, at work, or in our extended families—where the double is particularly active. There is a tricky synchronicity that occurs between the doubles in long-term relationships. When our own double begins to intrude into our consciousness, we may resist owning it as part of who we are, and in this process we can become more finely tuned to the double of the other. Qualities that once attracted us in the other now begin to show a shadow side. For example, perhaps I once saw him as so smart and deep thinking; now I see that really he is a pompous know-it-all. Or she appeared so charming and witty; but now all I experience is her superficial self-importance.

With partners, colleagues, and family members it is easy to slip into assumptions about the other and into unconscious habits of interaction. Have you ever had a recurring argument with someone where a higher part of yourself could imagine you both leaving the room and going out for a pleasant walk while these lower parts of the two of you enact this habitual squabble? You know perfectly how it will all proceed and how it will end. And yet you are caught in a kind of negative force field. Our doubles are at work here, and the only way to get off this endless track is for our "I" to wake up and do something different. It can be hard enough to resist the strength of our own double; in addition the other's double may try to impede any changes we introduce into the pattern. But whenever we can find the strength to look our doubles straight in the face, they lose power over us. Then perhaps we will find more compassion for the stuck places in both ourself and the other, as well as more encouragement for our journey of mutual development. A bit of humor can go a long way here, too!

Although my understanding of the double has been shaped by Rudolf Steiner's ideas, I have been intrigued over the years to see how often this aspect of our nature is portrayed in ancient myth and modern story. Two among many examples come to mind as I write. I recently saw a production of Shakespeare's *The Tempest,* and I was very moved near the end by the tender way this particular Prospero was able to say of Caliban, before freeing them both from their years together on the island, "This thing of darkness I acknowledge mine." In *The Picture of Dorian Gray,* Oscar Wilde gives an especially harrowing image of the double of a man who contrives to stay eternally young and beautiful while living an ever-more selfish, deceitful, and debauched life.

As we head into our forties, it becomes increasingly necessary that we recognize the workings of our double, and that we are willing to take up these challenges to self-knowledge and transformation. As long as we resist accepting that we have an inner self with which to guide our further maturing, we remain at the mercy of outer events to nudge us toward greater wakefulness. Of course from a deeper perspective, our higher self is very involved in those outer promptings. It keeps trying to wake us up to the possibility of more active personal responsibility and self-determination. We have moments of awakening, and then we fall back into our well-worn habits; we take a step forward with great effort, and then can slide back so easily. If we are willing to recognize how deeply seeded our resistance to change really is, we will also know how important some kind of inner practice now becomes. There is a new urgency to make an inner commitment to some form of meditation, conscious self-reflection, or prayer.

FORTY-TWO TO FORTY-NINE

The forties are an energetic time of life, falling as they do under the influence of the time we spent before birth in the Mars sphere. If we have experienced an inner awakening and an enhanced sense of self-responsibility as we come toward this phase, then we are now likely to feel energetic and self-reliant, able to take initiative with clear direction and enthusiasm. If we resist taking ourselves more in hand, these years may find us ever more involved in relational combat, asserting our personal power, and criticizing others. As mentioned earlier, it is in these years that we are again dealing with astral forces, working with our "I" to further transform and bring order to the swirl of our emotional life.

The forties are sometimes referred to as a time of second puberty, and this is more likely to play out with those who give little attention to genuine self-reflection. We see people who seem to be pursuing ever more self-gratification or who regularly blame others when they are challenged at work or at home. There are those who willingly use others for their own aims, or blindly ignore consequences they could easily anticipate if they were not so caught in their own narrow self-interests. Without a willingness to work honestly on oneself, the double will only grow stronger throughout these years.

In the previous chapter I mentioned that many women face the particular challenge of balancing their feminine and masculine sides during their thirties. I have observed that this inner need arises more often for men during this phase in their forties. I first began paying attention to the question after reading in earlier descriptions of this phase, mainly written by men, that it was an especially difficult time of life. But as I, and many women with whom I was working, moved into our forties, there seemed to be a breathing out, and a new sense of energy and freedom. Admittedly these were women who were consciously trying to work on themselves and who took their inner lives seriously. But also, articles began appearing in newspapers and magazines about the vitality and passion for life that women in many different walks of life were feeling as they entered their forties. Those who had had children early now felt able to dive into their careers with renewed strength; those who consciously chose to have children later brought a mature responsibility to their decisions. Those for whom work was a primary focus were advancing in their careers through the opportunities opened up by the women's movement.

But I observed that men in their forties were often burdened by job and home responsibilities, worried about money, tired of pushing their way up the career ladder, and sometimes disappointed that they had not reached the success they had imagined. As the astral and etheric forces that accompanied the building up of physical strength during the first half of life begin to slowly recede, we can all feel ourselves less physically vital, and new vulnerabilities begin to intrude into our consciousness. Our material culture does not really value vulnerability, seeing it as an expression of weakness. I would like to maintain, instead, that it is a quality that is much needed in our times. By midlife, most women have learned to deal with physical vulnerability, and also to value its inner side and the way it opens us to new possibilities of growth and insight.

But for many men this intrusion of what can be called a more feminine quality can be confusing and even threatening. They may feel a shift away from a strong outer or work-centered orientation and wonder what this will mean for their future. If the ambitions of one's thirties no longer hold such appeal, what hope does life offer?

Many men in long-term partnerships begin now to want to pay more attention to their relationships. But often, their partners—who may have tried for years to engage these men more fully in the relationship—are themselves now busy with their own interests and careers. "Where were you when I needed you?" is a frequent, if often silent, retort as the partner heads out the door. Or fathers may now want to spend more time with their children, but the kids are older and do not necessarily want to spend Saturday with Dad. There can be a sad lack of parallel needs as a tender, initially perhaps even naïve, side of a man is trying to be born, while the rest of the family is moving in a more outward direction. What is asked for if the family is not to fall apart is an active and renewing interest in each other and also new levels of both mutual and self-acceptance while important inner and outer growth is taking place.

In popular culture there has been much discussion over the years about whether a midlife crisis is an inevitability of aging. Certainly we see many forty-five-year-olds sporting a flashy new car, a youthful haircut, or a fresh relationship. And we all know someone who has gone through a particularly hard passage in these years. It is my observation that everyone comes up against something that challenges the "I" to take further steps in maturing. For one person it will be an accident or illness, for another the loss of someone close. There may be a betrayal, or the unexpected end of a job. Of course, what becomes most significant for our evolving life story is how we meet these difficulties: do we go through the pain or grief with courage, honesty, and integrity, or do we reactively defend ourselves and strengthen the power of our double? In our different ways we all become aware that time is passing, that life is more complicated than we imagined, and that we are indeed growing older.

My generally very upbeat husband was in a strangely somber mood on his forty-sixth birthday. Eventually he stated in a sad voice that he had just realized that he was now fourteen years away from sixty. He felt he would not have time to fulfill his many dreams. I resisted the urge to laugh at this unusual melancholy, but I could not help pointing out that if he wanted to worry about getting older, he was only four years from fifty. But no, it was sixty that was haunting him—interestingly to me now, two seven-year periods away from where he then was. It had only just really hit him that time was in some way finite and that his creativity might fade with the years. This heralded a genuine experience of midlife darkness for him. I am happy to report that this mood passed in time; in fact, he now enters his seventies with vitality and creative initiative he could never have imagined in his forties.

For most people these years through the forties are very full. We are deeply in the midst of multiple responsibilities—at work, at home, perhaps with children and with aging parents. How we meet the challenges of these years will strongly color the years to come. Are we able to take seriously the call to self-knowledge that this phase poses with resounding echoes? Are we coming closer to an essential core of our being, and are we allowing this inner self the space

"In the greatest confusion, there is still an open channel to the soul. It may be difficult to find because by midlife it is overgrown, and some of the wildest thickets that surround it grow out of what we describe as our education. But the channel is always there, and it is our business to keep it open, to have access to the deepest part of ourselves."
—SAUL BELLOW, from his foreword to
The Closing of the American Mind by Allan Bloom

it needs to grow? Or are we running with gasping breath from the shadow of our earthly mortality?

FORTY-NINE TO FIFTY-SIX

For many people this next phase comes with a sigh of relief. The intensity of Mars begins to subside and Jupiter offers a wider and potentially wiser view. This is another expansive middle phase, and for many it brings a second peak in one's creative life. We may feel a renewed inner vitality; and it is now possible to view our own experiences and the world in which we live with greater objectivity.

In my work with the Biography and Social Art training program we often engage the course participants in their own life research. One year as we were discussing life phases, we divided people into groups based on the phases they were in at the time. We asked each group to gather their own questions and to build together a picture of their particular phase. The group of those between forty-nine and fifty-six met in my office, and the raucous laughter spilling out into the hallway made all my colleagues wish that they could be in there, too. The group happened to be all women, and all were near the end of this phase. Their life experiences were extremely different: two long-married, two never-married, one separated, some with active careers, others actively searching for a next step. All had met profound challenges in life: a parent's suicide, a husband's betrayal, loss of one's country, and trauma with a grown child, to name only a few. Yet the shared enthusiasm for life at this point was tangible, and the sense of common experiences very real. When the group spoke about their discoveries with the rest of the students, this is what they presented:

HYMN TO JUPITER

YES!
Yes, our bodies need a bit of attention
some vitamins perhaps, or a diet
that finally agrees with us.
Occasionally, we need an early night's sleep
but quite often we can thaw a bag
of frozen peas on our heads
as our mood's fire sparks around us.

Yet our soul is filled with a new kind of
strength and determination.
We now—finally—decide for ourselves.
We go on a trip around the world without our family.
We are taking courses that truly interest us.
We decide against odds, to whom we open our doors.
We decide calmly, with new confidence
and without guilt.

We are in fact enjoying life.
We are joyful just to live
and we don't get bogged down so easily anymore.
Space and light are different now
and we have grown beyond our skin.
Our breath is reaching the horizon.
We have embraced the cuts, the wounds, the scars
and we heal our souls
with forgiveness of ourselves and of others.
Gratitude, tolerance, boundaries
give us a new sense of being.
We can now look into the mirror
and accept who we are!
It is about four o'clock in the afternoon.

I imagine that there is much in this portrayal that could also speak for the experiences of men in this phase—the out-breath, the self-determination, the gratitude, and awareness of self-learning, including what was brought about through suffering. Many people describe not caring so much about what others think, and a sense of an inner buoyancy that defies the now obvious physical reality of aging. It is in these years that we are anticipating the emergence of the Life-Spirit through the transformation of the etheric or life body. These years offer a deepening experience of life that transcends physicality.

For women these years and the last ones of the previous phase are generally the time of menopause. Hot flashes demand our attention; and many women learn to attend to what is happening when they occur. And what of the soul flashes that also flame up with surprising force? Can we learn to read these sudden mood swings? Can we find our center, ever and again, within the changes our body is undergoing? As energy is being released from our physical body, do we also experience soul and spirit liberation? As our physical fertility comes to an end, can we begin to recognize new possibilities of conception? One of the great benefits of the women's movement has been to bring the experiences of menopause into open discussion. What had for so long carried the false stigma of an end to femininity could finally be seen as a profoundly important passage toward a deepening experience of human wholeness and an opening to new levels of creativity.

The gap that began at forty-two—between people who take their own inner development in hand and those who continue to cling to a purely material reality—manifests in this next phase in ever more obvious ways. Those who resist regular self-reflection can become increasingly threatened by the next generation. These are the people who hold on to power and are constantly talking about how things were "in our day." They are critical of others, often boastful and insistent on their own authority. Many become progressively more rigid in their thinking and activities, and often, daily experiences become very compartmentalized. There can be a decided lack of real life in the increasingly desperate effort to avoid aging. The image of Botox is very powerful: taking in a toxic substance in order to eliminate the wrinkles that hold our life story, with the result that genuine facial movement, as an expression of interest and feeling, is constricted. Life is as if frozen.

At the other end of the spectrum of ways of being in this phase, we find people who are less attached to the details of every day and find their sense of meaning and life from a different source—be it an inner confidence, a new appreciation for the mysteries of the natural world, a love of art, or a spiritual awakening. In the face of life's challenges they exude self-assurance, trust, joy, and leadership. Their social skills have become more conscious over the years, and they willingly make space for younger colleagues. These people show a generosity of spirit in their support for and interest in others; their creativity finds new scope in being of service, for example as mentors and guides for the next generation.

When I was in my thirties and beginning my work as an adult educator, a colleague who was in his middle fifties came to a workshop I offered. Afterward, he told me that he would never have approached the subject the way I did—indeed, he was quite shocked when I began—but that I had arrived at the same place he would have aimed for, and that I should keep on following my own instincts and trust my ideas. The generosity of his interest was truly supportive for me as I was finding my way into teaching, and it remained as an inspiring hallmark when I anticipated this phase of life.

Several lines from William Butler Yeats's long poem *Vacillation* capture this mood of quiet blessing that is a potential gift of these years:

> My fiftieth year had come and gone,
> I sat, a solitary man,
> In a crowded London shop,
> An open book and empty cup
> On the marble table-top.
> While on the shop and street I gazed
> My body of a sudden blazed;
> And twenty minutes more or less
> It seemed, so great my happiness,
> That I was blessed and could bless.
>   W.B. YEATS[5]

---

5   Yeats, *The Collected Works of W. B. Yeats,* vol. 1, p. 255.

Of course in real life, no one is ever fully evolved or completely unevolved, totally awake or eternally asleep. Whatever phase we are in, we are all in process; but as we age, the force of our habit life becomes stronger and changes take serious effort. Often we feel a tension between our more awake side and the parts of us that do not want to move. It is easy to be inwardly lulled to sleep when our days are busy and distractions are everywhere. But life continues to throw its punches and so we are ever and again invited to wake up and take more responsibility for our actions and our inner growth.

In recent years—and surely related to the timing of when the baby boomers began entering their fifties—there has been a growing body of research about the possibilities of renewal in the years after fifty. For example, in *The Third Chapter,* Harvard professor and sociologist Sara Lawrence-Lightfoot explores, as the subtitle states, the "passion, risk, and adventure in the twenty-five years after fifty." Through interviews and visits with forty diverse women and men, she examines the motivations, the vulnerabilities, the insecurities, and the accomplishments of people between fifty and seventy-five who are pursuing new learning opportunities and new careers as part of a search for greater meaning in their lives. In spite of the individual differences in her subjects' lives and dreams, she discovers a kind of common path that "moves forward and circles back, progresses and regresses, is both constant and changing. The developmental terrain grows more layered; patience trumps speed; restraint trumps ambition; wisdom trumps IQ; 'leaving a legacy' trumps 'making our mark'. And a bit of humor saves us all."[6]

Third Moon Node

At the very end of this seven year phase, as we are approaching fifty-six, we experience our third Moon node. Once again the Earth, Moon, and Sun are aligned as they were at our birth. Often we find ourselves inadvertently reviewing different aspects of our life. Perhaps we feel there is some task we have forgotten to do. We may find ourselves wondering, "What *was* my true life intention?" Over the years I have noticed that often some strong and surprising event happens to

6   Lawrence-Lightfoot, *The Third Chapter*, p. 173.

people as this phase is coming to a close: they may become ill, experience a job change, suffer a loss, have an accident, or be otherwise provoked or invited into an unexpected decision or step forward.

FIFTY-SIX TO SIXTY-THREE

The next phase begins very much in the mood of the third Moon node experience at the end of the previous period. These are the years that show the influence of Saturn, that faraway planet personified in myth as Father Time carrying his scythe, in order to reap what has been sown. There is now a growing inclination to look back on the life we have lived so far. From deep within our will, resound questions about what we have left undone, or what still remains for us to do. Are there unattended relationships we need to take care of? Dangling threads that need to be woven more carefully into the fabric of our lives?

It was surprising to me as I entered this phase to feel a great interest in connecting with friends from my youth. One day, as if to show me that this was not just something living in me, I found a message on my office voicemail from my college boyfriend, with whom I had not spoken in over thirty-five years. Of course, I called him right back and it was lovely to be able to share news of our lives after so long. More recently Facebook and other forms of social media invite friends of earlier days to reconnect, stimulating memories, renewed interest, and sometimes even second-time romances.

But this is also a serious and more contractive phase of life, with challenges to the will that may carry echoes from as far back as early childhood. Some people are only now able to address wounds that were long papered over in the protective myth of a happy childhood. The uncaring mother or the abusive father may still haunt our unconscious habits of withdrawal, deception, or attack. Life themes we thought we had dealt with may continue to push us toward greater consciousness. These challenges come from deep within, resounding with spiritual intention. It is in these years that we begin to lay the foundation for the future development of the Spirit Body, as a transformation of the physical body.

And there are trials that meet us from without as well. In these years many people will experience the loss of friends or older relatives, or perhaps a forced early retirement. Illness may also be a factor, sometimes coming as the distressing fruit of earlier life habits such as smoking or ways of eating. Although in the rashness of youth we may have felt invincible, Father Time still approaches us, however unbidden.

As in the previous two phases, we can now see clearly the different ways people meet the task of self-development. Those who continue to resist the call to self-knowledge tend to hold on ever more tightly to their social position, work responsibilities, and even possessions. Many try to look and act younger in sadly foolish ways. Some become suspicious of younger colleagues or family members, fearful of losing their grip, and increasingly bitter about their own aging. It is as if the soul itself becomes pinched and the spirit trapped.

The early sixties can be a particularly vulnerable time for people whose self-identity has been strongly bound to their work accomplishments or to their physical vitality. In their dread of aging they may cling to the ways in which they felt alive and important when they were younger. If they do not find new possibilities of experiencing their own worth, they may become susceptible to various promises of shallow revitalization. For example, a relationship with a younger person who still glows with youthful life force offers the ultimately false hope of staving off the reality of aging. Flattered by the admiration for their apparent wisdom or maturity, some older people fall into situations where their vanity is stroked and they feel momentarily young again. Even devoted spouses can be tempted into what they rashly may see as a compartmentalized adventure, until the heartache and disruption that follow only further a sense of personal diminishment. The pathos of this was succinctly captured in the classic film *Moonstruck*, when the older wife, played by Olympia Dukakis, confronts her straying husband with the zingy one-liner, "No matter what it is you're up to, Cosmo, you're still going to die."

In the other direction are the people whose soul and spirit are becoming ever freer from the confines of the body, even as they may

---

SUITCASE EXERCISE • Recalling the exercise described in chapter
1 about the intentions you packed into your bag as you pre-
pared to come to Earth, reflect now on what is in your bag that
you did not bring with you at birth. What have you acquired
in your time on Earth so far? What are you taking with you as
you head toward your later years? What do you still hope to
develop/to be able to put in your bag and take with you across
the threshold of death?

---

attend to the importance of staying physically fit. They are no longer as
driven by outer circumstances and can be more patient and inwardly
creative. Their maturity is a benefit to coworkers and friends. Generosity seems to grow in both thoughts and deeds. Many now begin to
share treasured family possessions with the next generation—to give
things away while they themselves can still enjoy this living legacy.
Though life continues to be very full, there seems to be more time—to
tell a story to a grandchild, to mentor a struggling young colleague, or
to stop and deeply appreciate a glorious autumn tree or the particular
quality of a cardinal's redness against the snow.

At sixty Mary Oliver wrote an evocative and glorious picture of
her own ongoing activity in a long poem, appropriately named *Work*.
Here is a woman in her full maturity knowing and loving her true calling to observe the world around her—to study it and stare at it and
feel into it. As she says, "I am a woman sixty years old, and glory is
my work." And so she sings of the veil that just begins to lift, the veil
that is rent, and the "light, light, and more light" behind it. The poem
is much too long to quote here, but I strongly recommend reading it.[7]

As we move into our sixties, in addition to the looking back that
so often occurs, questions about the future also present themselves.
For many people this becomes a time to plan for life after retirement.
Do I have enough financial resources for perhaps another third of my
life, much of it without employment? If I retire, who will be left? Who
am I without the external props of identity that have sustained me for
so long? What, and who, will support me as I age?

---

7   Oliver, *The Leaf and the Cloud*, pp. 9–15.

Of course most people continue with their jobs throughout this phase and well into the next one. But questions about the future come into consciousness, from outside and from within. The reality of aging cannot really be denied; the autumn of life is gradually yielding to the coming of winter, and there is an inevitable wondering about what lies ahead.

THE LAYERS

I have walked through many lives,
some of them my own,
and I am not who I was,
though some principle of being
abides, from which I struggle
not to stray.
When I look behind,
as I am compelled to look
before I can gather strength
to proceed on my journey,
I see the milestones dwindling
toward the horizon
and the slow fires trailing
from the abandoned camp-sites,
over which scavenger angels
wheel on heavy wings.
Oh, I have made myself a tribe
out of my true affections,
and my tribe is scattered!
How shall the heart be reconciled
to its feast of losses?
In a rising wind
the manic dust of my friends,
those who fell along the way,
bitterly stings my face.
Yet I turn, I turn,
exulting somewhat,
with my will intact to go
wherever I need to go,
and every stone on the road
precious to me.
In my darkest night,
when the Moon was covered
and I roamed through wreckage,
a nimbus-clouded voice
directed me:
"Live in the layers,
not on the litter."
Though I lack the art
to decipher it,
no doubt the next chapter
in my book of transformations
is already written.
I am not done with my changes.

—STANLEY KUNITZ, *The Collected Poems*

CHAPTER 8

WINTER WINDS: SIXTY-THREE AND BEYOND

Approaching the subject of the years beyond sixty-three, I find, for a variety of reasons that I cannot stay within the framework of seven-year phases. Of course there are real differences between the sixties, the seventies, the eighties, and the nineties, but a strong seven-year rhythm is no longer as relevant. It is as if the uniqueness of each individuality begins now to shine—some brightly, some muted—but each one a distinct star in a vast universe of twinkling light.

As has been elaborated in previous chapters, Rudolf Steiner suggests that our experiences in the planetary realms through which we passed on our journey toward incarnation continue to influence us throughout the seven-year cycles leading up to sixty-three. These evolutionary planets dressed us and blessed us for our life here on Earth, not only with personality traits that will emerge over the years, but also by helping to set the stage—the appointments as some say—for important people, opportunities, and challenges we will encounter along the way of our life. Now, as we move through our sixties, we are in some way set free from that pre-birth legacy. The bindings that have held our life together begin to loosen.

In chapter 4, I mentioned how Rudolf Steiner says that by sixty-three—and even more so by seventy—we have encountered the main intentions with which we entered this life. Of course we now are carrying the many consequences stemming from how we met that destiny plan here on Earth, how we have taken up the offerings for development set up by our higher self. The ramifications of our earlier decisions and actions will continue to show themselves throughout the rest of our life, for example in our personal habits and in our on-going relationships. In this regard, the idea of being set free must not be taken too literally or narrowly.

As also stated in previous chapters, the transition around age sixty-three is often fraught with challenge. It is possible that in the time surrounding this milestone, we may face a direct encounter with some of our more unattended destiny intentions. It is as if we are offered, yet again, an opportunity to wake up to a developmental theme we meant to work on but whose prompts we may have basically ignored or pushed aside. Those who have had a loose relationship with truth may find themselves suddenly exposed in a series of white lies, not one of which was consciously intended to harm others but that, in their accumulation, threaten to derail other worthy attributes and accomplishments. Those who took false pride in outer appearances may, through an illness, be invited to meet themselves and come to know others in deeper and more significant ways. Or perhaps a lifetime of unchecked complaint and blame now yields unexpected isolation and loneliness as the sustaining rhythms of life begin to shift.

As I write this chapter, I am nearing my sixty-seventh birthday, and so am halfway between sixty-three and seventy. When I was younger, I had no qualms about holding forth enthusiastically about phases that were way beyond my age at the time, but as I have grown older I have sometimes shuddered at remembering those youthful declarations. Now I feel more cautious. I do not want to speak too boldly about what I have not been through myself. This is not to say that my own experiences would necessarily represent those of others, but at least they provide a foundation for my observations of life around me. They ground me. On the other hand, I have long been interested in questions of aging and have been privileged to know many deeply reflective older people who have shared much with me. So I venture carefully into these later years, knowing that personally I still have so much to meet and to learn.

I am reminded here of listening to an interview with Joan Erikson at ninety, where she apologized for what she and her husband Erik, the well-known developmental psychologist, had said about old age. The eighth stage in their system of life stages dealt with late adulthood; they called it "Wisdom," which they saw as the fruit of practicing integrity over despair. In the interview she spoke of how they had assumed that the very old would feel wise and integrated; but now, at ninety and living herself with a variety of pains and uncertainties, she said, "We hadn't been there, we didn't know..."[1]

None of which is to say that wisdom is not a potential fruit of aging. But even in these years beyond sixty-three, attention and consciousness are needed for the self-reflection and inner development that can allow the grace of wisdom. We are invited to look back and forward with quiet responsibility, even as we practice living in the present moment; inner and outer space are needed. In an earlier interview Joan Erikson had reflected on this question: "What is it to grow wise?" and offered the perspective that only the old can become truly wise, but that only some of them actually will.

Chapter 7 addresses the echoing resonance between the phase from fifty-six to sixty-three and the very first phase of childhood going right back to one's birth. Another perspective on our experience of passing through the transition around sixty-three is to consider what may be resounding from the circumstances surrounding our entry into life. As I thought of the outer and inner upheavals I experienced between sixty-two and sixty-four, I could not help remembering the stories of my own very traumatic birth and challenging early months. Having ruptured my mother's uterus, I should have died, but did not because my mother happened to be in the hospital for a check-up, and an immediate cesarean section could be performed. At sixty-three, I was profoundly surprised to find myself landing, again precipitously, in an unexpected inner world where I had to find my bearings in quite new ways. Of course, I do not mean to suggest anything causative between experiences at birth and at this transition around sixty-three; nevertheless, we may observe that our way of meeting important thresholds, or the kinds of events that surround such passages, may be strangely linked.

While writing the preceding, I had a very stimulating conversation with an older friend, who offered additional perspective on this

---

1   "A Conversation with Joan Erikson at 90," Davidson Films, 1995.

transition and the post–sixty-three years. She feels that one way to look at the idea of being a "child of the gods again," of being in some way set free, is to see sixty-three as an actual birth into a whole new level of our life journey. As the O'Neil's state in *The Human Life*, we are "fully born, finally! It has taken all this time to become genuinely human."[2] Now we step forward on a new road, one with different milestones and pitfalls, with wider views but the furthermost boundary, our own particular land's end, in shadow. Hopefully we can take up the journey ahead less bound by the petty details of our life story— like the "litter" Stanley Kunitz refers to—and more able to experience the "layers" of true human development.

Mary Catherine Bateson in her important book *Composing a Further Life* offers a contemporary view of the changing face of aging. She identifies what she calls Adulthood II as a stage between what we normally think of as adulthood, with all its pressing responsibilities, and old age. People in this stage still have energy and want to continue learning from a place of greater freedom, and they have much to offer to the future from the wealth of their life experiences. She characterizes aging today as "an improvisational art form calling for imagination and willingness to learn," and speaks of men and women, particularly in the years of Adulthood II, as "artists of their own lives, working with what comes to hand through accident or talent to compose and re-compose a pattern in time that expresses who they are and what they believe in."[3]

In reflecting on experiences that come our way from the mid-sixties on, it is interesting to consider whether we feel that new roles and skills begin to be asked of us. Sometimes surprising steps present themselves to our evolving "I"; curious new qualities are called forth. A volunteering job asks us to listen in unfamiliar ways; a trip opens us to an interest in some field of art or history we had never before considered; or a health issue calls into question how we enact our relationship to traditional medical authority. Could these developmental challenges bring with them premonitions of growth that may in some way belong to a future life? This idea should not be

---

2   O'Neil and O'Neil, *the Human Life*, p. 14.

3   Bateson, *Composing a Further Life*, pp. 19 and 24.

taken too literally, and yet we can ponder what seeds are being sown as we find ourselves exploring quite unexpected capacities. Can we imagine this as preparation for the future, a future extending even beyond our death?

I want to share a personal example that is still very much in process and still enveloped with questions. Since our middle sixties, my husband and I have found ourselves returning again and again to teach in China. This is not something we ever imagined. Although we are teaching subjects with which we have long been active, the settings, the language, and much of what is really asked of us there are decidedly new. Much is different in our ways of working and relating. And further, at quite another level than the official tasks asked of us, we have experienced ourselves at times standing out (and taller!) where there are literally no other Western people. We are even approached again and again to have our picture taken, often for some stranger's mother who has never before seen a person from the West. What are these kinds of experiences awakening in us? I do not have answers yet, but when I am in China, I am keenly aware in large and small ways of being on a surprising growing edge.

Of course I am not suggesting that everything arrives quite newly in the post-sixty-three years. Many years ago, I had a conversation with a wise older friend, then in her early nineties, who advised me to be sure to tell people in my biography workshops that they needed to have hobbies or real interests they wanted to pursue when they retired. She had observed that those elders who had been looking forward to some activity after retirement were much more likely to have fulfilling later years. It did not really matter what it was that invited their interest—playing an instrument, practicing a sport, gardening, learning a new language, travel, taking a woodworking class, bird watching, volunteering, writing poetry—what mattered was that people were engaged in their own future. Those who simply ended work without an imagination of anything they cared about pursuing were often quite lost and would frequently fall into a monotonous routine of empty days. Those following an interest would invite ever new sides of themselves to come to expression.

The interplay—perhaps even a kind of tension—between the ongoing aspects of who we are and the possibility of newness is often noticeable in the years leading up to seventy. Change is in the air; winter is announcing itself with early mists that alter the shapes of things on the horizon. The light is changing, the winds become sharper, but the midday Sun still offers warmth. Although many people continue to work full- or part-time throughout and beyond these years, out of choice or economic necessity, a gradual process of feeling more inwardly free often emerges within the outer activity. The judgments of others hold ever less weight. One friend extolled with a happy sigh: "I am done with accommodation." For those with reasonably good health, who find their own ways of exercising body and soul, and who maintain an active interest in the world around them, these can be years of unexpectedly rich fulfillment and accomplishment.

As I look around at my peers in their late sixties and seventies, for the most part I see vibrant active people. As a demographic we are healthier, more fit, and more engaged in the world than we generally remember was the case for our parents or grandparents. I witness real enjoyment in life—traveling to far corners of the Earth, perfecting a tennis or golf game, helping a non-profit initiative get off the ground, or finally gathering thoughts and questions into an article or a book. Many people happily describe how they are pursuing new interests or deepening personal research without a driving work-related motivation, but simply for the joy of learning. I do not think I am being overly positive when I say that many of us genuinely look forward to the future. I even see a surprising confidence that our bodies will not let us down too soon.

In spite of, or perhaps hand in hand with that confidence, many people in these years will come to an acceptance of the fact that some part of their body hurts—a knee, a hip, the lower back, a shoulder, or wrist—and that this is not likely to improve very much. Nevertheless, many would agree with Maya Angelou who said in an interview by Oprah Winfrey on her seventieth birthday, "I've learned that even when I have pains I don't have to be one." She also spoke of how she finds getting older "exciting." And Will Rogers, according to one of those lists of quotes on aging that spin around the internet, is reputed to have said: "One of the many things no one tells you about aging is that it is such a nice change from being young." Indeed, for many people there is a growing spaciousness of soul, liberation from the demands of job performance and fully scheduled time, and an energetic opening to new creativity.

Less fortunate are those who find themselves lost without the scaffolding of a job or their position in the eyes of others. Then these years can herald ever more complaint, bitterness, regret, and loneliness. The inner invitation to warm-hearted self-reflection may then be sidestepped and silences filled with media noise or all-consuming new diversions. Here again we see the two basic directions in which people can go forward: those who continue to take responsibility for authoring their ongoing stories and approach their aging process with interest, in contrast to those who feel increasingly the victims of time's passage, rejecting the call to self-knowledge and letting their souls contract with their declining physical capacity. Perhaps it is rare for anyone to be fully on one side or the other of this divide; we all tend to meander our way, more and less awake within the process of aging and the possibilities of maturing. And still, it matters that we try to both review with gratitude the life we have lived and to attend responsibly to how our later years progress.

As we grow older, and as we reflect on the wholeness of our lives, can we face, accept, and reconcile the joys and the accomplishments, the disappointments and the losses? It is in how we live this question that others and we ourselves experience the mark of our true "I" as it has been evolving through our biography. Are we now able to love, to forgive, to look forward with interest? Or are we judgmental, vindictive, pinched, and complaining? Or have we simply given up?

Today there is much research being done toward a greater understanding of the aging process. Life expectancy has increased worldwide, and with the baby-boom generation moving in ever-greater numbers through their sixties, gerontology has become its own booming field. It is interesting to note that gerontologists acknowledge several distinct aging processes: chronological, biological, psychological, and social. With some interesting parallels my own thoughts revolve more around considerations of body, soul, and spirit and how the expression, health, and inter-connection of these different aspects of our human nature continue to evolve through each individual's chronological aging.

In chapter 4 there is a diagram that shows the line of the physical body descending from the vitality of midlife toward its eventual death and return to the mineral world. In contrast, the spirit line ascends, slowly excarnating through old age, returning the "I" to its true home in the supersensible world. The soul's trajectory is ever more dependent on each one's own developmental steps. Tied to material reality and closely aligned with the state of the physical body and worldly success, the soul may feel as if it, too, is descending toward death. On the other hand, when gradually freed from an excessive dependence on physicality, the soul in the last decades of life can heed the call of the "I" and ascend what has been popularly referred to as the "staircase" of the human spirit.[4] This image of a stairway going up captures the possibility of awakening to the spirit through one's own inner efforts.

From a physical perspective there is an inevitability about the aging process. While a committed exercise program will influence our sense of fitness and, of course, individuals differ greatly in the health of their bodies and what is often called the luck of their genes, it is also a universal fact that physical vitality diminishes with the passage of time. As we move into old age, the different parts of our body that have served us throughout the years, most often without our conscious knowledge, begin to announce themselves and ask for some attention. Suddenly there are numbers to remember—cholesterol, blood pressure, PSA, or bone density. How much medical intervention do we need, do we want? We are faced with decisions that at a younger age we never imagined would actually come our way: is it time to have a hip replacement? How do I lower my cholesterol? Why is my body letting me down like this?

---

4   Jane Fonda, TED Talk: *Life's Third Act*, Dec. 2011, http://www.ted.com /talks.

This grand vessel, the body of our Earth experiences, begins to show wear and tear. While some will find a quick exit from the body through an accident or heart attack, others may experience a prolonged illness that brings with it the challenge of ongoing and perhaps more conscious inner growth. For many the movement toward physical frailty is very gradual. Along the way, some of the most noticeable changes have to do with the senses. Accompanying the progressive diminishment of our life forces is a general weakening of our sensory functions.

Older arthritic hands experience more dimly what the sense of touch can offer. Cataracts, glaucoma, and macular degeneration alter how we see the world around us. Impaired hearing brings changes in the objectivity of perception, often isolating people behind a curtain of misunderstanding or nodding complacency. As our sensory capacities of smell and taste diminish, it becomes harder to differentiate the aromas and odors that waft our way, or the delicate flavors and fine seasonings in the food we eat.

These changes that happen to our sense organs are often subtle and slow. Indeed, we may resist for a long time acknowledging that anything is different. This is particularly common with hearing loss, where out of a vain resistance to aging or to using a hearing aid, unfortunate verbal misinterpretations become ever more common. The burden is shifted to others, and they are blamed for mumbling, or even for whispering as if to exclude the compromised hearer from what is being spoken. Too often those with hearing loss try to cover for their diminished hearing by withdrawing from active participation in social conversation. We can only hope that before this sad self-protection leads beyond miscommunication to unnecessary isolation, the problem can be met with a willingness to seek help.

It is also possible to have a quite different experience with someone whose hearing is very impaired but who is, nevertheless, able to pick up what really matters through an intensity of listening that has little to do with physical ears. In this case the soul seems to reach beyond the physical blockage and hear with inner ears. Likewise there are very old people whose reduced vision appears to have stimulated another way of looking, of attending with a heart interest that yields deeper seeing and true insight. In this ability to move beyond the limitations of an aging body, we see the mark of an individual's soul and spiritual growth.

Steiner spoke not only of the traditional five senses but of twelve: touch, life, self-movement, balance, smell, taste, sight, temperature/warmth, hearing, language, concept/thought, and the sense of "I" (of the other). Many other researchers today also speak of more than the usual five. An appreciation for this wider range of sensory experience is very important in working with children, and it also enhances our understanding of what happens as the senses lose strength in old age. My purpose here is not to elaborate on all of these senses, but to indicate with a few examples the kinds of challenges that aging presents. For an excellent description of the twelve senses see *Our Twelve Senses* by Albert Soesman. In *The Fulfillment of Old Age*, Dr. Norbert Glas explores the soul-spirit transformation that is possible in old age as the physical sense organs lose vitality.

As one ages, it is easy to recognize how the sense of movement is gradually curtailed. The effortlessness of exercising the limbs, of moving the physical body becomes compromised, and for many this can feel like a deep loss of personal autonomy. Nevertheless, in spite of the outer constraints, some elders are able to find an inner freedom, a soul-spirit movement that lives through their power of imagination. My mother, in her mid-seventies, once gave me a profound image of this when I called to check in about her day. The physical activity she had so valued all her life was by then limited because of a painful bone disease; but that evening she replied enthusiastically to my question about her day, saying, "I went to China." To my puzzled query about what she meant, she chuckled and then elaborated: "In the mail today I received one of those travel brochures for a trip around China. Well, you know how I always wanted to visit China, but as I looked at the flyer, I realized that this is no longer possible for me. So I just decided to spend the day going anyway. I got out my maps, my encyclopedia, some history books, a world poetry collection, my cookbooks, my art and flower books...and I made my own journey. I had such a lovely day!"

Another story about my mother: this time from her mid-eighties, when she was living at the Fellowship Community in Chestnut Ridge, New York, where attention is given not only to the physical care of the older residents but also to their soul and spirit dignity and needs. By then she was confined to a wheelchair and had very limited use of her left side. Her sense of life, of wellbeing in her body, was a daily challenge. In spite of this, she always looked forward to the rhythm of putting away the silverware after the dishwashing from lunch was finished. Although with her damaged hand it took her perhaps an hour to do a job that a coworker could have done in a few minutes, there was a living understanding among the caregivers of her need to be useful. When she felt she could still be of service to others, she could rise above her aching and constricted body with genuine soul equanimity. Other residents would fold laundry, or were active in the weavery, the greenhouse, or the woodworking studio. Nowhere was time efficiency the dominant priority; there were real tasks to be done for the community, and they were tailored to be both possible and genuinely enlivening.[5]

In considering the steady decline of sensory acuity that occurs with aging it is easy to see how our physical nature is interwoven with soul and spirit developments. These three aspects of our being do not exist in isolation, however neatly we might want to characterize their differences. The body, even as it grows weaker, continues to be the vessel for the spirit's encounter with Earth. The spirit persists in guiding the body and soul into realms of experience that only the Earth can offer, which includes the pain of illness, the suffering of loss, and the possibility to rise above bodily limitations. The soul goes on mediating between body and spirit, gathering its essential human experiences from which the spirit will harvest its earthly learning.

The interconnection is very clear when we look at one of the most common experiences of getting older: an increasing forgetfulness. In general, we remember what affected us intensely, what

---

5   For more on retirement communities such as the one described, contact The Fellowship Community in Chestnut Ridge, NY (www.fellowshipcommunity .org) or Camphill Ghent, NY (www.camphillghent.org).

touched our feelings deeply. With aging and the gradual withdrawal of our life forces, our soul receives weaker impressions from the stimulation coming through our senses. Recent events may not be as deeply imprinted, and so short-term memories are less available. We may not be able to find our keys or recall a recent conversation, even as richly detailed memories from earlier years resound ever more frequently in reflective moments. Not long ago I attended a poetry reading by a woman in her late eighties who introduced several of the poems with stories from her childhood. I think she spoke for many older people when she looked out at the audience and said warmly, "Forgive me if I look back to childhood, but I have to."

As we age, we have more possibility to observe the wholeness of our life, to see in retrospect how apparently disparate events and curious details rearrange themselves like puzzle pieces into a strangely integrated totality. Perhaps we begin to perceive a mysterious working of some greater will behind the particular events of our biography; our sense of a higher self at work in our developing story can deepen. Our unique journey is there for our contemplation, if we are open to the work of life reflection. We can all be helped in this effort if those around us take the time to ask about our experiences.

In recent years graduates of the Biography and Social Art program that I directed for many years, have begun interviewing elders about their lives. This has identified several common developmental threads of aging, but more important for the interviewers was to observe how enlivening the conversations were for both parties. Even though some of the older people began with the statement that there was nothing very interesting about their lives, most of them perked up at having someone listen with genuine engagement to their stories. Cheeks grew pink, postures straightened, and laughter and tears were openly shared. Of course we all know the challenge of hearing the same, often unsolicited, stories from older friends and relatives; nevertheless, to bring a conscious approach and a genuine invitation to reminiscences can be a gift to all.

I have mentioned before the great contribution that StoryCorps is making to this effort of bringing people into communication across generational divides. A few years ago my son Stefan gave me a StoryCorps interview for my birthday, truly one of the most heart-warming gifts of my life. At that time he was a new father himself, and there in the tiny recording booth in Grand Central Station, our own parent-child bond moved to new levels of connection and under-standing. Dave Isay characterizes this work he founded this way:

> StoryCorps is built on a few basic ideas: That our stories—the stories of everyday people—are as interesting and important as the celebrity stories we're bombarded with by the media.... That if we take the time to listen, we'll find wisdom, wonder, and poetry in the lives and stories of the people all around us.... That we all want to know our lives have mattered.... That listening is an act of love.[6]

It is moving to notice how much the reminiscences of elders are especially loved by young grandchildren. Nor do children tire of the same stories again and again, of how Granddad crossed the ocean as a young boy and had to learn a whole new language, or how Grandma built a hideout in the woods with an old crate she and her friend dragged behind their bicycles from the local dump. On the subject of grandchildren, I must insert here the whole-hearted joy they awaken in so many older people. There is often an unanticipated sense of freedom in the love that elders feel for their grandchildren. Again and again I hear others describe what I know in my own heart: the deep bond, the ever-renewing pleasure, and the surprising, heart-opening patience that time with grandchildren invites.

Being the older person I now am, I have digressed somewhat from my subject of the changes in memory. Once thoughts of my grandchil-dren captured my attention, like the poet I quoted, I can only say, "I had to!"

A few years ago I comforted myself with the thought that the phone numbers and flower names that were disappearing from my ready recall were simply making room in my consciousness for more significant thoughts still to come. Now, like so many of my peers, I sigh with relief when I read articles about the normal memory lapses of aging, even while furtively checking the lists of symptoms for more

---

6   Isay, *Listening is an Act of Love*, p. 1.

concerning possibilities. As he has with so many of the adventures of daily life, Billy Collins captures with warmth and gentle humor the apparent inevitability of advancing forgetfulness:

FORGETFULNESS

The name of the author is the first to go
followed obediently by the title, the plot,
the heartbreaking conclusion, the entire novel
which suddenly becomes one you have never read, never even
    heard of,

as if, one by one, the memories you used to harbor
decided to retire to the southern hemisphere of the brain,
to a little fishing village where there are no phones.

Long ago you kissed the names of the nine muses goodbye
and watched the quadratic equation pack its bag,
and even now as you memorize the order of the planets,

something else is slipping away, a state flower perhaps,
the address of an uncle, the capital of Paraguay.

Whatever it is you are struggling to remember,
it is not poised on the tip of your tongue
or even lurking in some obscure corner of your spleen.

It has floated away down a dark mythological river
whose name begins with an L as far as you can recall

well on your own way to oblivion where you will join those
who have even forgotten how to swim and how to ride a
    bicycle.

No wonder you rise in the middle of the night
to look up the date of a famous battle in a book on war.
No wonder the Moon in the window seems to have drifted
out of a love poem that you used to know by heart.

                              —BILLY COLLINS[7]

---

7   Collins, *Questions about Angels.*

It is part of our living ever longer, that many older people will in fact receive the dreaded diagnosis of some form of dementia. As a culture we have much to learn about how to care for the intact spirit inhabiting an ever frailer body and a soul with diminishing consciousness. How can we imagine into the inner reality of someone who can no longer engage as before in the activities and interactions of everyday life? What is happening for the spirit during this protracted journey toward death?

A friend who has worked extensively with very old people told me that she often observes them exhibiting a kind of participatory consciousness, similar to how a young child picks up a parent's mood without direct communication. Those nearing the end of an experience-filled life seem at times to be awake to the world of living thoughts even when conscious attention to everyday verbal exchanges is no longer happening. The person we have known may seem ever more veiled, perhaps unable to speak out or act with clear determination, but we may be able to perceive a different level of attention. My friend recounted her experiences of hearing a mainly silent person in her care suddenly speak, apropos to nothing obvious, using a word or phrase—like mushroom, music, or marriage—that had just been part of my friend's own silent pondering.[8]

A former playwright and Jungian analyst named Florida Scott-Maxwell began keeping a notebook of thoughts when she was in her eighties. These undated entries offer deep and painfully honest reflections on her experiences of aging. Here is one:

> I don't like to write this down, yet it is much in the minds of the old. We wonder how much older we have to become, and what degree of decay we may have to endure. We keep whispering to ourselves, "Is this age yet? How far must I go?" For age can be dreaded more than death. "How many years of vacuity? To what degree of deterioration must I advance?"... Death feels a friend because it will release us from the deterioration of which we cannot see the end. It is waiting for death that wears us down, and the distaste for what we may become.[9]

---

8   From a conversation with Davina Muse.

9   Scott-Maxwell, *The Measure of My Days*, pp. 138–139.

EXERCISE • Models of Aging: Reflect on two different older people you have known, one whose ways of living with aging inspire you, and another whose approach to old age is depressing or distressing for you. Picture each one in as much detail as possible. Observe inwardly how they relate to themselves, and how they interact with others. What interests do they have? What activities do they engage in? What are the qualities they manifest that inspire or distress you?

Like many of my friends, I hold the silent wish that I will be able to die before I lose touch with my familiar sense of self. I think we all want to deepen as we age and to continue as an active support for friends and family members; we look forward to seeing how the next generation will solve some of the problems that stumped our best efforts; we may even have every intention of sorting through the odds and ends of life accumulating in the attic or in our desk drawers. But we do not want our later years to erase the memory of who we were in our prime. And so we meet questions of control and self-autonomy. There is no easy road map through the end of life, only the possibility—and the yet unknown gifts—of meeting each day with as much presence and interest as we are able.

APPROACHING DEATH

The prospect of death looms closer as the years go by. For some this is a source of great fear, for others it offers the comfort of release. Often it brings tenderness into everyday experiences—for example, toward encounters with those we love or the beauty of the natural world. How we approach the idea of dying has very much to do with what imaginations we hold for what comes after death. One person is convinced that there is nothing there, that if we have any after-life it is only in the legacy of our deeds and the memories of those who knew us. Another has vague ideas of ongoing energy, while others have deep faith in their images of heaven. Those who have a feeling for reincarnation anticipate death as a passage, a transition, a kind of birth, and the return of one's spiritual essence to its true home. And still, whatever our ideas or our faith, they often exist side by side with the apprehension of not really knowing.

In the following poem W. S. Merwin expresses the mystery within a quiet acceptance of what will come when it comes:

FOR THE ANNIVERSARY OF MY DEATH

Every year without knowing it I have passed the day
When the last fires will wave to me
And the silence will set out
Tireless traveler
Like the beam of a lightless star

Then I will no longer
Find myself in life as in a strange garment
Surprised at the Earth
And the love of one woman
And the shamelessness of men
As today writing after three days of rain
Hearing the wren sing and the falling cease
And bowing not knowing to what

—W. S. MERWIN[10]

I am grateful for how poets are willing to enter the mysteries surrounding the end of life, how their imaginations find words to express, and to appreciate what our reason so often tries to avoid. After the death of her long-time partner, Mary Oliver had this to say about the experience of coming toward that transition: "The end of life has its own nature, also worth our attention. I don't say this without reckoning in the sorrow, the worry, the many diminishments. But surely it is then that a person's character shines or glooms."[11]

Often the old would like to discuss their concerns, their fears, and their imaginations of dying, but they hold back to spare loved ones the distress of facing the losses ahead. The severing of relationships as

---

10 Merwin, *The Second Four Books of Poems.*

11 Oliver, *Our World*, p. 73.

we know them is sad to anticipate and then when it happens, is often surrounded by intense grief. Nevertheless, if we do not cling to what for many of us have become outmoded, materialistic images of death, it is also possible to face the passing of an old person, perhaps especially someone we dearly love, with a mood of celebration for the long life and the unique gifts of this particular human being.

More words from Florida Scott-Maxwell:

> Love opens double gates on suffering. The pain of losing good is the measure of its goodness. Parting is impoverishment. Reason gives no solace. The going away of someone loved is laceration... If I could only see far ahead, assess what will happen, but I can do nothing. So I ape a false cheer, and gradually my sorrow becomes a dumb facing of Fate, until sickened by acceptance I feel a change taking place. A hint comes of some melting or hardening—which is it?—and at last I reach an inner citadel where there is a wounded quiet, knowing strength.... Perhaps near the core of our being—are we ever near that unknowable centre?—one is beyond pain and pleasure. Is it possible that we approach the place where they are one? Is this to say—"Thy will be done"?[12]

Here we see the spirit reflecting, still exploring new threads of understanding and meaning. Often there is a strong desire to come to terms with one's life experiences, to find a new level of resolution and acceptance. One last quote from Florida Scott-Maxwell captures this important inclination toward life review:

> Age is a desert of time—hours, days, weeks, years perhaps— with little to do. So one has ample time to face everything one has had, been, done; gather them all in: the things that came from outside, and those from inside. We have time at last to make them truly ours.... You need only claim the events of your life to make yourself yours. When you truly possess all you have been and done, which may take some time, you are fierce with reality. When at last age has assembled you together, will it not be easy to let it all go, lived, balanced, over?[13]

---

12 Scott-Maxwell, *The Measure of My Days*, pp. 42–43.

13 Ibid., pp. 41–42.

ꝙ

Each one of us will have to discover our own way through the years of aging, to our own particular moment of dying. Some will try to make this journey as consciously as possible; others may blindly catapult across the threshold of death. Whether or not we have worked purposely on facing and trying to digest our life experiences, there is much evidence that a review awaits us after our death. Throughout history different world religions and mythologies have described, often in abundant if not also terrifying detail, an afterlife of judgment and purification. Western art and literature surround us with vivid pictures of purgatory, heaven, and hell. Even in our very materialistic times people who have had near-death experiences consistently describe an encounter with a panoramic review of the whole of one's life.[14]

Rudolf Steiner spoke often about the reality of life after death, or more precisely, life between death and rebirth. He characterized, from a variety of perspectives, the stages along the way between one life and another.[15] In the first few days immediately following physical death, Steiner suggested that the etheric or life body remains united with the astral body of the departing person. This is when the panorama of the whole of the life occurs. In a near-death experience, where the physical body first separates from the other three bodies and then some form of life-saving intervention reunites them, the etheric body can still retain a memory of the life tableau.

In the case of a person who dies, first the physical body is cast off, then after about three days the etheric body is also released. The "I," still connected to the astral body, now finds itself needing to extinguish the desires and pleasures of earthly life that continue to encumber it even though there is no longer a physical body with which to fulfill them. Here begins a new phase in the process of soul purification; without physical sense organs the "I" must liberate itself from the sense-bound longings and attractions that were formed on Earth.

---

14   The classic text on near-death experiences is *Life After Life* written in 1975 by Raymond A. Moody, Jr.; another, more recent bestseller on the subject is Eben Alexander, MD, *Proof of Heaven*.

15   See Steiner, *Theosophy*; *An Outline of Esoteric Science*; *Life between Death and Rebirth*; and *Staying Connected*.

A further aspect of this purification occurs as the still connected "I" and astral body review the now completed earthly experiences. This involves a detailed working backward through one's whole life, from the moment of death back to birth. This retrospective includes experiencing one's deeds in life from the perspective of the others on whom they had an effect. In particular, our selfishness, meanness, lies, and all the pain we caused are there to be re-encountered, to be felt now as others suffered them. Perhaps it is not hard to see how from this review, resolves begin to be built toward a future life on Earth. Our eternal self, in consort with higher spirit beings, gathers and reworks the fruit of our learning in order to invite future possibilities of redemption and further growth toward an ever more whole human becoming.

How are we to assess information like the preceding if we have no direct experiences of life between death and rebirth? I personally find the evidence from near-death experiences to be very compelling, and I have also been moved by images offered in art throughout the ages. For example, I recently saw the classic film *Wild Strawberries*, by the Swedish director Ingmar Bergman, which tells the story of an aging doctor who is to be honored for his long career. He decides to drive from Stockholm to Lund, where the award will be given, and during the long car journey, accompanied by his daughter-in-law and three young hitchhikers, he has a variety of experiences and dreams that offer him a review of his life. He encounters good things that he had done, people who loved him, and others who treated him badly. He also meets situations where he himself lacked courage or acted selfishly or unkindly. Especially in the dream sequences he encounters stark images of how his actions affected others. It is as if he is given a foretaste of what Rudolf Steiner suggested awaits us after death.

When the work of after-death purification is completed, Rudolf Steiner suggested that the astral body, like the physical and etheric before it, is also discarded. Now the "I" is at home in a world of spirit being: "During the life between birth and death, our surroundings speak to us through the organs of our bodies, but once we have discarded all our bodies the language of our new surroundings speaks directly to the 'innermost sanctuary' of the I."[16]

---

16 Steiner, *An Outline of Esoteric Science*, p. 88.

As spiritual fruit of the now cleansed former life, the eternal "I" retains what Steiner refers to as a kind of extract, like a seed from its experiences in the sensory world. This will be worked on further in the new spiritual environment the "I" now inhabits. Steiner characterized this world, and the further journey the spirit will take, in a variety of ways. In previous chapters I referred to his descriptions of different planetary realms where spiritual forces flow toward the Self, helping it rebuild and reconfigure the fruits of its earlier lives and prepare for a new life on Earth. This formulation of destiny is a long and complex process, and I encourage you to study it more deeply through the texts I have cited. I am only pointing in a most contracted way to this picture of the continuing journey the eternal human spirit makes beyond the death of the physical body and how the life just lived has ongoing influence on further lives to come.

Rather than elaborating more on Steiner's wide-ranging ideas on what occurs after death, I want to close this chapter with a look at some of the important changes in care for the dying that have been occurring in recent years. As a response to the many advances in medical technology surrounding childbirth in the second half of the twentieth century, particularly in developed countries, there was a groundswell of interest in "natural" childbirth; and in spite of increasing regulations, the appeal of home births continues to grow. Something similar has been happening in recent decades in relation to care for the dying, after-death care, burial practices, and memorial celebrations. Throughout the twentieth century, at least in the West, care for the dying became ever more technological and materialistic; traditional rituals surrounding death often seemed to lack genuine spiritual substance. Especially with the beginning of the twenty-first century, conversations about the threshold of death have become much more nuanced. I have also noticed an increase in articles, books, and other media attention that seem to indicate a growing desire to meet death more openly and actively.

In order to have a say about the levels of life-sustaining technology they want at the end of life, ever more people are signing living wills or other forms of advanced health care directives. Hospice care, green burial, and home care for the recently deceased are gaining much deserved attention. Movements like Crossings, or in my community, Sacred Undertaking, are bringing dignity and a deepening consciousness to the care of those who have died, as well as offering support to families facing the threshold between life and death.[17]

As we come to experience that death is not a final ending, we may change how we relate to those who have died and even begin to explore ways to continue nurturing our relationships with the "so-called dead," as Rudolf Steiner often referred to them.[18] Many people experience the value of a three-day wake, spending time with the body of the one who has died, sharing stories and memories with family and friends. Even with the grief of loss, funerals can be true celebrations of a life. Telling the person's biography, with living images of the gifts and the challenges that were part of this journey, is important for those attending the funeral and also, I believe, for the one who has died. More than once I have had the privilege of sharing someone's life story at a funeral or memorial service. It has felt as if my beloved people were present, experiencing the honor of the event, receiving the overview of their earthly lives as heart-filled encouragement along their further spirit way.

Beyond those immediate days after death and the funeral, there is much else we can do to foster an ongoing relationship: prayer and meditation, of course, but also inviting our friends on the other side to be with us as we read texts that are alive with spirit, and generally trying to be open to what communication may come to us from across the threshold. For example, what makes one of my dead suddenly come to mind as I am going about my day? Is this a prod, or a gentle request for my attention? When I inwardly pause to quietly say hello, I often find myself smiling within a strong sense of connection.

Steiner gave a picture that has been inspiring for me in my efforts to stay connected with people I care for who are no longer here on Earth: he suggested that we offer something very important to our loved ones when we vividly remember specific events we shared with

---

17   Sacred Undertaking, Great Barrington, MA, http://homefuneraldirectory
      .com/; also http://www.crossings.net; http://homefuneraldirectory.com.

18   Steiner, *Staying Connected.*

them. He said that for the dead, experiencing these memories, moving through the pictures we recall, is in some way similar to how enlivening it can be for us to experience works of art, perhaps when exploring a museum, or entering a beautiful architectural space, or listening to a piece of music. Steiner expressed it this way: "Our thoughts of love, our memories, and all that passes through our soul in connection with those no longer with us in the physical world create for the dead in their world something analogous to artistic creations in ours."[19] Just as art lifts us above the natural course of life, so, too, do our memories give something extra to the world of the dead, something uplifting, moving, and needed.

The dead are not really gone from us but only from our material perception. And we, too, will continue to exist on a spiritual journey after our death. Spirit and matter are aspects of one world, not two separate impenetrable spheres. Living on Earth our spirit being evolves through the opportunities offered by physical existence. After death and before a next incarnation we digest what we have learned and prepare our return to Earth, where once again, we will find our own unique way through the rhythmic cycles of growth in the natural world and in our human becoming.

19   Ibid., p. 112.

The sphere of the spirit is the soul's true home,
And we will surely reach it
By walking in the path of honest thought;
By choosing as our guide the fount of love
Implanted in the heart;
By opening the eye of soul
To nature's script
Spread out through all the universe,
Telling the story of the spirit
In all that lives and thrives,
And in the silent spaciousness of lifeless things,
And in the stream of time—the process of becoming.
—RUDOLF STEINER, *Verses and Meditations*

Meditation is old and honorable, so why should I not sit, every morning of my life, on the hillside, looking into the shining world? ... Can one be passionate about the just, the ideal, the sublime, and the holy, and yet commit to no labor in its cause? I don't think so.
—MARY OLIVER, *New and Selected Poems*, vol. 2

CHAPTER 9

TAKING ONE'S SELF SERIOUSLY:
GOING AN INNER PATH

Throughout this book I have referred to the importance of self-development, of taking ourselves seriously as beings of body, soul, and spirit. In considering life phases, I mentioned the challenges we inevitably meet, at the very least by mid-life and on into old age, to grow in self-knowledge and personal responsibility. The ways that our temperament or our gender influence our behavior also invite our attention. If we want to avoid experiencing ourselves as victims of arbitrary bad luck, or even recipients of random good luck; if indeed we seek to discover elements of deeper meaning in our lives, then we have no option as we grow older but to engage in some form of reflective inner work.

By including a chapter on inner development in this book, I do not want to suggest that there is one particular way to take up the call of soul-spirit work. Nor do I consider myself an authority on this subject. But I have been a seeker all my life. It is my experience that in very individual ways, most modern people sense an increasingly insistent call to acknowledge an inner core of self that is both invisible and real, both uniquely one's own and strangely universal. If we do not blot out this call—for example, with overwork, with recreational or pharmaceutical substances, with the distractions of media and the virtual world—then we are challenged to listen to promptings from a non-material dimension of reality. Our soul has much work to do by way of personal development; our spirit, too, seeks to gain new strength along an inner path.

In my twenties my interest was drawn to self-improvement, and I must admit that initially some part of me thought I was doing inner work just because I recognized its importance. I found the idea that life itself was a form of meditation very appealing. I also had a strong sense of social justice and I wanted to be of service. It took several years before I knew from the inside that if I wanted to be truly useful in the outer world, I had to devote real time and energy to my inner journey. I needed to attend to unexplored dimensions of myself and become more awake to the multi-dimensional facets of reality around me. And I needed to live more responsibly with the relationship between myself and the world—with all the social, environmental, and spiritual interconnections and consequences inherent in such a relationship.

Several years ago I was struck by all the gyms that began appearing on city streets. They seemed to sprout up on every vacant corner, and there behind the often very large windows were office workers and retired people, artists and teachers, moms and dads, all toiling away on stationary bicycles, or jogging on treadmills. These gyms and exercise centers are open long hours, allowing people to drop in at their "leisure" for a class or a workout. As I observed this rigorous attention to health and wellbeing, I found myself wondering why it seems so much easier to honor the needs of the physical body than those of the spirit. Why is it more difficult to carve out even ten minutes for an inner practice than to spend an hour at the gym? The benefits of physical exercise are clear, but I kept finding myself imagining a very different kind of wellbeing center—The Inner Gym. It is not likely that I shall ever found one myself, but I do feel it could be an important social initiative. (If this idea strikes an entrepreneurial chord in you, please take it and run with it!)

An Inner Gym would be a place to drop in for enlivening body, soul, and spirit activity. Rather than spinning or running in place, people could experience biography exercises that would illuminate events and patterns along their life journey. Cardio-vascular routines would be replaced by stretching consciousness toward living heart thinking. Nature observations would give access to organic rhythms of growth and the miracle of diversity, and in the process awaken unexpected reverence. Instead of listening to the loud and pounding beat of an anonymous musical taste, there would be space for inner quiet, and encouragement to listen for an inner sounding. There would be art activities, because the arts invite deepening perception—of color, tone, form, or balance—and provide practice in the work of transformation. And there would also be opportunity for gentle, healing, and playful movement activities.

Some of the activities in this Inner Gym could be pursued through classes, others in conversation with a trained biography worker, a new slant on the idea of a personal trainer. Activities would be available for drop-ins, and also for those seeking committed practice over time. Groups could form that would offer participants mutual support. The space itself would be beautiful, colorful, inviting, and confirming.

It is very clear that people today are exploring many pathways along their inner journeys. Some seek a conscious path of spiritual development, perhaps delving into diverse traditions as they forge their own meditative practice. Others deepen themselves through dedication to activities such as nature study, artistic practice, journaling, prayer, or works of service. In forging my own inner path, there are practices and guidelines that I have found helpful, attitudes and ways of working that encourage me to be more awake to the wondrous and challenging dimensions of life on Earth, and to the gifts and the needs that surround me. One way of looking at this chapter is to see it as my effort to describe a few of the activities that could be experienced in an actual inner gym.

As I have stated throughout this book, already as a young person I was drawn to Rudolf Steiner's ideas about the nature of the human being and the evolution of human consciousness. I soon came to understand that Anthroposophy, as he named his work, was much more than a body of knowledge to be studied; indeed I began to experience it more significantly as a path of awakening consciousness. The word *Anthroposophia* comes from the Greek *Anthropos,* or the human being, and *Sophia,* meaning wisdom, as well as the name for the Goddess of Wisdom. Anthroposophy has been translated as "wisdom of the human being," or "awareness of our humanity." However, I think it also implies "the human being coming to wisdom," in fact to cosmic wisdom.

In speaking about the inner path Steiner avoided saying there was only one right way to proceed. He articulated spiritual truths as he experienced them and spoke of the consequences of different activities rather than demanding adherence to one prescribed practice. He offered suggestions in the mood of, "you could try this," expecting that his listeners would have enough self-knowledge to discover ever and again their own areas needing attention and each evolving next step along the way of the emerging higher self. Even when he made declarations from his own spiritual research, he enjoined his listeners not to just believe him, but to do their own work of spiritual discovery. In the beginning I felt challenged by the responsibility to forge my own ongoing direction, but I also deeply appreciated this profound respect for individual freedom and the dedication to the idea that anyone working with integrity and commitment could find his or her own way forward.

My inner practice, or what I can also call my journey into meditation, has evolved over many years. As I reflect on this now, I recognize three overlapping spheres of attention. There are activities that invite me to look back into the past, others that center me in a living experience of the present moment, and still others that open me to something unknown coming from the future. Of course, the past, present, and future are not fixed points in our consciousness; and I do not want to portray them as exclusive domains. Perhaps someone else would place one or another of the exercises I will mention into a different sphere. I am merely trying to organize my thoughts within a vast subject. I am helped in this effort by Rudolf Steiner's mighty Foundation Stone Meditation, which calls the human soul to three great practices: spirit recalling, spirit sensing, and spirit beholding. This imagination provides a focus for what I want to describe.[1]

---

1   Steiner brought the Foundation Stone Meditation at the re-founding of the Anthroposophical Society, December 1923. There are many translations of the meditation; I refer to the one by members of the Association for the Arts

1. Practice Spirit Recalling

How have I come to be who I am? What has created the miracle
of the human body? What forces have been at work in the extraordinary diversity of life forms found in nature, or in the creation of
mountains, oceans, or deserts? What mysteries are at work in the
development of human consciousness, in the unfolding of history, in
the evolution of the universe? So many questions about our personal
lives and about the social, environmental, and spiritual dimensions of
the world around us invite us to become explorers of creation itself, in
all its manifold expressions and processes.

We are called to look back in myriad ways, and so we begin to
study. We consider the research and understandings of others, and
the ways they express their thoughts shape our own possibilities of
understanding. Much of education is about orienting us in the world
of space, elaborating the foundation we stand on and the body we live
within for our earthly activity. We can practice nature observation
and let it lead us into experiences of natural law at work. We can do
biography exercises that unlock doors into our own story of becoming. We can reflect on planetary influences or consider the laws of
karma. In quiet meditation we can begin to open ourselves beyond
our normal ways of knowing and reach dimensions of spirit reality
that are veiled by our everyday consciousness.

Remembering and *recollecting* are other words for this work of
looking back. This is not a pursuit for the intellect alone, and it is not
only about memory, but about *re-membering*—bringing the pieces of
our reality together in our consciousness, trusting the details to reveal
a deeper truth, holding phenomena side by side that may at first reveal
no connection, and allowing the forces of creation to begin to speak
within us.

There are many inner exercises that can aid us in relating spiritually to what is coming over from the past.[2] One that has become a

---

of Speech and Drama in North America, in the brochure "The Foundation
Stone Meditation" of the Anthroposophical Society in America (1998). For
further study see Zeylmans Van Emmichoven, *The Foundation Stone.*

2   Detailed descriptions of exercises on an inner path can be found in Rudolf
Steiner's *How to Know Higher Worlds.* Many useful exercises can be found

valued part of my daily practice is reviewing my day before going to sleep. Perhaps we are naturally inclined to do this, but is it possible to go beyond the normal way we tend to look back on daily events, replaying again and again our feelings about a mistake we made, a special conversation, or an injustice we suffered? As long as we are stuck in that groove, or even in wishing we had done something differently, we cannot perceive the deeper working of our will throughout the day, nor the import for our "I" of what occurred.

As we review the day, can we try to see ourselves as strangers, observing what took place from outside, without a running commentary of judgments, regrets, or pride? Steiner suggested that we do this review in a backward direction, from evening to morning; "we visualize things correctly, but are not bound by their sense-perceptible sequence."[3] This immediately takes us out of an automatic replay; we have to be more awake in viewing images from the day, in observing what the actual causes were of what we experienced as consequences. By watching the day unfold backward, our normal habit of experiencing time is altered and we also strengthen our capacity to see inner images.

Doing the daily review should not take long; indeed, with practice just a few minutes is enough to view the flow of your day from the present right back to the beginning of the morning. But what can so easily happen is that we lose focus and find ourselves stuck rehashing some knotty part of the day, dreaming off on an unrelated topic, or perhaps even falling asleep still propped up in bed. Without a further detour of berating oneself, the best thing to do when such lack of attention occurs is simply to return to the review. Once our backward glance reaches morning, we can enter sleep without a lot of tag ends hanging over from the day just passed. We are ready to enter the spiritual world that sleep opens up for us.

There are, of course, many other ways to practice spirit recalling: for example, reviewing the passage of the year in our garden, trying to selflessly reflect on a difficult social issue, meditating on an historical

throughout his lectures, such as "Practical Training in Thought," printed in *Anthroposophy in Everyday Life*.

3   Steiner, *An Outline of Esoteric Science*, p. 319.

event, or remembering people in our biography who opened doors for us. Such reviewing activities can enhance our sense for the majesty of the creative forces through which we have come into being and strengthen our trust in the foundations of earthly existence. When I make space for these kinds of reflections, I experience gratitude arising within me—for the Sun that warms me, the ground that holds me, the work I love, the dear people in my heart, and even those who have hurt me. All have been part of my becoming; all inspire the unfolding of my greater will. I feel that I am part of cosmic and karmic mysteries that are so much larger than I can rationally understand, but I also know that in my own small way I am endowed with great gifts and meaning-filled challenges. With both humility and reawakened responsibility I experience myself alive and growing within the ever-evolving world of matter and spirit.

2. Practice Spirit Sensing

It is especially in our feeling life that we know ourselves in the present moment, that we sense our aliveness within the ongoing flow of time. But how do we truly attend to the fullness and integrity of this moment within the streaming rhythms of life? How can we be awake to what is happening, now? How do we honor a present feeling, without succumbing to the drag of the past or the pull of the future? The phrase *spirit sensing* is sometimes translated as *spirit awareness* or *mindfulness*. The aim of mindfulness is well known in many spiritual traditions; how can we practice the centering attention needed for this presence of heart and mind? What is the experience of *presence*?

If I carefully observe a flower, a child, a sunset, or an idea, I may, through the work of recollection, be able to approach the creative forces behind its existence. In the very act of observing, I may also experience awe and wonder at the particular miracle before me: the form and growth patterns of the flower, the rosy-cheeked exuberance of the child, the impossibly juxtaposed colors of the sunset, or the complexity and dimension of the idea. When with genuine interest I pause to really take in what is before me, my feeling unites with what I am meeting. But so often in our busy lives, burdened by all we are carrying and worried about what lies ahead, we just hurry along with a fleeting glance of surface recognition. We miss the true miracle of the moment; we fail to be present to what is right in front of us.

Rudolf Steiner speaks of a fundamental mood of soul that is the starting point for any genuine path of spiritual development: "an attitude of reverence, of devotion to truth and knowledge."[4] This feeling must be awakened ever and again, in the present moment; it is not enough that we felt reverence yesterday or plan to feel it tomorrow. I think that as modern people we must acknowledge that feelings of reverence or devotion are not always easy for us. We are well schooled in critique, in finding what is wrong with a person, an idea, the weather, or the economy. Even young children have games to find the flaws in a picture and are taught to look critically at strangers and at what they do not already know or understand. But inner work cannot develop in a healthy way if its necessary starting mood is far from our everyday habits of relating to the world. If we have gone through the day finding fault, how can we be open to genuine spiritual perception in fifteen minutes of inner practice? I ask this even as I know the contradiction in what I am saying, for I can recall many times when I have been amazed by the nearness of genuine wonder, if only I stop, make an inner reversal, and really look—at the colors of wilting flowers on my table, or the endless ingenuity of the squirrel on my birdfeeder, or the gentle generosity on my husband's tired face.

But we need to be awake to make such an act of inner reversal. Otherwise unconscious habits of dismissal actually diminish our humanity, precluding an openhearted encounter with the world and a healthy approach to spiritual development. There is much about modern life that needs our critical attention, but how do we educate right judgment without fostering doubt, negativity, and fear? How do we nurture wonder and allow room in our souls for awe and respect? We need to prepare ourselves for inner vision through devoted attention to what is worthy of our respect. Large life events—childbirth, accidents, attending to someone at death—come to us, gracing us with awe-inspiring experiences of spirit presence. It is more challenging to open ourselves to feelings of wonder and devotion in the seemingly small offerings of daily life. Yet all around us are inspiring people,

4   Steiner, *How to Know Higher Worlds*, p. 16.

important ideas, and natural wonders. When we meet them with open interest for the truths they embody, we invite a deeper knowing.

Another prerequisite for inner work that Steiner mentions in the first chapter of *How to Know Higher Worlds* is the need to create moments of inner quiet in which one practices distinguishing the essential from the inessential. Like reverence, inner quiet is not a given in our busy, noisy, wired, and distractible lives. We need to build pauses into our days, moments to reflect and realign ourselves with what really matters. Discerning what is essential requires consciousness and an open heart; events, thoughts, or feelings do not come with labels announcing their significance, nor is the determination an intellectual process. We learn to be discerning through practice, and this learning needs an inner tranquil space in which to grow strong and confident. Then we may begin to hear the hidden meaning and the connecting rhythms resounding through life around us.

But so often we have a running monologue filling our consciousness. Worries, to-do lists, advertising jingles, replays of a challenging conversation.... It can be difficult to stop the stream of words, images, snatches of song. Even when we sit down for a moment of quiet, the buzz goes on. How to stop the incessant noise, the distractions that inhibit our attention from going where we want it to be? The more we tell ourselves to be still, the more outrageous the disturbance can become. And then our foot begins to itch, and a fly drones at the window. It can be helpful to momentarily acknowledge each distraction, bringing it to rest with a nod of attention. Sometimes working with a settling image can be helpful: imagining a shepherd gathering his sheep for sleep, or the Sun disappearing behind a darkening hill, or a boiling pot of soup coming to a simmer and then to rest. We are aiming to quiet the clamor of our everyday self so that our higher self can attend to true spirit sensing. In his excellent book, *Meditation as Contemplative Inquiry*, Arthur Zajonc refers to this as giving birth to our "silent self."[5] Only in a state of inner tranquility can our higher self be truly receptive to the invisible workings of spirit.

Many kinds of exercises help us to find a quiet center and an inner wakefulness for meditation, for spirit sensing. At different stages

---

5   Zajonc, *Meditation As Contemporary Inquiry*, p. 30.

along my inner path, I have found a group of six exercises to be essential. Steiner described these exercises many times, referring to them as accompanying activities needed to balance out the one-sidedness of other meditative practices. At a preliminary level they help us stay centered in our thinking, willing, and feeling, and also in the practice of positivity and openness. This work is strengthening to our everyday self, for example enhancing self-confidence, focus, and stability, and it is also vital for a balanced emergence of our higher self.[6]

These exercises are often described as control of thinking, control of will, control of feeling. For myself I have found it useful to approach them as centering activities. The idea of "control" can sometimes make us rather fierce, but we need to approach this work on ourselves in a friendly way. Thinking, feeling, and will are all activities of the soul, and at any point our "I" may be off balance within them, or only partially present in how they are working in us. For example, when listening to a friend relate a recent adventure, have you ever found yourself inwardly composing a grocery list or reviewing a conversation you had over breakfast with your daughter? Or perhaps this splitting of attention happens when you are studying, praying, or meditating on a well-known verse. How often is our mind filled with thought clichés, dead thoughts we carry along from yesterday, or someone else, or the media? In the realm of the will, perhaps you set out to rake the leaves but on the way are distracted into sweeping the entryway, which reminds you to sort through the mail. Then the phone rings and, before you know it, it is too dark to work outside and so the leaves join the list of unfinished tasks. In these instances there were thoughts going on in you and deeds that you accomplished, but where was your conscious "I"? Do you ever find yourself wondering if anyone was "home"? *How* could I have thought that, or *who* did that? If we want to trust ourselves to be centered and awake in the present moment, we need to practice being actively there. The following exercises are a great help in centering ourselves

---

6   Steiner, *An Outline of Esoteric Science*, pp. 310–316 and Steiner, *Start Now!*, pp. 109–118. Detailed descriptions of the exercises can also be found in Zajonc, *Meditation as Contemplative Inquiry*, pp. 67–89 and in Lipson, *Stairway of Surprise*. I also wrote about them as an aid for parents in *More Lifeways*, pp. 11–20.

within our essential soul activities, in preparing us for the possibility of spirit sensing.

Thinking

The first exercise addresses thinking and involves inwardly reflecting on a simple, man-made object such as a cup, a spoon, a needle, or a matchstick. We bring our voluntary attention to the thoughts that belong to the object: its function, form, origin, what it is made of, how it was made, how it was distributed, perhaps even comparing a spoon to a fork or a cup to a bowl. We try not to jump from thought to thought, but rather to follow in our mind's eye, as far as we are able, the actual thought forms that are made physically manifest by this object. Although working with this exercise may encourage us to look more carefully at the small objects that surround us, while doing the exercise itself, we do not have the object in front of us, but with closed eyes try to picture it clearly. This is schooling for our attention as well as practice in objectivity.

The exercise need not take more than five minutes, but it does need to be done regularly, perhaps beginning with a one-month commitment to do it every day. Especially at first it is not uncommon to drift off and find yourself inwardly recalling a disagreement with a colleague or remembering a recent social event. If this happens, just go back to the object, since reflecting on how you got distracted is still off topic. It is possible to stay with the same object for several days or choose a new one each day. What is important is that you are active in your current thinking, not passively running through what you thought yesterday or randomly grabbing for bits of information you know about the object. As you make inner space for the objective thoughts inherent in what you are considering, the essence of the object can begin to speak.

Will

The second exercise moves us into the domain of the will. It can be very useful before taking this next step to first review your day from the perspective of where you were in your will. What moved you through the day—your own desires, outer obligations, the wishes or needs of others? Did you have a plan? Were you scattered, or driven, or aimless? How did you meet unexpected challenges to your intentions—with flexibility, passivity, rigidity, consciousness? Are you carrying a backpack laden with unfulfilled resolves that weigh you down day after day? Such self-assessment generally suggests the usefulness of this second exercise. There is much about the will that is truly mysterious; we are basically asleep to whole dimensions of what moves us through our days, what makes us do what we do. Nevertheless, we can practice being more centered in forming and fulfilling our intentions.

The exercise for the will is deceptively simple. It involves deciding on an intention and then actually following through with it, every day. You choose a specific time in the day when you will do an insignificant action that takes only seconds to accomplish—like scratching an ear, twisting a ring, looking out the window—and when the time comes, you do it. The simplicity of the action precludes the excuse of not having enough time for it. We choose something unnecessary because this is conscious practice in building a capacity, and the only aim is to fulfill our self-appointed task. Feeding the dog or watering a plant demand our action through their own objective needs, and so do not count for this exercise. Clearly this is not about clock time or about obsessively watching for the moment, nor would it be appropriate to set your phone or digital watch as a reminder. You could, however, decide to do your task after brushing your teeth in the morning or last thing before heading to bed. What is important is to begin listening to an internal prompt to action. When you first try this exercise, it might go well for a few days, and then suddenly you realize that a week has gone by and you never remembered it at all. How could this happen? Where did the intention go? And how many much more meaning-ful resolves have similarly disappeared from your consciousness? The importance of paying attention to how we follow through with self-determined aims shows itself to us ever and again.

$\wp$

The next exercise is about our feeling life, but before I address it, I want to share what happened to me as I was working on these pages. It was a quiet Friday and I spent several hours editing earlier paragraphs and writing about the mysterious and often slumbering will. After that I made notes on how I wanted to describe the feeling exercise in a way that would make it clear that the effort is not about stifling genuine feelings, but rather about finding one's own center from which to express them with authenticity and equanimity. Then, I accidentally deleted everything I had done. How could this have happened? What sleeping will lurked in the "don't save" click that instantaneously erased hours of work? What followed was my very authentic feeling reaction… you might have heard me expressing my distress with a complete lack of equanimity! When I calmed down, I called my writer son who with sweet sympathy assured me that if I had clicked that particular prompt, there was nothing to be done but start again. And so I did, still with enthusiasm for these exercises that I know foster centeredness and build capacities of attention, but humbled enough to need to tell you that I also know that the work is never done!

Feeling

The third exercise invites us to practice equanimity in the expression of our feelings. How often when we feel something strongly, do we react out of pure habit? We lash out with anger, we fall into self-pity, we are taken over by weeping or stricken with fear. The feeling can so overwhelm us that we are "beside ourselves." How can we find our center within what the feeling is telling us, and from there express what is needed? This exercise is not meant to curtail the experience or the sharing of genuine feelings—there are times to cry, times to express joy or anger—but to encourage us to find appropriate ways to communicate them with inner equilibrium. Appropriate not by some abstract standard, but in relationship to the situation in which we find ourselves. When we let a feeling resound within us, it can reveal deep truths that are easily lost in a reactive or habitual expression. Our feelings are messengers, telling us about the world, and we need an open inner space and a quiet pause in which to receive the message and find our authentic response. As suggested in approaching the will exercise, it can be very useful to look back on your day from the perspective of your feeling experiences. When were you aware of your feelings? Did you express yourself honestly or did you mask your true feelings? Were you thrown off center or reactive, unresponsive, shut down, or hollow? Did the way you communicated your feelings serve your relationships, or lead to unexpected consequences?

Rather than entailing a particular task, this exercise is about bringing consciousness into our feeling life. As practice, you can review a situation in which you recognize that you "lost it," bringing attention to what set you off, and then also imagining how you might have acted from a place of greater inner balance. Or perhaps you see a time when you felt nothing, when a kind of inner dullness prevented you from perceiving what was happening around you. It has been my experience that this kind of attention to daily experiences gradually began to help me be more aware in moments when I am on the edge of reacting from habit or temperament, tiredness, or irritation. I cannot say that I always find equanimity at such times, but when I pause enough to remember that my automatic reaction rarely serves anything good, in that instant of heightened consciousness, I sometimes find a more measured and creative way to express what matters. In previous chapters I have spoken about the *double*, that unconscious part of our reactive life that so often shadows our best intentions. I have found this exercise to be particularly helpful in alerting me to when my double, with all its old, undigested, and stuck parts of me, would keep me from living fully in the present moment. When I can remain centered within and responsible to my true feeling experiences, my double loses its grip on my behavior and I am more alive and connected to the world around me. There is much to be enjoyed and much to be suffered in modern life; our sensitive and trustworthy presence is well served by the practice of this exercise.

Positivity

I have mentioned how easily we modern people can slip into a critique-oriented approach to the world: we see what is wrong with the political situation, with our spouse, with our child's teacher, or with traffic on our commute to work. We are saddened by a friend's diagnosis of cancer and engulfed by a sense of loss. The fourth exercise is about practicing positivity even in the midst of a problem that cannot, and perhaps should not, be ignored. Calling on our awakened thinking and equanimity of feeling we now go another step to search for something worthy, some sliver of goodness within what is perhaps objectively difficult. As with the other exercises, it can be very useful to review your day from the perspective of positivity versus negativity. Were you at any point aware of being caught in a cloud of negativity? Or engaged in gossip, or general complaint? Did you have moments of appreciating someone's behavior or ideas? If so, how did that feel? Were there moments when you felt jealous or judgmental? What about your assessment of yourself? Did you get caught in critiquing your hair, your weight, your job, or lack of ambition?

This exercise challenges us to go beyond first impressions, to seek out and be faithful to a core of goodness in another, to move beyond partisan prejudices. In describing this exercise, Rudolf Steiner often related a Persian legend about Christ walking with his followers when they came upon the remains of a dead dog. The others drew back in disgust, but Christ looked more closely and commented on the dog's beautiful teeth.[7] This was not a denial of the rotting carcass, but its own positive statement. The challenge of this exercise is to be on the lookout for "beautiful teeth" in our daily experiences. As a way of practicing we can bring to mind something that is a genuine problem for us—pollution, teenagers' excessive texting, the continuing unrest in the Middle East, or a bossy colleague. As we inwardly observe the situation, we try to find some thread of hope or beauty or decency within what is difficult or threatening to us. Ultimately we want to be able to catch ourselves in the moment of falling into automatic negativity, or to have the courage to broaden out a conversation that is reveling in complaint or gossip. Are we able to explore a fuller picture from a centered place within ourselves? Often by searching for something we can admire, the context for our negative feelings widens and we can approach the challenge in a more holistic and heart-centered way.

Openness

The fifth exercise calls on the willingness of our "I" to be open and centered, ever and again, in meeting something new, such as an idea

---

7   Steiner, *An Outline of Esoteric Science*, p. 315.

that seems impossible, an unexpected quality in someone we know well, or a reconceiving of ourselves. Without overturning everything we already know, can we practice a readiness to keep on learning, receptivity to a different perspective, even acceptance of being wrong? Here again, it is useful to look back to see where you have been open and where closed. Can you see where habit, fear, or prejudice determined how you met a new idea, a person, or a social situation? Do you ever find yourself thinking, "That's ridiculous" or "Not how I do it!" or "He is always so..." If you find moments where you have entertained something new, what prompted this? Was it someone else insisting, your own conscious effort or interest, or a shock of recognition? Are you able to experiment with ideas that shake up your orderly world? Can you be open to contradiction, with trust that a deeper truth may be presenting itself to you? It is easy to become caught in tradition, in daily routines, and familiar mental pictures, particularly as we age. Young children bring fresh interest to everything they meet; but as adults we have our favorite habits of thought, interpretations of the world, and behaviors that provide security and are part of how we know ourselves. And so we can get stuck, as if we have finished growing. In our thinking and use of language this leads to cliché; in our resistance to otherness we find the root of all prejudice.

We need to work with objective thinking and activated will to practice openness. Can we explore diversity, genuinely opening ourselves to difference? Can we find examples where we recognize that we shut down and at least in retrospect open the gates that imprison our ideas or our behavior? So often we are expected by others, and even by ourselves, to react to certain moral, social, artistic, or political ideas in well-established ways. But what if instead we listen for something new in what others contribute and in how our own thoughts could evolve? For example, we may hear a younger person enthuse about what feels to us like the reinvention of a well-oiled wheel; instead of closing off with a patronizing nod, can we honor this freshness of discovery with a readiness for an unexpected nuance? Can we catch ourselves in moments where daily habit would close us down? Many years ago at a fortieth anniversary celebration, the husband of the couple being honored spoke about how he and his wife found something surprising in each other every day. In my late twenties at the time, I remember looking at that old couple and wondering how such a thing could be possible. Now, after forty-five years of my own marriage, I appreciate the ever-renewing effort (even if not done daily!) and the heart-stretching rewards behind such a statement. The practice of opening ourselves and continuing to learn throughout life enriches our daily experiences, enhances our creativity and trust in discovery, and prepares us to meet ever-new dimensions of reality.

Harmonizing

After working with each of the preceding exercises, we are challenged to attend to their different spheres of activity in a balanced way, as part of our ongoing inner practice. Often people introduce one per month into their daily activity, trying also not to neglect the ones that came before. The sixth exercise involves harmonizing the different activities on a regular basis. If we take seriously the injunction to know ourselves as a foundation for our inner work, then we will recognize which domains need particular attention at any moment. Where am I becoming off center? If I see that my thoughts are often scattered, I know I need to focus for a time on being more centered in my thinking. If I find myself not finishing anything I set out to do, taking up the will exercise will offer support. Perhaps I recognize an excessive reactivity in my feeling life, and so the third exercise needs particular attention. Likewise if I find myself getting caught in negativity or regularly rejecting new ideas or experiences, I can strengthen my "I" with the fourth and fifth exercises. I have often thought of these exercises like the five points of a star. The sixth exercise is the star itself: it comes into being when inter-connecting lines join the five separate points. This weaving together of the different parts is greater than one plus one plus one, and so the whole begins to shine, to ray into the world from our unique and centered self.

As we practice the various exercises, we build capacities. Like practicing musical scales so that our fingers are free to really play music from the heart, or doing physical exercise so that we are healthy and strong, working with these six basic exercises strengthens our "I" to be more fully present in our activities in the world and in our encounters with the multi-sided challenges of life today. Many years ago John Davy, a friend and colleague at Emerson College in England, interviewed Elisabeth Kübler-Ross for an article he was writing. She had just completed her important book, *On Death and Dying*, and John was interested in how she articulated what she had identified as commonly experienced stages gone through by those confronting a serious illness or the death of a loved one. He recognized in these trials that people meet in intense life circumstances, the same spheres of activity that the six exercises address: *denial* that this bad news can really be true, is an inability to hold the thought of what is happening; *anger* is a rebellion of the will at its apparent lack of control; *bargaining* ("I promise to give up smoking if only I can live until my daughter's wedding") is an effort to find equanimity in the turmoil of feelings; *depression* stems from an inability to see anything positive in the difficult situation; and *acceptance* brings an openness toward the unknown ahead. John was interested to learn that the chapter in Kübler-Ross's book that followed the description of how people move through the five stages was called "Hope," an attitude born of finding inner balance and peace with what destiny has in store.[8]

I know from my own experiences with grief how real these steps are and how they overlap and recur at different levels in the process of restoring inner equilibrium. I agree with John's insight that this is an archetypal progression, essential to healing and to supporting our developing soul and spirit. Voluntarily working with the six exercises tills the soil of these domains of activity within us. There are, of course, many other exercises that also serve the deepening of our capacities of perception. I chose to specifically mention this group of six because I know they work. They help us meet what comes to us in life with inner confidence and resourcefulness, and beyond this, they strengthen our emerging higher "I" as it awakens to new possibilities of spirit sensing.

℘

---

8   This comparison between the six exercises and the stages identified by
     Kübler-Ross is elaborated upon in John Davy's article "Discovering Hope,"
     The Anthroposophical Review, vol. 5:2, 1983, pp. 27–32.

3. Practice Spirit Beholding

What is it to *behold* and even more to *behold spirit?* In the word *beholding* is the implication of seeing, even the suggestion of something grand or unusual, something worthy of our effort to look. But it also requests that we make space, a hold, in our inner being for what is coming toward us. We could be looking to the future, or across the threshold of normal perception. We are facing the yet unknown, but so often what we already know and all we carry as legacy from the past, in our thinking, feeling, and ways of being block an open view. We may be too full to receive anything new. In our answer-oriented times, how can we ourselves become a living question? How can we practice an inner stillness that is open to beholding the revealing light of spirit?

Rudolf Steiner's first major book addressed the question of human freedom through an exploration of the nature of thinking and how conditioning, schooling, tradition, and our own previous experiences can keep us bound to the past. Steiner located the potential for freedom in what he called moral intuition. The title of the book has been variously translated into English as *The Philosophy of Freedom, The Philosophy of Spiritual Activity,* and most recently *Intuitive Thinking as a Spiritual Path.* Taken together these three titles remind me of the call to practice spirit beholding, on my path of spirit awakening and also in my daily life. Is it possible to live so openly with a question or a decision that needs to be made that I can freely intuit the answer? Can I calmly behold the "right" solution for this particular situation, not through any outer or inner coercion but because I recognize it is the right course, however it may contradict conventional wisdom, rational assessment, or even my own wishes? In this sense beholding is also a kind of listening in to spirit aims—my own karmic intentions and/ or broader cosmic realities. Can I freely bring my light of thinking to a spiritual truth I now perceive?

Have you ever been in a situation where you had no idea how to go forward, no imagination for a next step, when everything you knew coming over from past experiences seemed useless? This could be during a situation of physical danger, a trial in a relationship, a conversation with a client, or an apparent teaching disaster. My experience at such times has been that if I do not run away, there comes a moment when I have to let go of trying to control what will happen. My inner self can only ask for help, as a silent prayer. Then, when I have relinquished even fear, as I stand in a state of complete unknowing, an answer comes. I know what to do. Moreover, I feel tremendous gratitude. In that instant I know that I am held by spirit guidance, and I am humbled by the realization that I could ever have forgotten that it is always there. I have come to feel that part of the practice of spirit beholding is asking more consciously for help, not waiting for dire moments of need, but practicing getting all my clever ideas out of the way and allowing an open space for something to come toward me.

There is a writing exercise that can stimulate this sense for spirit presence in our lives. I have done this with classes and in small groups, but it could also be done on one's own. In involves writing a letter to your angel, saying honestly what is on your heart and asking for guidance if you have a question. I do not mean to assume that each of you reading this considers yourself on letter-writing terms with your angel, or even that you feel you have one. You could also think of this as writing to your higher self. Take it in a playful way, and just write "Dear Angel" and go from there. Then put the letter aside and go do something else. After some time, perhaps an hour, sit down again and without rereading your letter, begin a letter back to yourself, from your angel. You may be surprised at what this invisible presence has to say to you, and the love and support that are expressed in the reply. At the very least this kind of exercise can activate an inner dialogue between your everyday self and a higher part of your consciousness.

Of course, there is a danger with exercises like this that we focus on ourselves, that we enhance our modern tendency for self-centeredness. My experience is that the angel reply may actually have startling reminders to get over our narrow concerns, to move beyond the smallness that can so easily fill our days. How else can we practice the selflessness that is necessary for real spirit beholding? Nature observation is a way to school our objectivity, as is child study or attention to temperaments. What is particularly important is that we learn to withhold our likes and dislikes from our observing, for they only offer insight about us and nothing essential about what we are studying.

As previously mentioned, exercises in observation may involve looking into the past and also attending openly to what is currently before us. We may reflect on the creative forces that have brought this object of nature or human ingenuity into being, and we may also be filled with reverence for what we are now experiencing. There is the additional possibility of beholding what is not yet fully manifest. Carefully following a plant as it develops through the spring, in quiet observation or with simple pencil sketches, is a schooling in selfless development. As we bring our attention to the plant day after day, we begin to notice the small steps of growth that belong to the fullness of its evolving being. We open ourselves to beholding its essence. Or in a different kind of inner observation, a thoughtful teacher or parent holds daily images of a child in order to open a view to his or her potential. It is a gift, both to the adult and to the child, to perceive the spirit coming into being in the young person; it takes attentive self-discipline to not impose one's own hopes and ambitions onto the child's development, but to selflessly serve this being's healthy becoming.

It seems to me that artistic practice is another way toward awakening spirit beholding, at least when art is not made as a merely materialistic product. In the act of creating, an artist is in conversation with a chosen medium and the work of art coming into being. There is a listening for what would be composed, or a looking into the world of color and form for what the painting would become. A novelist or playwright inwardly beholds the characters as they interact and evolve; this is part of finding the words and narrative form that will embody them. In poetry the rhythm and meaning of language may describe the visible world, but the poet's art is to perceive and communicate invisible realms of soul and spirit as well.

Many meditative exercises begin with carefully building up an image, for example from nature, our biography, a feeling experience, a word or phrase, or perhaps a symbolic picture. After concentrating on the self-created image, holding it and attending to its resonance in our feeling life, we can go a further step by then clearing away the picture we have formed, inwardly turning from it, without diminishing our inner attention. If we can remain alert in empty consciousness, and without expectation, an after-image may present itself to our beholding. Arthur Zajonc describes in very helpful detail this process he refers to as a movement between focused and open attention.[9] A similar process is at work in what we call spiritual research, when we live deeply with a question, offering it selflessly to the light of spirit. We cannot control when or how responding thoughts may begin to sound in us, but our open attention at the edge of not knowing invites their revelation.

The open attention needed to truly behold is not intellectual work, but heart work, as Rainer Maria Rilke expressed so well in a poem called *Turning Point*. Here is an excerpt from that longer poem:

> For there is a boundary to looking.
> And the world that is looked at so deeply
> wants to flourish in love.
>
> Work of the eyes is done, now
> go and do heart-work
> on all the images imprisoned within you; for you
> overpowered them: but even now you don't know them.[10]

There are many different ways of attending to our inner lives, of building an inner practice that opens us to the mysteries of the created world and the spirit reality that infuses it with being. I have barely touched the surface of possible approaches in this chapter. Within the three practices to which the human soul is called by Rudolf Steiner's Foundation Stone meditation—spirit recalling, spirit sensing, and spirit beholding—I have located several exercises that offer guidance along our path of inner development; these are activities that can awaken us to a deeper knowing of ourselves as beings of body, soul, and spirit. Looking back at one's day or immersing oneself in the wonders of the manifest world bring us closer to the forces of creation at work in the universe and in our own lives. Exercises that awaken reverence or invite inner quiet, as well as those that center us in our soul activities of thinking, feeling, and will, encourage us to live more

---

9   Zajonc, *Meditation as Contemplative Inquiry*, p. 39.
10   Rilke, "Turning Point" from *The Selected Poetry of Rainer Maria Rilke*.

fully in the rhythms of time and in our true feelings of the present. Learning to bring stillness to the many swirling thoughts that fill our busy consciousness allows us to open to a world of spirit being and to enliven our thinking with divine presence.

Many people today pursue an inner practice in order to find peace and stability in their lives and to strengthen themselves in achieving their dreams. This work on oneself is vitally important to balance the chaos and stress that is so prevalent today and to heal the deep wounds that many adults carry over from childhood. And then beyond this focus on self-reflection and inner balance, is where the more selfless work of spirit attending can begin. I share Rudolf Steiner's characterization of meditation as inward contemplation and converse with the spiritual world, as a way to supersensible knowing. We each will prepare the ground for such development in our own ways. For some, prayer opens a way to spiritual listening; others work with sacred texts and verses that offer bridges beyond our more personal concerns. Even a sentence can become a stimulus for rich contemplation. Long ago a phrase from Emerson jumped out at me from a now-forgotten text: "Every wall is a door." This became a profound stepping-stone on my meditative path. And Steiner's *Calendar of the Soul*, with its weekly meditative verses, stands out as an ever renewing invitation to contemplate throughout the course of the year our human relationship with the living being of the Earth.[11]

There is no substitute for individual inner practice, but many activities that we share with others can support the development of focus, openness, and connection. As one example of this, I want to share a deepening experience I had with my sister Linda after she was diagnosed with cancer in the late 1990s. We lived several hours away from each other, but we wanted to involve ourselves in a meaningful activity that was not directly related to her illness. Over the years we had enjoyed writing together, creating exercises to remember events and places from our childhood. That our memories of shared experiences were always so different had helped deepen our mutual

---

11   Steiner, *Calendar of the Soul;* there are numerous translations and editions of these verses, first presented by Steiner in 1912.

understanding, as well as our appreciation for the reality of our different temperaments.

With the crisis of Linda's illness we decided to try writing together as a daily practice. Each evening one of us would call the other. We would together choose a word that had somehow sounded in our experiences of that day. Then we would hang up and write about our chosen word for ten or fifteen minutes. When we were finished writing, we would call each other again and share what we had written. The words we chose ranged from the most mundane to the sublime—doorknob, laundry, beauty, family, honesty, friend, dragon, intimacy, eternal, goddess.... Nothing was too lowly or too exalted, and every word revealed unexpected treasure. We did this shared writing for almost a year, not every day, but never with more than a few days' gap between our efforts.

I mention this joint experience because it was so simple and yet so rich. The daily process never took more than half an hour. Individually and together we found this shared commitment to be a great gift and a renewing joy. For me the writing was a chance to go inside a word, to quietly let a concept begin to speak to me. Linda was often more imaginative; sometimes her writing would become a story, a dialogue, or a riff on the spelling or sound of the word. Our voices grew stronger as the months went by. We loved hearing each other's pieces and experiencing how our very different approaches and styles would somehow combine to suggest a greater whole. The world kept opening up more and more; the cancer could not shut life down. In those moments of exploration and sharing, we touched into spirit truths, and Linda's illness lost its overwhelming hold on the future.

I had not reread our writings in several years, but I dipped into them as I began to write about our experience. My initial intention in mentioning this time in my life was to encourage others to take up this focusing and opening writing activity with a friend or relative. But as I meandered my way through some of our notebooks and loose scraps of paper—we never even considered writing on a computer—I came across our offerings on the word *threshold*. These seem to me related to this chapter, to this question of an inner path, and so I am inserting them here. They are personal and they reach out to broader truths. They were never edited but stand as expressions of a moment in time, with all their run-on sentences and the dashes and dots of spontaneous writing. The only omission is that I have condensed the last two paragraphs of Linda's piece, because she mentioned living people, and I cannot ask her for permission to include that. She died in March 2007. Many conversations she and I had over the years echo throughout this book, and so I am particularly happy to include some her own words as well.

"THRESHOLD," BY LINDA NORRIS (AUGUST 11, 1999)

Thresh—to me—means to harvest something in order to prepare it for the next step in the process of its meaning, its destiny. Hold means—to me—to stop for a moment and know something specific. A threshold then could be a place in your life where you are ready to harvest an aspect of yourself that you have been growing within you or working on. And you must know it and hold it up to your inner, higher eyes and mind and with the help of the spirit of your heart, work/weave that knowledge into your present consciousness and never put that knowledge down again. It must become part of the teacher or the priest or the healer within you—for the benefit of others who have not made it to that threshold yet. And at all times that knowledge must be disseminated with hope.

As a child, talking and walking and thinking are all thresholds to cross. The I of all of us crosses thresholds every day in our journey of becoming an individual who chooses a moral code and ways of living our life. Being born, literally, is a huge threshold. We leave a home we've probably been comfortable in. Being born, inside ourselves, to ideas and feelings and doing activities from our thoughts is a threshold. Being brave in any way, where we would rather choose the known, is crossing a threshold. Dying—letting go of Earth and present home and familiarity—that is a threshold. Going to sleep is a letting go and a crossing of a threshold.

It seems I've cried at important thresholds of my life. I cried as a baby—for I must have missed the angels—and I got drugged for those tears. I cried when Pooshie and Chief, our dogs, were lost—and I was rewarded with a dream of where they were. I cried from hating myself so—and I was rewarded at eighteen by permission to stop my medicine taking—and this was a new threshold opportunity for me. I didn't cry much when my Father died—I refused to cross that threshold of grief—as years later I did the same with my Mother. And not crossing that threshold of grief to knowledge of the intimacy of myself, has contributed, I feel, to my present cancer and my own self now being near the threshold of this grievous place I know as death.... This is sad and sorry to me now—for not crossing thresholds leads to ill health. If you will not try consciously, then your body will do it in some way for you. Karma and the lives of our soul and spirit journey—it's all about crossing thresholds....

There is always something of a surprise at every threshold.

"THRESHOLD," BY SIGNE
(ON HOLIDAY IN CANADA, AUGUST 11, 1999)

There are two bridges near where we are staying here in the north woods. One is a single lane, with two wooden tracks for car wheels over a foundation of boards laid side-by-side. Along the sides are metal cables and below the River Rouge passes in rapids. There are rocks and white water and at either end of the bridge is a stop sign to halt the coming traffic for the one lane passage. The other bridge is a covered one—a red tunnel with a peaked roof highlights the one lane passage. Here there is a gate, like at a railroad crossing to hold the traffic for passage one way or the other.

These bridges are for me images of threshold—of that space between here and there that must be passed. There may be peril in this transition, at least there is the call to heightened attention. We are asked, if not forced, to pause before embarking, before crossing over. With one we can see the dangers below, with the other we must enter a dark passage, we hear the rattle of our crossing as we head for the opening of light.

And what of the threshold to the spirit? We cross it at death, and yet it is there inviting—or perhaps blocking—our passage everyday into a world of supersensible perception. I have sometimes thought we build the threshold with exercises and the work of inner development, of self-knowledge: we create the foundation from which to bridge across to another land, we lay the stones that mark our journey—like the wooden or marble threshold between rooms or under a doorway marks the place of passage. And yet, though this building work must matter, the threshold is always there.

Steiner says we must meet a guardian at the Threshold to really pass over with consciousness—an encounter with all the stuff of ourself that is unworthy, proud, vengeful, vain, angry, jealous...all that we ignore in building our earthly self-image. Now we must see it, accept that we are this, release that sense of self that holds us together in daily life, if we would awaken to true spirit knowing. Our shame at this encounter holds us back...we stop...we turn aside in fear...or when the time is right we head across with nothing to hold onto. Except a far-off light, a focus against the inner beasts that claw to pull us back, against the shaking passage—the biting winds of doubt, the rocks of fear, the rushing streams of hateful, tormenting feelings. The one true light ahead. Is it only my wishful thinking that feels its warmth?

In other ways I see thresholds everywhere. These seem to me more like veils, or curtains, or like the hanging rugs that act as room dividers in an Arab courtyard. They can be lifted, pulled aside, even removed to reveal a new depth, a fuller space, other beings or activities. It's like this in a conversation, or walking in the woods, or in drawing a picture, or pondering a thought—suddenly (or maybe gradually) a wider, richer, fuller world is there than at first glance. An opening occurs, some threshold is dissolved, and then (and this I think is quick) the veils move back in place and ordinary life resumes.

~

There is another way of attending to inner work that I would still like to mention before ending this chapter. In *How to Know High Worlds*, Rudolf Steiner spoke about conditions for an esoteric or inner life. He introduced these requirements as spiritual facts; whether and how they might be applied is left to each individual. These are areas for attention well known to any genuine spiritual schooling; indeed they are implicit in many of the practices I have already mentioned. Organized this way they offer a clear reminder that can never grow old, of activity that will never be finished.

CONDITIONS / REQUIREMENTS FOR ESOTERIC TRAINING

1. *Attend to the improvement of your physical and mental or spiritual health.*
2. *Feel yourself to be part of the whole of life.*
3. *The conviction that thoughts and feelings are as important for the world as actions.*
4. *The conviction that our true nature does not lie without but within.*
5. *Steadfastness in following through on a resolution once it has been made.*
6. *Develop the feeling of gratitude for all that we receive.*
7. *Understand life as these conditions demand.*[12]

I have worked with these conditions in waves over the years. It is repeatedly humbling for me to realize how forgetful I can be, how such obvious prerequisites to my wellbeing and my further development can slip from my consciousness. And so I take them up again when I recognize the need for the prompting they offer. I have used them as a morning encouragement and as an evening focus for review. I generally attend to one at a time for perhaps a month, and I experience how they build on each other as I move along. Each time I return to them I am amazed at how such direct statements can open into so many nuanced directions for my self-transformation.

Inner development is after all about transformation, and not only of myself. We work individually on ourselves in the service of true human becoming, which also includes our stewardship of the Earth that is our home. Our story and the Earth's story are one. Increasingly we human beings are responsible for our further evolution; we have become co-creators with the divine world. The earthquakes, tsunamis, and severe weather events of the last decade seem to me to be calls from the Earth

---

12 Steiner, *How to Know Higher Worlds*, ch. 5.

to take our responsibility more seriously. I do not feel we will be able to solve the global dilemmas we face—the social, environmental, political, and economic challenges—with our worn-out ways of thinking and acting. We need an awakened spirit attention that would invite the moral intuitions that can meet the problems of the present and the future.

And so we practice, and practice again, that we may awaken our essential self and selflessly offer our capacities to the challenges of our times. I know that I can only do real inner work from a place of inner freedom; no one, not even I myself, can make me meditate. I can only do it out of my own free will. Until then it is no more than a good idea. And I can only do it as an act of love. Surely love, as freely willed activity, is the true purpose of our inner work—love that unites and forgives and supports, that knows our essential connectedness within nature and spirit. All else is coercion, or duty, or wishful thinking. I am painfully aware of my daily inadequacies, and yet I also trust that through my efforts I am gaining strength to face the forces of fear that would storm toward me. I want to meet the threats, the doubts, and conflicts that abound today with an open, unafraid heart. I know this sounds idealistic, and I do not minimize the powers of egotism, deception, greed, and prejudice in the world and still within me; but I would give birth to my higher self and this I know can only be a deed of love. I want to make space for, honor, and attend to an eternal, indestructible Self, membered as it is within an evolving spiritual world.

The human heart can go to the lengths of God.
Dark and cold we may be, but this
Is no winter now. The frozen misery
Of centuries breaks, cracks, begins to move;
The thunder is the thunder of the floes,
The thaw, the flood, the upstart Spring.
Thank God our time is now when wrong
Comes up to face us everywhere,
Never to leave us till we take
The longest stride of soul we ever took.
Affairs are now soul size.
The enterprise
Is exploration into God.
Where are you making for? It takes
So many thousand years to wake,
But will you wake for pity sake.

—CHRISTOPHER FRY, *A Sleep of Prisoners*

CHAPTER 10

LIFTING THE VEIL

There is a myth that I have been living with for many years. As with any true story, I never grow tired of it, nor does it ever stop offering me new insights and new questions. I call it true not because it is recorded history or a biographical anecdote, but because it speaks to deep truths I recognize around me and within me. When I first read it over thirty-five years ago, I knew I needed this mysterious story with its provocative images of contemporary life and of my own soul state. At first I related to it more through feeling than any clear understanding; as the years have gone by, it has posed me many questions in my efforts to glimpse its deeper meanings.

In chapter 2, I mentioned my conviction that myths from all over the world express truths about how human beings relate to themselves, to nature and to the divine world. Their images are not to be taken literally, and no one myth contains the whole story. Nevertheless, in their often puzzling soul and spirit pictures, they offer us something important about the time and place in which they were told and the consciousness of the people living then.

The story I want to share is a modern myth, first told by Rudolf Steiner in a series of lectures addressing myths from a variety of ancient cultures. It speaks of the New Isis—not the goddess as she was known in ancient Egypt, but in her current state. It is not a new rendition of an old myth, but a very modern tale about Isis in this new age. It is founded on a picture of evolving human consciousness, particularly in how we understand and relate to divine realities, and suggests that spiritual beings themselves also evolve over time. Steiner tells the story very carefully, asking his audience to listen with openness and impartiality. He speaks with humility, stating that he can only begin to characterize the basic elements of this new story.

For many people today even the monotheistic idea of one God is challenging, never mind what may seem like a return to primitive beliefs in a panoply of gods and goddesses. I can imagine that for some readers it may be difficult to consider a story about a goddess in contemporary times. There is a phrase from a lecture by Steiner that has echoed in my thinking for a very long time: "for everyone resembles the god he (*she*) understands."[1] What do we understand today of divine workings? And what might such resemblance have to do with the question of human becoming, for an individual and also more broadly in an era such as our own?

It was part of twentieth century cultural development that increasing numbers of people began to question the image of God as an old man with a long white beard. Some determined that "God is dead," perhaps a liberating thought in the development of one's individuality, but over time a view that leaves little with which to identify except cold materialism; unless, of course, one takes up the challenge to re-enliven the godly within oneself, not through dogma or belief, but as a conscious deed. From the middle of the century onward increasing numbers of people began searching other traditions for warmer or more comprehensive images of the spirit. For example, various people have looked into Hinduism, Buddhism, Sufism, Daoism, Kabala, and many indigenous practices from all parts of the world in an effort to forge a spiritual understanding for themselves that offers inner sustenance and inspiration. Some women, feeling the one-sidedness of male-dominated religions, turned to earlier forms of Goddess worship in their search for something to resemble, while still others embraced witchcraft. Within and outside of Christianity people also began to speak more about Mary, and even more so about Sophia, once revered by the Greeks as a being of Wisdom, by the ancient Hebrews in the Old Testament[2] as a partner to God before Creation, and still remembered in the word philosophy (*philosophia*—love of wisdom).

The widespread nature of this searching speaks of a desire to understand ourselves in relationship to a spiritual world of which

---

1   Steiner, *The Gospel of St John*, p. 191.

2   In Proverbs 8 and 9, Wisdom tells her story (especially in 8:22–35).

we sense we are a part. Throughout history different cultures have experienced the divine world through the lens of their own life circumstances and needs, and they have connected themselves to the spiritual beings they perceived, for inspiration that would work into their daily lives. In our age, how can we find a way toward a living spiritual understanding that does not undervalue the strong sense of individuality that has developed over so many centuries? And how do we understand the call that so many individuals feel today, to a new possibility of selfless reconnection with nature, spirit, and each other?

In chapter 2, I also mentioned the old myth of Isis and Osiris that was so important to the ancient Egyptians. Isis was revered as the "epitome of all the deepest thoughts the Egyptians were able to form about the archetypal forces working in nature and in the human being."[3] There was a veiled statue of Isis in the temple at Sais with an inscription that guarded her deep mysteries: "I am the All, I am the Past, the Present and the Future; no mortal has yet lifted my veil." The world of divine reality she guarded could only be known after death or by those who had a deep understanding of spiritual life, particularly those initiated into the Mysteries after long training. Without such preparation an ordinary mortal, bound to the matters of everyday life, could not lift this veil to the spirit and remain alive in the face of such majesty.

Here is a retelling of the New Isis Myth, in my own words but very close to how Steiner related it.[4]

THE NEW ISIS MYTH

The story takes place "in the age of scientific profundity, in the midst of the land of the Philistines." On a secluded hill, there was a remarkable building that was open to visitors at convenient times, even though few people noticed it. In a central place in the building was a large statue of the Representative of Humanity surrounded by adversarial beings. This statue, however, was actually a veil for another, invisible statue—behind the visible statue was a statue of the new Isis, the Isis of a new age.

---

3   Steiner, *Ancient Myths*, p. 61.

4   Ibid., ch. 3; also in *Isis Mary Sophia*, pp. 191–202.

Some people in this age of abstract thinking determined that the visible statue represented or signified the new Isis, but this only showed their complete lack of real understanding. The figures in the visible statue were artistic renderings of their own true realities, and behind them was the real new Isis. In special circumstances a few visitors had experienced the new Isis behind the visible statue and had seen that she was asleep. At very special moments some were able to read the inscription that stood clearly there: "I am the Human Being, I am the Past, the Present, and the Future. Every mortal should lift my veil."

One day, and then again and again, another figure approached the sleeping new Isis, somewhat like a visitor. And she considered this visitor to be her benefactor, and she loved him. One day both the new Isis and her visitor believed in a particular illusion: she had an offspring and she considered her visitor to be the father. He also thought he was the father, although he was not. This visiting spirit was, in fact, the new Typhon, who had been known as Set in ancient Egypt. He believed that if he took possession of the new Isis, he would secure a special increase in his worldly power.

The new Isis had an offspring, but she understood nothing of its nature. She moved it around, dragged it into far-off lands because she thought that this was what she must do. She trailed her offspring through different regions of the world until it fell into fourteen pieces, through the very power of the world.

When the new Typhon became aware of how the new Isis had dragged her offspring about until the world had broken it into fourteen pieces, he gathered the pieces together into a single whole. With his vast scientific knowledge he made a single being again out of the fourteen pieces, but this being obeyed only the laws of the machine. It appeared to have life but it obeyed only mechanical laws, and because it had arisen out of fourteen pieces, it could reproduce itself fourteenfold. And the new Typhon could give an image of his own countenance to each one. Now each of the fourteen apparent offspring of the new Isis resembled the being of the new Typhon.

And the new Isis had to watch all these strange events, half-divining the miraculous changes that had occurred, aware that she had dragged her offspring about and that she had somehow brought all this to pass. Then one day she was able to receive her offspring once again in its true form. She received it back in its genuine form from a group of nature spirits, from nature elementals. Her offspring had been stamped into the offspring of Typhon only through an illusion, and now as she received it back in its true form, a tremendous, clairvoyant vision dawned upon her: she realized that although she had become a new Isis, she was still wearing the cow horns of ancient Egypt.

The power of her clairvoyance now summoned back perhaps Typhon himself, perhaps Mercury, and through the strength of her clairvoyance he was obliged to place a crown on her head, to set it where the old crown that Horus had seized from her so long ago had been, in fact, on the spot where the cow horns now stood. But this new crown was only of paper, covered with all sorts of scientific information, and yet it was of paper. So now the new Isis had two crowns on her head, the cow horns, and the paper crown adorned with all the knowledge of the age.

One day, through the power of her clairvoyance, there arose within her the deep meaning, "as far as the age could reach," of what is described as the Logos in the Gospel of St. John. The deep meaning of the Mystery of Golgotha arose within her. Through the strength of this mystery, the power of the cow horns took hold of the paper crown and transformed it into a golden crown of genuine wisdom.

~

Trying to interpret a myth runs the risk of destroying the magic that makes it so powerful. Nevertheless, the images in this story call out to be at least briefly considered. And they pose provocative questions. It is not difficult to feel how the age of scientific profundity refers to our own time, full as it is with logical, materialistically literal, and self-important theories on everything. Few today have the eyes or the inclination to see invisible statues of present-day spiritual beings. People familiar with Rudolf Steiner's work will, however, recognize the description of the building on the hill with its statue, *The Representative of Humanity;* in January 1918, when this story was told, the first Goetheanum was being constructed in Dornach, Switzerland, as a center for the developing anthroposophical movement. A large sculpture like the one described was intended as a centerpiece in the building.

The statue, carved by Rudolf Steiner and Edith Maryon, survived the fire that destroyed the building a few years later, and is now in the Second Goetheanum, constructed after Steiner's death. The wooden statue is massive, over twenty-four feet tall, with a large central figure, *The Representative of Humanity,* balancing different forces of evil that beset human development. There are beings that tempt us away from our human work on Earth, offering us light, warmth, and spirit bliss, puffing us up with self-importance and pride; there are also powers that would contract us in pain, suffering, and cold isolation, that would bind us to the material Earth. This latter kind of evil thrives on fear and manipulation, hoarding, and deceit.

Why would a statue, *The Representative of Humanity,* the essential spirit core in us all, with the different adversaries held at bay, be a veil for the new Isis? How is she to be found behind that dynamic work of balancing polarized qualities of evil? A first step is clear: only those who truly look will find her. The inscription declares that this new Isis is herself the human being, a divine presence as a picture of our soul; and it challenges every mortal to lift the veil. Now is the time for us to open to the spiritual dimensions of our past, present, and future, time to lift the veil of slumber. For here at the beginning of the story, the new Isis, as human being, is asleep. The excerpt at the beginning of this chapter from the play *A Sleep of Prisoners* by Christopher Fry echoes the inscription with a timely question: "But will you wake for pity sake?"

Another figure, reminiscent of the jealous usurping brother in the ancient Osiris–Isis myth and now gifted with modern technological know-how, visits the new Isis and she considers him her benefactor and loves him. In our digital age what powerful illusions and virtual experiences do we love and consider as true supports? In the story, illusion surrounds the relationship of Isis and Typhon: both think he is the father of her offspring, although he is not. Who is the true father of this offspring? Is this a contemporary virgin birth—remembering that the original meaning of *virgin* was one who is complete within herself, and not only a reference to sexual chastity? Typhon yearns to possess the new Isis, to gain more power for himself. Who is she really? What power is he after? She is still asleep to the nature of her offspring. Like any modern mother, she drags her offspring around—to the mall, to the movies, to day-care—because of some dim sense that she must, in order to survive, or to be sure her child is "ready" (for what?), or just because everyone else is doing it. Or perhaps it is each of us who drags our inner spirit self around, into the enticing, demanding, and stressful world that encompasses us. But with all the chaos and stimulation, the spirit child falls into pieces.

In the myth, Typhon now marshals his scientific and mechanical skills to reconfigure the fourteen dismembered pieces of the offspring into a whole, as if putting together the parts of a machine. Then with a push of pride he clones his creation into fourteen apparent beings, each bearing his countenance. These kinds of technological feats, and an at times blind adherence to the laws of the machine, surround us today, but in 1918 they could barely have been imagined. When do we fall under the spell of mechanical images of life, and where do we try to impress our countenance, our mark of pride and personal influence on what we do in the world?

In a different mood, how familiar is the confused, half-conscious sense of responsibility that the new Isis feels as she watches what is happening to her offspring? Do you sometimes feel a dim personal accountability for the struggles and the suffering around and within you, but not know how to make things different? What to do when this passive sense of connectedness is coupled with an absence of will? To truly wake up, Isis must perceive a new dimension of reality and enter the world of formative forces where elemental spirits of nature are at work. This can offer her a knowing of her offspring in its genuine form. Is this a reference to our need and our possibility in this age of the consciousness soul, to awaken a capacity of living thinking—or what can also be called spirit vision or etheric perception—in order to consciously perceive the supersensible life forces behind the veil of lifeless matter?

As the new Isis awakens to the true nature of her offspring, she also realizes that she is still wearing the cow horns of her ancient Egyptian stature. The lingering power of this old way of being and knowing summons the return of her visitor who is obliged—a further clue to her innate power—to place another crown over the cow horns, a paper crown covered with all the scientific data of the age. This is for me a strangely amusing image: Isis with two crowns on her head where once she had worn her true Goddess crown. In ancient Egypt her son Horus, enraged that she had freed his wicked uncle from imprisonment, had snatched that crown away, replacing it with the cow horns. This horned crown, echoing her ancient, all-encompassing wisdom, is now encircled by a paper crown of endless information. The image of these two crowns, sitting uneasily atop her head, feels familiar to me. As modern people we can intellectually study the ways of ancient initiation, the steps to earlier forms of enlightenment; and ringing our yearning for that wisdom from the past is the ever-available internet, inundating us with the facts that feed our current desire to know ever more. It often feels that these old and new ways of knowing are uncomfortable with each other—important as they both are to our present and future, they speak different languages to different parts of our being, and tell of different domains of reality.

In time, and in a way appropriate to the times, the clairvoyance of the new Isis becomes strong enough for her to understand the meaning of the Logos, as referred to in the opening of the Gospel of St. John: "In the beginning was the Word, and the Word was with God, and the Word was a God." The Logos, the Word, has been understood also as the Christ being, and in the story the term "Mystery of Golgotha" addresses the incarnation, death, and resurrection of Christ, Golgotha being the name of the hill where the crucifixion took place.

Steiner spoke often about the Christ being but not in any denominational or dogmatic way. He addressed Christ's connection to all of humanity and pointed to his significance in many different religions, although sometimes he was known by different names. According to Steiner, Christ's universal presence cannot be owned by any religion, for his deed of sacrifice has spiritual import for all the Earth and all human beings. His earthly mission of selfless love has hardly begun to be articulated or understood. As a spirit of the Sun, Christ entered a human body at the Baptism in the Jordan, lived on the Earth for three years, and went through death and resurrection in order to unite his divine presence with our ongoing human destiny.[5]

I am very aware that for many modern people, referring to the name of Christ is an obstacle to considering ideas like those expressed here. The history of Christianity is riddled with narrow interpretations of so great a mystery, and sadly also with prejudice, intolerance, violence, and abuse. Next to that, it must also be said, stand centuries of devoted prayer, piety, compassion, and service within various Christian traditions. A similar problematic polarity can be found in the histories of all the major religions. Can we conceive of the Christ being unhampered by any particular religious doctrine or practice? Can we recognize in his deeds of sacrifice and resurrection something fully inclusive that speaks to the spirit within us all? Can we imagine this Spirit of Love connected to our own indivisible self? And do you listen, as I do, for what the next, more all-embracing name of this universal spirit of humanity will be? This question has lived in me for many years, but it was spurred on when I once read that Isis had been known as Isis for over 3,000 years. That is a very long time, but the statement also suggests that she, or any divine being—just like reincarnating human beings—has been and will be known by other names in other times.

Returning to the story, it was when Isis awoke to this deep mystery of Christ's incarnation, death, and resurrection that the cow horns could take hold of the paper crown and transform it into a golden crown of genuine wisdom. Through an inner awakening to the power of divine love, the spiritual contributions of the past could join with the learning of the present and so be of service to a truly human future. This picture speaks to where we stand in our present time. Can we now wake up to the spirit within and around us? Can we transform our ways of knowing with a newly enlivened spiritual consciousness? In Steiner's words:

> Even though the power of action that is bound up with the new
> Isis statue is at first weak, exploring and tentative, it is to be

---

5   Steiner spoke often about the significance of the Christ being in earth evolution. See, for example, *Christianity as Mystical Fact,* lectures on the Four Gospels, *The Fifth Gospel,* and *Reappearance of Christ in the Etheric.*

the starting point of something that is deeply justified in the impulses of the modern age, deeply justified in what this age is meant to become and must become.[6]

I have barely touched upon the many deep questions that live within a myth like this, a myth that we modern people are in the process of fulfilling. As with any myth or fairytale, the different characters are all part of our own individualities; they live within our soul potential. We are mother, father—illusory and real—and child, visitor and visited, broken and whole, false and true, unknowing and wisdom-crowned. In this New Isis myth we are called to lift the veil, to recognize our spirit core, to face the counter-forces within and around us that distract and dull our attention, and most urgently of all to develop new powers of perception and love.

Two years after telling this story, Rudolf Steiner himself began to identify the new Isis being with the name Sophia, most explicitly in a series of lectures called, *The Search for the New Isis, Divine Sophia*.[7] In these extremely moving lectures, Steiner speaks of the Christ being's deep and enduring relationship to the Earth and all humanity, even though we have lost the ability to know, to intuit, the true nature of this universal spirit. In our times, if we would awaken our capacity of intuition in the face of this great mystery, there is a preliminary step: "It is not the Christ we lack, but the knowledge and wisdom of the Christ, the Sophia of the Christ, the Isis of the Christ."[8] We need to find a new relationship to this age-old, but ever evolving feminine principle of bearing; we need to bear new responsibility for our own soul reality, that we may come to know the true spirit within us.

With the mechanistic consciousness of our materialistic age, we can easily lose sight of divine wisdom spread out through all the universe. We become captivated by technological wizardry, mathematical abstractions, and the "facts" of weight, measure, and number; and these can blind us to the deeper mysteries within the beauty of a rose, the magnificence of the starry sky, the raging power of a forest fire, or our own

---

6   Steiner, *Ancient Myths*, p. 66.

7   Two of the lectures are also printed in *Isis Mary Sophia*, pp. 203–226.

8   Steiner. *The Search for the New Isis, Divine Sophia*, lect. 2.

essential nature. To become truly human we must discover a new relationship to divine wisdom, whether we choose to call this Sophia or not. Our devotion to natural science needs to expand to an interest in spiritual science as well. With all the objectivity that we have developed in our efforts to observe and understand the world of matter, we need now to open ourselves in clear consciousness to what lies beyond the threshold of physical reality. It is becoming ever more possible to approach this threshold between ordinary and supersensible perception, and if we would go this path in a healthy and conscious way, then each of us is challenged to awaken a new capacity of living imagination.

Serious social, environmental, and political problems surround us today, and we will not find the solutions we need with the same old ways of thinking that circle habitually round in deeply rutted and closed loops or that are grounded in selfishness, competition, and greed. Global warming, gun control, profound income inequities, partisan blockages in the US Congress, and perpetual unrest in the Middle East are but a few of the headline concerns of the twenty-first century. These issues have all been building for a long time, and they will not be significantly addressed until we are able, both individually and collectively, to meet them with a new kind of heart thinking. I do not mean this in any sentimental way; I mean a thinking that is alive, morally intuitive, free of the constraints of tradition, discerning, and lovingly open to the real needs at hand. This is a work for everyone. The solutions to the problems we face do not lie in abstract programs, but will only succeed when grounded on genuine individual responsibility. Even good ideas are hollow if the people espousing them are not trying to live them. Violence, selfishness, prejudice, and fear can only be addressed in the social world when individually enough people no longer give harbor to these forces in their souls, but rather do the inner work that can clear the way for new imaginations, for truly creative, independent, and spirit-filled thinking, feeling, and willing.

In chapter 9, I mentioned one of Steiner's foundational books, now in English as *Intuitive Thinking as a Spiritual Path: A Philosophy of Freedom*. For me, this book has been a lifetime guidebook for my own path of awakening. I have had the privilege of teaching it for many years; and in the process I have myself learned to value living

thinking, to appreciate and yet also try to open myself beyond the
influences of my upbringing, schooling, temperament, and life roles,
and most of all to trust my intuition. Steiner described this book of
his youth as "a biographical account of how one human soul made
the difficult ascent to freedom."[9] I appreciate this characterization
very much and have found in the careful process he builds throughout
the book, important landmarks and significant questions and challenges for my own journey of becoming more inwardly free. My road
has been long and winding, with unexpected obstacles and detours; I
have stumbled and made what have seemed at times like wrong turns.
The possibility of error is an inevitable companion on the path toward
freedom. Honest reassessments are a significant part of any movement
forward. I do not anticipate a once-and-for-all arrival, but I gratefully
receive the open vistas when they appear. And the fellow travelers
who have often pointed me in new directions. Amidst the rigors of
the trek, the joy along the way has been both surprising and profound.

The closing chapter of the second half of *Intuitive Thinking as
a Spiritual Path* addresses the question of the free individuality as
it relates to the many generic aspects that are part of being human.
How can one be free when we share characteristics with others of
like ethnicity, education, or social background? In this book I have
explored the universal nature of several different aspects of human
nature, such as gender, temperament, soul orientation, and life phases.
These different facets of our life on Earth can feel at times like the
broken pieces of the offspring of the new Isis—with each piece in danger of acquiring singular, and illusionary, importance when separated
from the whole. But when the various pieces come together in an individual life, the shared opportunities and challenges inherent within
each of them offer rich life learning. Rudolf Steiner spoke of the different generic components of our human experience as the "medium
through which we can express our own distinct being. We use the
characteristics nature gives us as a basis, and we give these the form
that corresponds to our own being."[10]

9   This is from a letter to Rosa Mayreder, quoted in *Rudolf Steiner on His
    Book the Philosophy of Freedom*, pp. 5–6.
10 Steiner, *Intuitive Thinking as a Spiritual Path*, p. 226.

On the long road of becoming our unique selves, we can find many clues to the mystery of this life on Earth by exploring how gender, nationality, or temperament, like heredity and DNA, have been the clay with which our "I" has molded an intentional vessel for its development. This magnificently constructed vessel, with all its many parts, is not itself my real "I," but rather its temporary home on Earth—temporary but vital on the way to becoming fully human. In different life phases we meet characteristic thresholds and so stand fully within the paradox of our earthly individuality and our universal humanity. Experiencing a joy or sorrow in our life, can we recognize that we came to Earth for this? Working through and beyond the commanding voices of duty, habit, fear, guilt, anger, or even good behavior, can we practice, ever and again, meeting what we intended to meet with an open creative heart?

Can we freely take the step we need to take with love for the mystery of destiny, with a grateful knowing that "This is mine"?

The wishes of the soul are springing,
The deeds of the will are thriving,
The fruits of life are maturing.

I feel my destiny,
My destiny finds me.
I feel my star,
My star finds me.
I feel my goals in life,
My goals in life are finding me.

My soul and the great world are one.

Life grows more radiant about me,
Life grows more arduous for me,
Life grows more abundant within me.

—RUDOLF STEINER, *Verses and Meditations*

Appendix

Biography Work with Others

B iography work, as a specific field of research and activity, has been steadily developing during the last several decades. Inspired by the work of Rudolf Steiner and Anthroposophy, people in many parts of the world have been exploring how this multi-dimensional approach to human life can serve healing and awakened consciousness in our times. In many countries, in addition to a variety of public offerings, there are now training courses for those interested in working as biography professionals. The following description of some of the ways of working is taken from the website of The Center for Biography and Social Art, of which I was a co-founder.

Biography Workshops and Classes

Biography practitioners offer workshops and classes on a variety of life themes, infusing the learning process with social art. Sessions might include short talks, biography exercises, work with story, nature observation, artistic activity, inner practice, and small-group conversations. One of the gifts of this way of working is a heightened appreciation for each unique life as it resonates within the context of universal patterns. Exploring biographical questions in small groups invites new self-understanding and also awakens interest in the experiences of others. In our ever-more virtual world, it fosters real meetings and genuine appreciation for the diversity of human striving and creativity.

A sampling of recent workshops or classes offered by biography practitioners:

Bringing Consciousness to Life
Forgiveness
Parenting as a Path of Development
Living a Life of Intention
Biography and Destiny
Family Matters
Karmic Resonances
Conversations with Your Higher Self
Life Stories: Unraveling Our Life's Journey in the Company of
    Other Curious Travelers
Life as an Ongoing Work of Art

BIOGRAPHICAL CONVERSATIONS

Sometimes we want to look at our lives from a fresh perspective, and we realize that we would like to do this in conversation with someone else. We are not in a crisis but there is a question that keeps surfacing, and we would like to explore its roots through our evolving life story. Perhaps the idea of seven-year phases intrigues us, and we would like to work with someone on how they have played out in our own life journey. Or we may be at a transition moment, and we want to gather some of the threads weaving through our life before stepping toward the future.

At the heart of biography work is the understanding that each life story is a unique revelation of intention and deep wisdom. For the biography practitioner, each "journey" is sacred and there is an understanding that the "traveler" is continually informed by both individual and universal truths. Biography practitioners bring a carefully structured process, artistic exercises, and true listening to life explorations. Often there will be an agreement to meet for several sessions. Ideally these conversations happen face-to-face, but it is also possible to do this by phone or with Skype.

BIOGRAPHICAL COUNSELING

The need or desire to work with one's biography in a more formal setting, with a specially trained professional, typically arises out of a crisis. One might have experienced a life-changing event, be struggling with a difficult decision, or realize that one is faced with thoughts, feelings, or behaviors that are confusing, overwhelming, and perhaps even harmful to oneself or others. Biographical counselors are trained in biography and social art in addition to their background in counseling and/or psychotherapy, and they can offer charting, dialogue, and art activities to encourage greater objectivity. This approach supports a renewal of strength, insight, and balance; the focus remains fully on one's biography, but with particular attention to experiences that seem to resonate with the central difficulty. The process requires devoted time in order to bring about meaningful inner and outer change.

BIOGRAPHY CONSULTATION WITH EXISTING GROUPS

Very often in collegial, faculty, or community groups, there is a wish to know each other more deeply, but there is neither time nor energy to hear long recitations of everyone's life story. In an efficient yet warm way, biography practitioners can offer helpful perspectives, questions, and exercises that bring renewed life into group interactions, and deepen interest and respect among colleagues. Activities can be built around specific questions belonging to the group; for example, one faculty wanted to look into their own childhood phases as part of deepening their curriculum discussions. Many general biographical themes—such as temperaments, gender, life phases, or soul types—can provide a background for strengthening working relationships.

BIOGRAPHY AND SOCIAL ART AS PROFESSIONAL ENHANCEMENT

People trained in biography and social art are bringing new perspectives and practices into many existing professions, such as art therapy, medicine, adult education, work with the homeless, care for the elderly, hospice, and death care.

For more information about biography work in the United States and for links to biography practitioners in North America, as well as to activities in other parts of the world, go to the website of The Center for Biography and Social Art www.biographysocialart.com.

Bibliography

Alexander, Eben, MD. *Proof of Heaven: A Neurosurgeon's Journey into the Afterlife.* New York: Simon and Schuster, 2012.

Anschutz, Marieke. *Children and Their Temperaments.* Edinburgh: Floris Books, 1995.

Baring, Anne and Jules Cashford. *The Myth of the Goddess.* London: Arkana (Penguin Books), 1993.

Bateson, Mary Catherine. *Composing a Further Life.* New York: Knopf, 2010.

Bloom, Alan. *The Closing of the American Mind.* New York: Simon and Schuster, 1987.

Bryant, William. *The Veiled Pulse of Time.* Hudson, NY: Anthroposophic Press, 1993.

Burkhard, Gudrun. *Taking Charge: Your Life Patterns and their Meaning.* Edinburgh: Floris Books, 1998.

Collins, Billy. *Sailing Around the Room.* New York: Random House Paperback, 2002.

——. *Questions about Angels.* Pittsburgh: University of Pittsburgh, 1991.

Davy, Gudrun, and Bons Voors. *Lifeways: Working with Family Questions.* Hawthorn Press, 1995.

Dillard, Annie. *An American Childhood.* New York: HarperCollins, 1987.

Feldman, Irving. *Collected Poems 1954-2004.* New York: Schocken Books, 2004.

Finser, Torin. *School as a Journey: The Eight-Year Odyssey of a Waldorf Teacher and his Class.* Hudson, NY: Anthroposophic Press, 1994.

Frost, Robert. *The Poetry of Robert Frost: The Collected Poems.* New York: Henry Holt and Co., 1969.

Fry, Christopher. *A Sleep of Prisoners.* New York: Dramatists Play Service, 1953.

Gilligan, Carol. *The Birth of Pleasure.* New York: Borzoi Books, 2002.

Ginzberg, Louis. *Legends of the Jews.* Baltimore: Johns Hopkins, 1998.

Glas, Norbert, MD. *The Fulfillment of Old Age.* New York: Anthroposophic Press, 1970.

Goethe, J. W. *Goethe's Botanical Writings* (tr. Bertha Mueller). Woodbridge, CT: Ox Bow Press, 1989.

———. *Italian Journey 1786–1787*. San Francisco, CA: North Point Press, 1982.

Graves, Robert. *The Greek Myths I*. New York: Penguin, 1960.

Hammarskjöld, Dag. *Markings*. London: Faber and Faber, 1966.

Healy, Jane. *Endangered Minds: Why Children Don't Think and What We Can Do About It*. New York: Touchstone, 1990.

———. *Failure to Connect: How Computers Affect Our Children's Minds—and What We Can Do About It*. New York: Simon and Schuster, 1998.

———. *Your Child's Growing Mind: Brain Development and Learning from Birth to Adolescence*. New York: Doubleday, 1984.

Hickey, Robert and Kathleen Hughes, *Find Your Seasoning, Find Yourself*. New York: Acropolis Books, 1984.

Hillesum, Etty. *An Interrupted Life: The Diaries of Etty Hillesum 1941–43*. New York: Henry Holt and Co., 1966.

Isay, Dave. *Listening Is an Act of Love: A Celebration of American Life from the StoryCorps Project*. New York: Penguin, 2007.

James, William. *Talks to Teachers on Psychology; And To Students on Some of Life's Ideals*. Create Space Independent Publishing Platform, June 11, 2012.

Jocelyn, Beredene. *Citizens of the Cosmos: Life's Unfolding from Conception through Death to Rebirth*. Great Barrington, MA: SteinerBooks, 2009.

Justice, Donald. *Night Light*. Wesleyan Poetry Program. Middletown, CT: Wesleyan University Press, 1981.

König, Karl. *Brothers and Sisters: The Order of Birth in the Family*. Hudson, NY: Anthroposophic Press, 1984.

Kübler-Ross, Elisabeth. *On Death and Dying*. New York: Simon and Schuster, 1969.

Kunitz, Stanley. *The Collected Poems*. New York: Norton & Co., 2000.

Lawrence-Lightfoot, Sara. *The Third Chapter: Passion, Risk, and Adventure in the 25 Years After 50*. New York: Sarah Crichton, 2009.

Lievegoed, Bernard. *Man on the Threshold*. Gloucestershire: Hawthorne Press, 1985.

———. *Phases: Crisis and Development in the Individual*. London: Rudolf Steiner Press, 1979.

Lipson, Michael. *Stairway of Surprise: Six Steps to a Creative Life*. Great Barrington, MA: SteinerBooks, 2002.

Matthews, Margli, Signe Schaefer, and Betty Staley. *Ariadne's Awakening: Taking up the Threads of Consciousness*. Gloucestershire: Hawthorne Press, 1986.

Matthews, Paul. *Slippery Characters*. Hereford, UK: Five Seasons Press, 2011.

Merwin, W. S. *Migration: New and Selected Poems*. Port Townsend, WA: Copper Canyon Press, 2005.

———. *The Second Four Books of Poems*. Port Townsend, WA: Copper Canyon Press, 1993.

Moody, Raymond A. *Life after Life: The Investigation of a Phenomenon—Survival of Bodily Death*. San Francisco: Harper, 2001.

Moore, Thomas. *The Planets Within: The Astrological Psychology of Marsilio Ficino*. Great Barrington, MA: Lindisfarne Press, 1990.

Neuman, Erich. *The Origins and History of Consciousness*. Princeton, NJ: Princeton University Press, 1954.

Oliver, Mary. *The Leaf and the Cloud: A Poem*. Cambridge, MA: Da Capo, 2000.

———. *New and Selected Poems,* vol. 2. Boston: Beacon Press, 2005.

———. *Our World* (photography by Molly Malone Cook). Boston: Beacon Press, 2007.

———. *Thirst: Poems*. Boston: Beacon Press, 2006.

O'Neil, George and Gisela O'Neil. *The Human Life*. Edited by Florin Lowndes. Spring Valley, NY: Mercury Press, 1990.

Plato. *The Republic*, Book 10 (tr. Benjamin Jowett). New York: P. F. Collier & Son, 1901.

Rilke, Reinar Maria. *Later Poems*. See also the blog: Gaiam Life, "Stream of consciousness," blog.gaiam.com/quotes/authors/rainer-maria-rilke?page=1.

———. *The Selected Poems of Rainer Maria Rilke*. New York: Random House, 1982.

Ritchie, George. *Return from Tomorrow*. Waco, TX: Chosen Books, 1978.

Roszell, Calvert. *Near-Death Experiences*. Great Barrington, MA: SteinerBooks, 1992.

Scott-Maxwell, Florida. *The Measure of My Days: One Woman's Vivid, Enduring Celebration of Life and Aging*. New York: Penguin, 1979.

Sheehy, Gail. *Passages: Predictable Crises of Adult Life*. New York: Bantam Books, 1977.

Smith, Patti and Signe Schaefer. *More Lifeways: Finding Support and Inspiration in Family Life*. Gloucestershire: Hawthorne Press, 1997.

Soesman, Albert. *Our Twelve Senses: How Healthy Senses Refresh the Soul*. Gloucestershire: Hawthorne Press, 1990.

Stafford, William. *The Darkness around Us Is Deep: Selected Poems of William Stafford*. New York: Harper Perennial, 1993.

Steiner, Rudolf. *Ancient Myths and the New Isis Mysteries*. Hudson, NY: Anthroposophic Press, 1994.

———. *Anthroposophy in Everyday Life: Practical Training in Thought, Overcoming Nervousness, Facing Karma, The Four Temperaments*. Great Barrington, MA: Anthroposophic Press, 1995.

———. *At Home in the Universe: Exploring Our Suprasensory Nature*. Hudson, NY: Anthroposophic Press, 2000.

———. *Autobiography: Chapters in the Course of My Life, 1861–1907*. Great Barrington, MA: SteinerBooks, 2006.

———. *Calendar of the Soul*. Spring Valley, NY: Anthroposophic Press, 1982.

———. *Christianity as a Mystical Fact: And the Mysteries of Antiquity*. Great Barrington, MA: SteinerBooks, 2006.

———. *Cosmic Memory: The Story of Atlantis, Lemuria, and the Division of the Sexes*. New York: Rudolf Steiner Publications, 1959.

———. *Education for Adolescents*. Hudson, NY: Anthroposophic Press, 1996.

———. *The Education of the Child*. Hudson, NY: Anthroposophic Press, 1996.

———. *The Fifth Gospel: From the Akashic Record*. London: Rudolf Steiner Press, 1995.

———. *Gospel of St John*. Hudson, NY: Anthroposophic Press, 1984.

———. *Gospel of St Mark*. Hudson, NY: Anthroposophic Press, 1986.

———. *How to Know Higher Worlds: A Modern Path of Initiation*. Hudson, NY: Anthroposophic Press, 1994.

———. *Intuitive Thinking as a Spiritual Path: A Philosophy of Freedom.* Hudson, NY: Anthroposophic Press, 1995.

———. *Isis Mary Sophia: Her Mission and Ours.* Great Barrington, MA: SteinerBooks, 2003.

———. *Life between Death and Rebirth.* Hudson, NY: Anthroposophic Press, 1989.

———. "Man and Woman in the Light of Spiritual Science," *Anthroposophical Review*, vol. 2, no.1 1980.

———. *Manifestations of Karma.* London: Rudolf Steiner Press, 1969.

———. *The Meaning of Life: And Other Lectures on Fundamental Issues.* London: Rudolf Steiner Press, 2005.

———. *An Outline of Esoteric Science.* Hudson, NY: Anthroposophic Press, 1997.

———. *Reappearance of Christ in the Etheric: A Collection of Lectures on the Second Coming of Christ.* Great Barrington, MA: SteinerBooks, 2004.

———. *Reincarnation and Karma.* Hudson, NY: Anthroposophic Press, 1992.

———. *Rudolf Steiner on His Book* The Philosophy of Freedom. Edited by Otto Palmer. Spring Valley, NY: Anthroposophic Press, 1975.

———. *The Search for the New Isis, Divine Sophia.* Spring Valley, NY: Mercury Press, 1983.

———. *Start Now! A Book of Soul and Spiritual Exercises* (ed. C. Bamford). Great Barrington, MA: SteinerBooks, 2004.

———. *Staying Connected: How to Continue Your Relationships with Those Who Have Died.* Hudson, NY: Anthroposophic Press, 1999.

———. *Theosophy: An Introduction to the Spiritual Processes in Human Life and in the Cosmos.* Hudson, NY: Anthroposophic Press, 1994.

———. *Verses and Meditations.* London: Rudolf Steiner Press, 2012.

Sturgeon-Day, Lee. *Biography Workbooks.* Prescott, AZ: Lifeways for Healing Education, n.d.

Sulloway, Frank J. *Born to Rebel: Birth Order, Family Dynamics, and Creative Lives.* New York: Pantheon Books, 1996.

Tannen, Deborah. *You Just Don't Understand: Women and Men in Conversation.* New York: William Morrow, 1990.

Tolstoy, Leo. *Leo Tolstoy's 20 Greatest Short Stories Annotated.* edited by Andrew Barger, New York: Bottletree Books, 2009.

Van Houten, Coenraad. *Awakening the Will: Principles and Processes in Adult Learning.* Forest Row, UK: Adult Learning Network, 1995

Whitman, Walt. *Leaves of Grass.* Radford, VA: Wilder Publications, 2007.

Wordsworth, William. *The Oxford Book of English Verse: 1250–1900.* Edited by Arthur Quiller-Couch. Oxford: Clarendon, 1919.

Yeats, William Butler. *The Collected Works of W. B. Yeats,* vol. 1. New York: Scribner, 1997.

Zajonc, Arthur. *Meditation as Contemporary Inquiry: When Knowing Becomes Love.* Great Barrington, MA: Lindisfarne, 2008.

Zeylmans Van Emmichoven, F. W. *The Foundation Stone.* London: Rudolf Steiner Press, 1963.

Acknowledgements

Many people have played a role in this book coming into being, some no longer on the earth but still very alive in my heart. I am grateful to my parents, Carl and Harriet Eklund for the warmth that surrounded my childhood and the legacy of exploration that guides me still. My sister, Linda Norris, was a companion through so much life learning, and I miss our hours together. Her spirit support has been ever present in the writing shed she gave me before she died. The many conversations I had with my friend and colleague Norman Davidson echo on in me and keep me searching.

It was with Christa Kaufmann (Hornor) that I first dared to trust what could awaken within a group of people interested in a common theme. I thank her for prompting what became such a central thread in my life. The years of women's groups that followed, eventually under the name *Ariadne,* prepared me for my later work in adult education. Although we now live on different continents, Dede Bark, Stephanie Cooper, Margli Matthews, and I have continued to meet throughout the decades and they are at the core of my becoming; our multi-layered conversations over so many years resound throughout this book. That Margli and I have been able to continue developing biography work together is a great gift in my life.

I feel enduring gratitude to the many students with whom I had the privilege of working in Foundation Studies at Sunbridge College and elsewhere; to those who shared their questions and insights at workshops; and to the participants in the Biography and Social Art program. All of them have inspired my devotion to human development and warmed my heart. I am also grateful to my colleagues over the years, and enriched by the ways we tried together to serve a better world. Thank you to my present colleagues in developing the Center for Biography and Social Art, for their creativity and commitment, and for the encouragement they offered me with this book. The Biography and Social Art program could never have developed without the friendship and guidance of Maria DeZwaan; many thanks for all she has brought to the work and to me personally.

Biography work is developing all over the world and I have learned much from many long-time friends in the work, including Karen Gierlach, Lee Sturgeon-Day, Rinke Visser, Josien DeVries, and my colleagues in the International Biography Trainers' Forum.

Many other friends have also been central in developing the ideas that this book addresses, especially Kathleen Bowen, Jennifer Brooks Quinn, Noela Maletz, Patricia Rubano, Joseph Rubano, and Patti Smith. Deep thanks to them, as well as to Susan Crozier and Waltraude Woods for reading early drafts and offering suggestions and encouragement. Much appreciation also to Wanda Root and Leah Walker for sharing poems and generous support, and to Robin Zeamer for her photographic eye. Special gratitude to Ann-Elizabeth Barnes for her steady belief in the book and invaluable editorial help. I take full responsibility for the stubborn places where I resisted good advice.

Many thanks to the people at SteinerBooks: to Gene Gollogly for his initial and abiding enthusiasm for the project, to Dianna Downing, Mary Giddens, and Jens Jensen for their care with the text. And thank you to the Foundation for Rudolf Steiner Books for much appreciated funding support.

My daughter Karin and my son Stefan have been my great teachers since my early twenties. The privilege of being their mother and accompanying them through so many years of mutual growth is a treasure in my life. And thank you also to those they brought into our family: Diane Crespo, Kaya Dillon, and Chenta Laury. I thank whatever wisdom guides my destiny for all of them. And also for Tessa Chao, chosen sister from our childhood. With Cyris and Talei Laury Schaefer, the youngest members of our family, I have been able once again to marvel first-hand at the miracle of life unfolding on earth. They bring me ever-renewing wonder and joy. And Chris—I have such deep gratitude for our long journey together. He never ceases to inspire me, challenge me, and keep me growing. His support for this book was unwavering: reading drafts, asking hard questions, smiling as he read my voice, and getting dinner when I was too absorbed to stop writing.

The title of this book is a living question for me, and my beloved people—family and friends, students and colleagues—are part of my personal, ongoing, living answer.

PERMISSIONS